Deter, Detain, Dehumanise

Deter, Detain, Dehumanise: The Politics of Seeking Asylum

EDITED BY

RACHEL SHARPLES
Western Sydney University, Australia

AND

LINDA BRISKMAN
Western Sydney University, Australia

emerald PUBLISHING

United Kingdom – North America – Japan – India – Malaysia – China

Emerald Publishing Limited
Emerald Publishing, Floor 5, Northspring, 21-23 Wellington Street, Leeds LS1 4DL.

First edition 2024

British Library Cataloguing in Publication Data
A catalogue record for this book is available from the British Library

ISBN: 978-1-83753-225-4 (Print)
ISBN: 978-1-83753-224-7 (Online)
ISBN: 978-1-83753-226-1 (Epub)

Printed and bound by CPI Group (UK) Ltd, Croydon, CR0 4YY

INVESTOR IN PEOPLE

To those who have spoken out, to those who have been silenced, and to those who have lost their lives under punitive and de-humanising policies and practices.

Contents

List of Images

About the Editors

Rachel Sharples is Lecturer in Sociology at Western Sydney University. She is the author of *Spaces of Solidarity* (Berghahn Books, 2020). She has written for The Conversation and the Forced Migration Review. She has published chapters in *Contemporary Perspectives on Human Rights Law in Australia* (Thomas Reuters, 2020), *The Modern Guide to the Urban Sharing Economy* (Edward Elgar Publishing, 2021) and the *Handbook of Migration and Global Justice* (Edward Elgar Publishing, 2021). She has received an Early Career Research Award for her research and writing and along with Linda Briskman convened the Politicisation of Seeking Asylum symposium in October 2020 which drew more than 500 attendees from across the globe.

Linda Briskman holds the Margaret Whitlam Chair of Social Work at Western Sydney University. She is co-author of the award-winning book *Human Rights Overboard* (Scribe, 2008). She has published more than 10 books, including the co-authored *Human Rights and Social Work* (Cambridge University Press, 2022), the co-edited *Indigenous Health Ethics: An Appeal to Human Rights* (World Scientific, 2021), the co-edited *Social Work in the Shadow of the Law* (Federation Press, 2018) and *Social Work with Indigenous Communities: A Human Rights Approach* (Federation Press, 2014). She has authored more than 100 academic publications on human rights issues and published in Arena, The Conversation and written opinion pieces in ABC's The Drum, as well as for international media outlets. She has won awards for her writing, research and advocacy.

About the Contributors

Hani Abdile is a writer and spoken word poet based in the country of the Gadigal people of the Eora Nation, in Sydney. She was forced to leave her home country of Somalia and came to Australia seeking protection in 2014. During her 11 months in immigration detention, she found healing in poetry and developed a love for writing. Her first book of 43 poems, *I Will Rise*, was published by Writing Through Fences in 2016 and explores how the power of our collective voices can help shape the world to be a better place, for the next generation.

Barat Ali Batoor is a multi-award-winning photographer and filmmaker. His photographs were exhibited across the world including the United States, Europe, Asia and Australia. His works have been published in *The Washington Post*, *Newsweek*, *New York Times*, *Wall Street Journal*, *The Guardian*, *Stern*, *India Today*, *Risk Magazine*, *The Global Mail*, *The Daily Mail*, *The West Australian*, *Strategic Review* and others. His documentary film *Batoor: A Refugee Journey* won an award for the 'Best Director' at the Melbourne Documentary Film Festival. The film was also nominated for the 2021 Walkley Documentary Award.

Behrouz Boochani is a Kurdish-Iranian writer, journalist, scholar, cultural advocate and filmmaker. His book, *No Friend but the Mountains: Writing from Manus Prison* won the 2019 Victorian Prize for Literature. He has also won the Special Award at the NSW Premier's Literary Awards, the Australian Book Industry Award for Nonfiction Book of the Year and the National Biography Prize. It has been published in 19 languages in 24 countries and is currently being adapted for both stage and screen. His most recent book is *Freedom, Only Freedom*. He was a political prisoner incarcerated by the Australian government in Papua New Guinea for almost seven years. In November 2019, he escaped to New Zealand and now resides in Wellington.

Kate Coddington is an Associate Professor in the Department of Geography and Planning at the University at Albany. She is a feminist political geographer whose research examines how the experiences of increasing numbers of forced migrants who fall outside the protections of asylum law illuminate changing dimensions of border enforcement, mobility and sovereignty. Current research involves exploring the role of public information campaigns in border enforcement, the gaps in refugee governance in the Asia-Pacific region and the role of impoverishment and destitution in migration control policies.

Michelle Jasmin Dimasi is an Australian anthropologist and writer focussed on refugees, migration and Afghanistan. She is the author of *Hope, Solidarity and Death at the Australian Border* with the foreword by UNHCR Goodwill Ambassador Khaled Hosseini (The Kite Runner) and all book royalties going to The Khaled Hosseini Foundation to help Afghanistan's humanitarian crisis. She has written for ABC News, *Newlines Magazine*, *Inside Story* and the *Canberra Times*. Today, she lives between Dubai and Kabul and previously resided in Saudi Arabia, Singapore, and on Christmas Island.

Claire Loughnan is a Lecturer in Criminology, at the School of Social and Political Sciences, University of Melbourne. Her research interests are in border protection, immigration detention and the modes, practices and effects of spaces of confinement and control.

Julie Macken is an Adjunct Fellow in the School of Social Sciences at Western Sydney University. She completed her PhD into the question surrounding Australia's abuse of those who came seeking the state's protection. She has worked as a Documentary Film Writer and Senior Writer with the *Australian Financial Review*; worked as Political and Media Consultant to Federal Labor and NSW Greens and has worked in media for Greenpeace and ActionAid. Her research focussed on the psycho-analytic drivers of Australia's abuse.

Julia Morris is Associate Professor of International Studies at the University of North Carolina Wilmington. She holds a PhD in Social and Cultural Anthropology from the University of Oxford, where she was a research student at the Centre on Migration, Policy and Society. Her research focusses on the political economy of migration and outsourced asylum regimes, from ethnographic fieldwork in Nauru, Australia and Geneva to research projects in Jordan and Guatemala. She has published widely and is the author of *Asylum and Extraction in the Republic of Nauru* (Cornell University Press, 2023).

Bosco Opi currently works for the University of South Australia in the Research Office. Prior to that, he worked for the Australian Department of Home Affairs on border protection for about a decade. He holds a PhD in Migration and Refugee Law from Flinders University, Faculty of Business, Government, and Law. His PhD thesis provides a decolonial critique of 'prolonged' refugee encampment in Kenya and Africa by extension. He is a decolonial scholar and the author of 'Borders Recolonised – The Impacts of the EU Externalisation Policy in Africa' (2021) published in the *Journal of Decolonial Discipline*.

Claudia Tazreiter is a Professor in Ethnic and Migration Studies at the Institute for Research on Migration, Ethnicity and Society, University Linköping, Sweden. She is the author of *Asylum Seekers and the State. The Politics of Protection in a Security-conscious World* (Routledge, 2017); *Fluid Security in the Asia Pacific. Transnational Lives, Human Rights and State Control* (Palgrave, 2016); and the *Handbook on Migration and Global Justice*, edited with Leanne Weber (Edward Elgar, 2021).

Anthea Vogl is an Associate Lecturer at the University of Technology Sydney Faculty of Law. Her research addresses refugee and immigration law, and racialised forms of regulation of non-citizens and the border. She is currently co-leading an Australian Research Council Discovery Project examining the privatisation of refugee reception and resettlement and she is the author of *Judging Refugees: Narrative and Oral Testimony in Refugee Status Determination* (Cambridge University Press, 2024).

Foreword

Let's start with this image: two tiny islands in the middle of a huge ocean and much further away, another big island, a continent. People who escaped persecution, discrimination and war sought asylum in the big island. But they got rejected and were banished to the tiny islands and jailed there. Politicians in the big island thought that by banishing them, they would be out of sight and out of mind. But years later, refugees in the small islands challenged the big island – mostly through art, writing and collective resistance like hunger strikes and protests which have become visible on public platforms. This is just an abstract of Australia's policy towards refugees in recent years and how refugees challenge it through narrating.

Refugees in Manus Island and Nauru have not only resisted in order to survive but built a knowledge of resistance or 'resistance knowledge'. This knowledge is the way refugees exist, resist and introduce themselves into the world. The knowledge of how refugees have resisted oppressive powers is a good way to analyse and understand Australian politics and society.

It is crucial that when we talk about these refugees, we recognise that they have distanced themselves from simply being victims of cruel refugee policies. Beyond being in a position of bearing witness to and experiencing cruelty, they have also created their own discourse and this is the main part of this resistance knowledge. When I talk of resistance knowledge, I don't just mean refugees, but also those people in and out of Australia who have been standing up for refugee rights and working with refugees, and who are also part of this discourse.

It is a collective resistance and collaboration to introduce a unique and radical perspective towards politics and Australia's political culture. It is an epidemiology of people who have been dehumanised for decades in the public and the prison camps.

Refugees in Australia's detention system have not only exposed the cruelty of this regime but have challenged the dehumanisation process and the idea that refugees are less than other people. Dehumanisation is the most important concept in this context that we should know and be aware of, because only through the process of dehumanisation is it possible to create such a tragedy. Dehumanisation begins in the context of language and fighting against this process still happens in the context of language. Refugees are first criminalised in language. They are introduced as a threat against national security in language first so that it's easier to normalise keeping people in indefinite detention and exile them, while the public accepts it. The concept of 'boat people', 'illegal refugees' and 'offshore processing centre' are keywords entered into the popular language to justify or normalise Australia's detention system. The established media have also used words like 'rapists', 'drug dealers' and 'potential terrorists' to describe refugees. The refugees in Australia have challenged this language and created their own.

This book is another attempt to challenge this prejudiced language. It tries to understand the differing aspects of Australia's detention system and expose the different layers of it. To understand this system, we need an inter-disciplinary approach, because Manus and Nauru happened in the context of Australia's colonial mentality. In other words, we can say it is the unconscious side of Australia. This book is not only academic but is also a part of collective collaboration and collective resistance knowledge. This is a critical piece of work to analyse the Australian detention industry and expose different layers of it, but at the same time, decolonise the language and narrative about refugees to create a fundamental change.

Behrouz Boochani

Acknowledgements

The idea of this book started with a symposium we organised in October 2020, *The Politicisation of Seeking Asylum: Manus Prison Theory and Australia's Response to Asylum Seekers*. We were looking for a way to build on a significant body of work that already existed around Australia's offshore detention practices and its treatment of asylum seekers. We decided on the broad theme of the politicisation of seeking asylum, because it spoke to the very deliberate and calculated approach governments have taken towards those seeking asylum, not only here in Australia but globally. We believe this issue is a multi-faceted one, that it does, and will, require a multi-pronged approach, and so we brought together speakers from a range of disciplines: political science, geography, law, sociology, social work, criminology, who often work in interdisciplinary ways, to bring their own knowledge to the problem.

Over 500 people attended the online symposium which took place deep into the first year of COVID-19. They came from many countries across the world. We want to thank them for turning up on such an important global issue, at a time when they could easily have claimed fear, uncertainty and exhaustion. We'd also like to thank our partners in that symposium, the Challenging Racism Project and the Diversity and Human Rights Research Centre at Western Sydney University and Academics for Refugees, and the presenters and panellists, who evoked thoughtful, passionate and innovative discussions: Alison Mountz, Behrouz Boochani, Omid Tofighian, Anne McNevin, Andrew Burridge, Maria Giannacopoulos, Claire Loughnan, Julie Macken, Claudia Tazreiter, Philomena Murray and Anthea Vogl. Many of these presenters have contributed chapters to this book, and we thank them for their commitment and continued support of this work. We'd also like to thank additional contributors who brought unique and powerful insights to the topic: Kate Coddington, Michelle Jasmin Dimasi, Julia Morris and Bosco Opi.

We felt strongly that this book should also include creative pieces from refugees and people seeking asylum. Barat Ali Batoor and Hani Abdile generously gave us their extraordinary written words that captured their experiences and hopes. Lived experience is vitally important to these discussions, but it also takes an incredible personal toll, and we appreciate the generosity with which Batoor and Hani gave their words and their time.

We'd like to thank the School of Social Sciences at Western Sydney University for their ongoing support of our work. This includes institutional, financial and collegial support. In particular, we would like to mention our colleagues and friends at the Challenging Racism Project, and Kate Huppatz and the School Research Committee.

Cymbeline Buhler and Lucy Fiske offered important editorial reviews and feedback which we thank them for. We'd also like to thank our publisher, Emerald Publishing, and, in particular, Iram Satti, Lauren Kammerdeiner, Daniel Ridge and Brindha Thirunavukkarasu. This was not an easy book to find a home for, and their enthusiasm and commitment to the ideas in this book were evident from day one.

Behrouz Boochani and Omid Tofighian were instrumental to the ideas generated in this book. Their critical thinking around Australia's offshore detention policies and the Australian government's treatment of refugees and people seeking asylum have brought important language and knowledge to this topic. We thank them both for their generosity and intellect and their support of this book. We are particularly fortunate to have Behrouz write the Foreword for this book.

And finally, we would like to acknowledge the many, many people seeking asylum who have suffered under the Australian government's detention policies. Those who have spoken out, those who have been silenced, those who lost their lives under this hardline, punitive and de-humanising policy and practice. Because they dared to hope for something better. Their courage and their humanity must be remembered and celebrated.

Introducing the Politics of Deterrence, Detainment and Dehumanisation

Linda Briskman and Rachel Sharples

Western Sydney University, Australia

The number of displaced people throughout the world steadily increases with the rise in global conflicts, internal oppression, and denial of human rights. Correspondingly, receiving nations are becoming increasingly immune to the contexts of suffering as borders tighten to prevent entry of those seeking sanctuary. Under the pretext of humanitarianism towards refugee flows, the reality is that bordering practices not only prevent people from seeking haven but also inflict cruelty and harm. It is within this global context that this collection of chapters emerges, with the focus on Australia as an unfortunate 'leader' in privileging border security over humanitarian considerations. Despite a robust advocacy movement, media exposure of denial of human rights, academic research and refugee voices, successive governments have not relented. There is a continuum of strategies, where government deterrence practices and the growth of the detention industry have sought to strip people seeking asylum of their humanity.

Overview

The chapters in this edited collection arise from an October 2020 global online symposium on the Politics of Seeking Asylum. The symposium and the collection were inspired by the Manus Prison Theory developed by Behrouz Boochani, who was detained on Manus Island in Papua New Guinea, and Omid Tofighian. With Manus Prison Theory Boochani and Tofighian articulated a philosophical undertaking with devastating real-world applicability.[1] It is an ideology that

[1]Boochani and Tofighian have written extensively on Manus Prison Theory and Australia's border-industrial complex, together and individually. Their work gives a far more thorough rendering of the theory than we do justice to here. For example, see *No Friend But the Mountains* (2020), *Freedom, Only Freedom* (2023), 'Manus Prison Theory' (*The Saturday Paper*, 2018), 'The Last Days in Manus Prison' (*Meanjin*, 2018), 'Behrouz Boochani and the Manus Prison Narratives' (*Continuum*, 2018) and Boochani's journalism in *The Guardian*, particularly around the closure of the Manus Regional Processing Centre in 2017.

Deter, Detain, Dehumanise: The Politics of Seeking Asylum, 1–8

Published under exclusive licence by Emerald Publishing Limited
doi:10.1108/978-1-83753-224-720241001

works to suppress the opportunity 'to know' about what was going on inside Australia's offshore detention facilities and the structural violence that fed it, but also to know the people who were being harmed. It describes a system, carceral by nature, intended to deter, detain and dehumanise through multiple intersecting dominations, submissions and oppressions; Boochani and Tofighian have used the term *kyriarchy* to help describe these functions.[1–2] Importantly, Manus Prison Theory positions this system as an extension of the Australian colonial-settler state, a stance that is examined by many of the authors in this collection as they seek to connect a contemporary system of politicisation and dehumanisation with foundational practices of violence and oppression.

There is a call to action that can also be found in Boochani's writing, something we have been mindful of in this edited collection. As Tofighian writes in his reflection at the end of *No Friend But the Mountains,* 'His [Behrouz'] intention has always been to hold a mirror up to the system, dismantle it, and produce a historical record to honour those who have been killed and everyone who is still suffering.'[2] In a small way, this book also intends to hold that mirror up, to expose the system that has underpinned Australia's border-industrial complex, and to dismantle it, in order to know and to practice a more humane approach to the right to seek asylum.

Most of the chapters in this edited collection are written by academics with a long-standing interest in refugee studies and with a critical approach to practices of deterrence, detention and dehumanisation. They each provide understanding and critical assessment of policies towards people seeking asylum as a series of systems, structures and operations that seek to normalise practices that betray human rights norms and a culture of morality. In this way, they point to a betrayal of what is expected in countries that purport to be liberal democracies and committed to the rule of law. In the Australian political context, the injustices meted out to innocent people who have been detained in the sites of Nauru, Manus and Christmas Island speak volumes to how far a government will go to deny entry into a country that claims to be advanced in supporting refugee settlement.

As we prepare this book for publication in November 2023, the Australian High Court has ruled that Australia's system of indefinite immigration detention is unlawful, overturning this long-standing practice. The ruling meant that those who have languished in indefinite detention, some for many, many years, without the government's preferred prospect of relocation to other countries, are mandated for release. The days that followed this ruling saw the media and both the ruling Labor Party and the opposition Liberal Party collude in portraying many of those released as hardened criminals. Stooping to populism, the Labor Government rushed measures through the federal parliament to further dehumanise and criminalise those they had been forced to allow into the community. These included surveillance through wearing ankle bracelets, curfews and strict reporting conditions.

The chapters in this book are not merely academic, but are presented in an accessible form of writing that engages with the politics that underpin the policies and practices of managing asylum. They are intended to pique the interest of

---

[2]Boochani, B. (2020). *No friend But the Mountains* (p. 373). Picador.

advocates and others in the community wishing to inform themselves about how the right to seek asylum has been politicised. Although the Australian context is centred, the volume touches upon how the politicisation of asylum has taken hold in other countries. This is an insidious and perhaps predictable outcome of Australia's offshore detention policy. Slogans, practices, policies, laws and government rhetoric get used for manipulation of public sentiment that has shaped Australia's response to people seeking asylum. They have now informed how countries like the United Kingdom, France, the United States, Greece, Italy and Poland are responding to their own refugee flows. The practice of offshoring and pushing responsibility for refugees away from Western states has also gained traction, with poorer source and host countries being drawn into the messy work that obfuscates human rights and accountability. Australia has developed the blueprint for the contemporary systems and operations of immigration detention. The increasingly evident risk we are now seeing is the way this is becoming an established norm in defiance of international obligations to protect human rights.

For a time, it was Western academic writing and the work of activists, not necessarily mutually exclusive, that dominated the asylum seeker space, particularly at the peak of immigration detention in Australia where the voices of those detained were directly silenced. Increasingly, film, art and other creative pieces have entered the public domain as well as academic writing stemming from the Global South. The power of lived experiences supplements the collection. When the writing does not draw on lived experiences, it largely draws on the author's attempts as allies to re-humanise those who have been dehumanised. The dehumanisation of people seeking asylum has become so normalised in the national narrative that it goes unquestioned. Some of the authors draw on refugee narratives to illustrate their arguments, while others who have borne witness to the suffering of those who seek asylum present their conversations and observations. With this in mind, we begin and end with autobiographical refugee stories. The conceptualisation of the book around themes of deterrence, detainment and dehumanisation, while not new, contains illustrative case study chapters that reveal current reflections into the structural framings of asylum. A feature of the interdisciplinarity of the book is that it values different styles of voice from social science disciplines to journalism to law and ethnographic observation. Furthermore, the positioning from a range of disciplines including sociology, geography, law, political science and social work reveals how different lenses converge to provide political analyses of oppressive structures and systems.

Despite the diversity proffered in the collection, consistent themes emerge. The first is a neo-colonial stance that goes hand in hand with the measures adopted by Western governments. Australia stands out as an example of a colonial grip. The trajectory from Indigenous dispossession, invasion and colonisation that set the scene for white Australia has never been totally erased, and the tropes of white Australia have not been eliminated. This has been reproduced in forms of neo-colonialism that result in exploitation in offshore detention where Australia has provided financial incentives to economically challenged countries to do its bidding.

The scourge of racism, a further emergent construct is a powerful force for exclusion. Corresponding with this is fear and panic about those 'not like us' who are seen as a threat not only to Australia's security but our way of life. Insidiously, racism is an enabler for deaths at sea. How the nation state rhetorically justifies lamenting deaths at sea while instituting harsh measures is a conundrum that the authors grapple with. Nation-states across the globe continue to invest vast sums of money into deterrence that repeats the cycle of drownings rather than providing safe means of passage as a solution. What is perceived as a crisis is in reality a continuum of displacement in an increasingly unequal and troubled world.

A further theme is the power of neoliberalism which has hold on how governments use capitalist ideology to justify the infliction of harms including outsourcing torture through lucrative contracts in the spheres of security, logistics and health. These align with Australia's ideological approach to people seeking asylum. Where there is an array of state and non-state actors, the capacity to pinpoint the sources of harm is obfuscated and commercial-in-confidence provisions disallow transparency and information flows. Within the neoliberal construct, money is no object even though the financial resources poured into deterrence, including detention, do not necessarily achieve the aims of the government or its citizens.

What is apparent from the contributions, each with their own specific research focus, is that although there are shifts in policies and practices and changes in government, the underlying ideologies that result in dehumanisation have been immovable. More broadly, states that portray themselves as bastions of liberal human rights, particularly in the West, are guilty of imposing inhuman practices that deny the humanity of the dehumanised and those rendered rightsless. The photos that accompany many of the narratives illustrate this intransigence.

The Collection

The chapters begin with a refugee story from accomplished writer and photographer, Barat Ali Batoor, whose own experience of seeking asylum inspired his writing. Through Batoor, we are taken into the precarious position of refugees in Indonesia where money changes hands to facilitate a journey to safety. Although filled with hope for a safe future, the fear of those in this limbo setting is palpable, balanced by reflections on what they have fled as an oppressed minority of Hazara in both Afghanistan and Pakistan. The roles of those known as 'people smugglers' in assisting passage to safety, precarious as this may be, is in sharp relief to government proclamations of those who move people as solely malevolent. What shines from Batoor's account is a determination to escape his persecution and to reclaim his future.

The following scene-setting chapter by Rachel Sharples and Linda Briskman provides a theoretical, historical and political overview of the racialisation of refugees in the Australian context. It does so through examining racialised bordering and how this intersects with criminalisation through a national security lens. An overarching policy through edicts of successive governments is the exclusion of refugees from the nation state by means of punitive measures that fly in the face of Australia's dominant portrayal to the world as a successful multicultural nation. This chapter also foreshadows chapters that follow by calling out the colonial mindset of the Australian state that originated with racialisation and brutality towards First Nations peoples, paving the way for excluding non-Anglo migrant groups that fell outside the national narrative of how the nation was constructed. This mindset enters the formal political sphere where politicians will do whatever it takes to buy votes for the purpose of retaining or gaining power, however illogical, untruthful or rights-denying. Within the neoliberal framework, the cost of outsourcing incarceration does not feature as a concern to the government that has also been able to convince other deterrence-minded countries to follow its duplicity through exporting policies that achieve human misery, a theme followed up in later chapters.

Julie Macken's chapter presents a provocation for readers by naming the practice of torturing people seeking asylum. Macken's long-standing experience as a journalist and political consultant, and her disillusionment that once the impact of policies and practices were widely known they would change, led her to examine the problem through an academic lens. Academia, alongside her position as a scholar and activist, allowed Macken to formulate a unique analytical lens. As with the chapter before and those which follow, a colonial mindset and the violence it involves is adopted to demonstrate a torturing nation. For Macken, a psychological framework is explanatory, and she crafts her analysis by drawing on the work of Sigmund Freud and Melanie Klein. The chapter's innovation is an endeavour to understand the workings of the nation state psychoanalytically. In this paradigm, the purposes of deterrence are both political and psychological and used to satisfy the unconscious needs of an uncritical electorate.

If deterrence is the goal that harsh policies and indifference to suffering are intended to produce, this is no clearer than in the chapter by Kate Coddington. Coddington exposes the problematic nature of public information campaigns aimed at preventing people from seeking asylum. Her contribution reveals how messaging directly feeds into deterrence measures by exposing and analysing messaging that pervades in Australia and internationally, with racist foundations not far from the surface. In Australia, the 'No Way' campaign was a clever rhetorical trick that aligned with the Stop the Boats refrain, signalling that those who attempt the journey to Australia by boat would not meet their goal of settling here. Messaging uses a variety of mediums, for example, posters and media, and is directed to diverse audiences, for example, would-be arrivals and the general public, but always with the aim of stopping people attempting boat journeys. Research, however, reveals that despite the unconscionable amount of funding poured into such campaigns, they have been largely unheeded by their primary audience. There is an important secondary audience, the Australian public, reinforcing the attempt to have electoral appeal for not only keeping borders 'safe' but craftily signalling fairness and humanitarianism. Although on a global scale, there are differing tactics used, they are commensurate with endeavours to deter boat arrivals and show that those who attempt such crossings will be punished.

The collection moves into the international sphere with the chapter by Bosco Opi. Opi writes from his own lived experience of the refugee camp and throws down the gauntlet to those who write about refugee policies and practices without such intimate knowledge. Writing from an Afrocentric lens, Opi's post-colonial critique takes us through the history of Kenya's encampments, preceding those of immigrants, that was not only introduced by its former coloniser Britain but has continued in the 'post-colonial' era. In theorising the camp as a site of neo-colonial power administered by Western organisations, his detailed description of conditions, surveillance and control illustrate what he calls borderphobia. The chapter places a critical lens over the role of the United Nations High Commissioner for Refugees, whose former brief as protector shielded it from culpability in keeping refugees encamped. The EU's complicity in extraterritorial policy is another exposé of power relations. As elsewhere, there is waning hospitality in Kenya that resonates with the impact of outsourcing and is relatable to camps funded by Australia, although at a different context and scale. Again, the ambiguity arises as to the divide in power between state interest and compassion, an unfortunate duality that masks violence in what Opi calls the colonial trap.

Claire Loughnan takes us into the realm of data. Who is counted and who is not. When it comes to counting those who have 'illegally' entered Australian territory, numbers dominate the political and media landscape, which arguably enables the Australian Government to amplify a fearful population. Here neoliberalism appears at play. Under the neoliberal project data and counting matters, but it is selective and protects complicit states by not counting lives lost at sea. This non-counting contrasts with the dehumanising classification and assignment of numbers to detained boat arrivals in immigration detention. The chapter also reveals the role of civil society in counting deaths through innovative and moving projects that refuse to allow the invisibility of those dying in attempts to seek asylum and restore some humanity to those who have lost their lives.

From there we move to the work of Australian writer Michelle Jasmin Dimasi whose extensive travels through troubled zones and experiences with death are portrayed in her aptly titled chapter 'Die Trying'. This chapter represents an ethnographic rather than an academic stance, by showing that when governments fail to act on death, activists can do so through the vigilance of observation and connection. From Afghanistan where she writes, Dimasi hears the howls of one man who lost a family member reminiscent of the grief of the aftermath of the boat crash on Christmas Island, signalling an emotion that was lacking from the official responses in Lampedusa and Christmas Island. Recounting her ethnography on both Lampedusa and Christmas Island she shows how ports of entry create perilous journeys for those who desperately seek freedom. A binding narrative is how residents and humanitarian groups have shown their humanity, often to no avail, as a contrast to what followed for survivors frequently detained and denied the safety and security that they rightfully sought.

In keeping with our undertaking to use creative forms of prose, law academic Anthea Vogl adds to the use of creativity by drawing on two exhibitions that distil events and stories highlighting the politics behind refugee representation. The first exhibition, *All We Can't See,* examines incident reports contained within the Nauru files, and juxtaposes these dispassionate reports with artists' illustrations of the incidents described. The *I Came By Boat* exhibition is somewhat contrasting in the telling of personal stories of those who have made Australia home and overcome the brutality to which they were subjected at the hands of the Australian Government. Ironically this exhibition is celebratory, in contradiction to the politics of representation in the national story, as shown in other chapters of this collection, which focus on denying entry and the hope of a liveable life. Vogl draws on Manus Prison Theory by seeing art and literature as a form of resistance to dominant tropes and the potential of a counter-genre. For those who have not witnessed the unbearable, there is a call to resist the normalisation of representations of refugees, and in particular the depiction of the dangerous border-crosser that so often accompanies government portrayals of people seeking asylum.

Adopting the concept of racialised assemblages, Julia Morris' chapter argues that outsourced asylum regimes exacerbate the subjection of both Indigenous and migrant communities to toxic practices and discourses. As an extractive process, such outsourcing creates a duality of discourses whereby people seeking asylum become destitute victims and the locals in 'host' countries are portrayed as brutish villains. Where solidarities have emerged between locals and those who are involuntarily housed in Nauru, this does not emerge in either government narratives or those of advocates, with a polarity that emphasises a divide rather than shared humanity. Again, the neoliberal approach of outsourcing dominates, with displacement taking place in sites for an extractive asylum industry. Nauru is a zone where encounters occur between disparate cultures but where shared exploitation is a binding phenomenon. Racialisation emerges here too as discourses of the 'inferior' dangerous refugee are transmuted in depictions of Nauruans as also racially inferior. The chapter details the consequences of the outsourced regime on both the local population and refugees, highlighting the discursive, intersectional and lived realities, and particularly the impact of representations on people seeking asylum. The toxicity of the industry is highlighted through interviews conducted by Morris during her fieldwork which also reveal the impact of racialisation. Morris' chapter serves as a warning to other countries intent on developing an extractive industry with political benefits for the sending country and economic benefits for the hosting country.

The last academic chapter combines looking back with possibilities for the future. As we near the end of the collection it is heartening to envision possibilities for an alternative future. Claudia Tazreiter critically examines what she denotes as carceral archipelagos not only present in Australia but now favoured by the United Kingdom and the European Union. Like many of the other authors in this book, her analysis traverses the themes of colonial practices and racialisation. In mounting her arguments, Tazreiter traces the historical moments that enabled such harsh practices to take hold, including the attacks in the United States on 11 September 2001 and the subsequent anti-Muslim sentiment, and in Australia the notorious *Tampa* affair where the roots of offshoring were propagated. As others in the book have also depicted, resistance is manifest through creative approaches, and particularly those with lived experiences who have made videos, films, written books and used social media. These give rise to an alternative politics to overthrow the rhetorical devices and 'ethical traps' by state actors to keep the population free from threats. The question remains for Tazreiter as to how to overcome the racial capitalist necropolitics whereby creativity and collaborative endeavours can assume to restore the diminishment of a human rights culture.

We finish close to where we began, with Hani Abdile's poem on the challenges of refugee flight to arrival. Complementing Batoor's refugee story, Abdile's work reinforces the importance of creative outlooks. Through her poetic narrative, we can see that despite the challenges that have been the focus of this collection, the journey's end can be filled with hope, an antidote to displacement and flight. The bonds formed by survivors of the journey, now in a new land, reveal their resilience and readiness to call the new land home. As Abdile poignantly writes, hope is the guiding star.

As editors, we make no apology for being passionate about naming the malice that has been imposed by Australia's offshore detention regime. How this has not only impacted those at the receiving end, but also how we construct the notion of a nation and its citizens. History has, and will, judge nations on how they treat minorities and the most vulnerable who reach their shores. Australia's legacy here will be a damning one.

We can end in despair, but we would rather offer some hope. Rehumanising the process of seeking asylum in well-resourced countries such as Australia has the potential to show the world that we can cease to normalise and legitimise unfounded border security fears and act with dignity and an ethic of care to people who are denied the safety and security to which Australians also aspire and largely experience. We can dismantle the system that has caused unprecedented harm and violence against one of the world's most vulnerable but also resilient populations. The chapters in this collection give an indication of where those efforts need to lie and as Behrouz Boochani states in his Foreword, collective collaboration and collective resistance are crucial.

A Desperate Search for Freedom

Barat Ali Batoor

Multi-Award-Winning Photographer and Filmmaker

In a humid atmosphere, beads of sweat traced paths down my neck as a group of 16 individuals including myself, were huddled around a crimson plastic mat. We were a mix of people in search of a safe place from Pakistan and Afghanistan, alongside four young Indonesian people smugglers. One of them, a neatly dressed Indonesian man sporting jeans and a designer T-shirt, offered biscuits and drinks from blue plastic pitchers. Squatting down, he meticulously counted the money. The Indonesian terms *Seribu*, *Dua ribu*, and *Tiga ribu* resonated as the men conversed in Bahasa, dividing the money into stacks of US$1,000. A nagging thought gnawed at me: 'I hope every cent is accounted for'. I couldn't help but wonder about the repercussions of getting caught and what lay ahead.

A surge of uncertainty hit me. The uneasy question lingered: 'What if our journey is exposed?'

As discussions continued in Bahasa, the money bundles were confirmed at US$16,000. This crucial sum would determine the next phase of our voyage from Sumatra to Jakarta. Glancing at my camera's time code (set to Pakistani time), the digits 11:30 p.m. blinked. We were weary from the 4½-hour motorboat trek from an unidentified point in Malaysia – a midpoint in our intricate journey.

Although our motorboat voyage across the muddy Malacca Strait had been relatively smooth, the irritation over stolen shoes and a T-shirt from my backpack, and the spill of a shampoo bottle inside, lingered. Nevertheless, my camera remained untouched, which provided a glimmer of solace.

Click after click, I documented the scene: the men orchestrating a symphony of thousands of dollars on the mat, a new angle, a friend wiping sweat off his neck. The transaction completed and the Indonesian men exchanged handshakes and urged us to rest. A few hours later, they would return to ferry us on a gruelling 21-hour van ride to an unidentified airport from where we were supposed to board a plane to fly to Jakarta.

Finding a corner of the room, I settled onto a mat, using my backpack as a makeshift pillow. I reflected on the journey so far, the hurdles we'd surmounted, and the uncertainties that lay ahead. Images of leaving Pakistan stirred within me, accompanied by thoughts of my car in Kabul and the deteriorating situation for Hazaras in Quetta. A potential encounter with Indonesian police loomed as

Deter, Detain, Dehumanise: The Politics of Seeking Asylum, 9–10

Published under exclusive licence by Emerald Publishing Limited
doi:10.1108/978-1-83753-224-720241002

I remembered crossing immigration checkpoints and securing passage through Thailand with a mix of employment and photography workshop letters.

An opportunity to attend the workshop in Chiang Mai had been the initial plan before things dramatically deteriorated for me in Afghanistan, but life's twists forced me to confront new challenges. Travelling from Thailand to Malaysia, I sought out another smuggler, someone who introduced himself as Nok. His offer to work with him was tempting, yet my objective remained to seek freedom, not financial gain. Journeying from Hat Yai to Su-ngai Kolok, passing checkpoints and an unexpected meeting with Sam, the Thai people smuggler who Nok introduced me to, I began to navigate this unfamiliar landscape.

Joining a growing group of asylum seekers in a makeshift house, I aimed my camera at my companions, capturing their faces, their stories and their shared uncertainty. Fate soon brought me face to face with Tono, a former acquaintance from Quetta, who had become intricately involved in the smuggling business. Our reunion held both surprise and melancholy, as I discovered the path his life had taken.

As our group grew and the moment of departure neared, the weight of our decision settled upon us. The news of Australia's new offshore policy created an unsettling backdrop, but my resolve to forge ahead remained unshaken. Going back simply meant death and being transferred to Nauru or Papua New Guinea seemed a better option at that time. Reflecting on the situation of people who lived on those islands, in detention centres, people who had lived with uncertain fates for 10 years or more seemed so cruel and tough to me. I am not sure how I would survive if I ended up in this situation of uncertainty, suffering under these inhumane immigration policies.

I spoke with my mother and told her about my decision. She cried over the phone and pleaded that I should take care of myself as this leg of the journey she heard was very dangerous. She had heard of a family where most of them drowned in the sea and only a young boy survived.

Navigating darkened roads, jungle paths and nerve-wracking encounters with authorities, our journey continued, driven by a shared determination to escape and reclaim our futures.

Chapter 1

'Create a Problem, Provide a Solution': The Racialisation and Politicisation of Seeking Asylum

Rachel Sharples and Linda Briskman

Western Sydney University, Australia

Abstract

When it comes to deterring and incarcerating people seeking asylum, there is a fusion between racialisation and politicisation. The bedrock is the colonisation of the nation now called Australia, where the dispossession of Indigenous peoples was a national project that later merged into the building of a state that lauded British heritage and the exclusion of migrants through the White Australia policy. This foundation of nationhood continues in a manner that challenges the myth of harmonious multiculturalism by determining who is deemed worthy and who is excluded. The centrepiece of racialised bordering is the immigration detention regime which is increasingly characterised by transporting people to offshore sites. This chapter argues through examples, how people seeking asylum have been racialised, dehumanised and criminalised, particularly through a national security lens.

Keywords: Borders; refugees; racism; immigration detention; politics; neoliberalism

Introduction

When John Howard uttered the now infamous edict 'We will decide who comes to this country and the circumstances in which they come' (PM Transcripts, 2001), he was establishing the direction of Australia's asylum seeker policy for the next

Deter, Detain, Dehumanise: The Politics of Seeking Asylum, 11–30

Published under exclusive licence by Emerald Publishing Limited
doi:10.1108/978-1-83753-224-720241003

two decades. Howard's utterance instigated a series of policies and practices that brought a more punitive and dictatorial approach to the right to seek asylum. At its core was the exclusion of the 'racialised' asylum seeker from the nation-state. Subsequent political leaders further entrenched this approach. In 2012, Labor Prime Minister Julia Gillard re-instated the 'Pacific Solution' by re-opening the offshore detention centres on Nauru and Manus Island, declaring the move necessary 'as too many lives have been lost at sea' (Medhora, 2015) – invoking the dual humanitarian concerns of compassion and fairness to mask what was otherwise a pragmatic and deceptive political decision to appease perceived voter discontent on the issue. In 2013, Labor leader Kevin Rudd announced that people seeking asylum who arrived by boat would 'have no chance of being settled in Australia as refugees' (SBS News, 2013) – setting a punitive exclusion of a certain type of mobility and person and denying a core principle of Australia's international obligations. In 2013, Liberal leader Tony Abbott used 'stopping the boats' as justification for militarised measures that pushed back asylum seekers from Australia's land and waters. This included towing boats carrying asylum seekers back into international waters and allegedly paying off people smugglers (Marks, 2015). Abbott stated he would do whatever was needed, 'by hook or by crook' (Hurst, 2015), to ensure he stopped the boats, the most obvious test yet of what Australians would tolerate in terms of tough action against people seeking asylum. In 2018, Liberal Prime Minister Malcolm Turnbull expressed a neoliberal commodification of asylum seeker bodies when he told US President Trump that '... in order to stop people smugglers, we had to deprive them of the product' (Jacobs, 2017). In 2022, Liberal Prime Minister Scott Morrison made perhaps the most blatant politicised comment on this issue, when on the morning of the 2022 Federal Election he announced the interception of a boat carrying asylum seekers from Sri Lanka and declared that if we wanted the boats stopped, 'You need to vote Liberal and Nationals today' (Karp, 2022).

Racialised Politics Past and Present

These are well-known incidents in the historical lore of Australia's contemporary approach to asylum seekers, but they are worth looking at anew in the way they illustrate the interplay between race and politics. Politicians have used all kinds of language to justify their treatment of asylum seekers – some of it presented as a manufactured humanitarian concern, a more blatant reference to capitalist neoliberal interests, or simply a desperate howl for political survival. Entrenched in these responses is the strong statement of exclusion that speaks to a politics of power and control over belonging to, and protection of, the nation-state. At the core of this politics is a restrictive and racialised immigration programme that excludes the 'racialised other' (in this case people seeking asylum), from the nation-state. In seemingly contradictory paradigms, people seeking asylum are caught between a protection gap and an enforcement gap (van Houte et al., 2023).

This is, of course, born out of what Ien Ang (2003) has called a fearful settler-colonial mindset, with historical links to the racialisation of the 'other' that is deeply embedded in Australia's national identity. Aboriginal and Torres Strait

Islander peoples can be seen as the original recipients of othering by white colonial forces, a practice that has also been utilised against 'unwanted' migrant groups – people from Muslim, Chinese and African backgrounds, for example. This could be seen as a provocative statement, for how can we prove this is an ideology and practice of racism and not one of 'national interest' and security, or economic and population management, or sovereignty, as is often purported. We do not claim that race is the only factor in asylum seeker policy and practice, though it is certainly *a* defining one, but rather that with a few exceptions, it has been largely under-examined in contemporary scholarship (see Huynh & Neyland, 2020), leading to poorer understandings of the drivers of seeking asylum and state responses to it.

Over the course of this chapter, we intend to discursively centralise race in the politics of seeking asylum. We will argue that Australia's asylum-seeker policy has racialised roots and that a key feature of the politicisation of asylum in the Australian context is the deliberate racialisation of those seeking refuge. There are two key lenses through which this can be argued. The first is an argument put forward by Michael Grewcock (2013) that the Australian state engages in systematic human rights abuses 'that inevitably rely upon and reformulate racist assumptions about "unwanted" migrants' (in this case asylum seekers) (p. 26). Using Grewcock's framing, we can argue that the indefinite detention of those seeking asylum and the ongoing psychological and physical harm associated with detention is a human rights abuse; and that the criminalisation of those seeking asylum through unsubstantiated claims of 'illegal entry' and other criminal activity is a systematic and institutionalised human rights abuse. We argue that racist assumptions underlie the construction of people seeking asylum as incompatible with the values that belonging to the Australian nation supposedly requires; and that bordering work that seeks to securitise Australia's national borders for the purpose of repelling 'unwanted' migrants is also based on always evolving racist assumptions about who has the right and privilege to cross borders and for what purpose.

The second and related argument is that the securitisation of Australia's borders is a means to apply the filter of 'race' to achieve political, economic and electoral ends (Smith, 2019), particularly around the movement of 'undesirable' migrants. The border then becomes the filter through which a sorting process can occur, a process that seeks to preserve the primacy of whiteness within the territorial bounds of the nation-state (Smith, 2019). This is largely facilitated by a process of sorting desirable from undesirable migrants, usually based on what economic contribution they can make to the Australian nation, and their capacity to assimilate into mainstream white Australia without posing a 'security threat'. This is evident in that the vast majority of people seeking asylum who travel to Australia by boat are from countries affected by geopolitical conflicts such as Afghanistan, Iraq, Iran and Myanmar, conflicts that Australia has played some part in, whether through military deployment, financial or development assistance or imposition of sanctions. Most asylum seekers are from the Global South, many are from minority groups in those countries and have experienced prolonged periods of persecution, displacement and denial of rights – meaning the intersectional factors of class, education and ethnicity also become filters through which Australia's racialised approach to immigration detention is practised (Phillips & Gottardo, 2023). Migration has always been a process of politics, determined by political and economic interests despite our attempts to frame it with a humanitarian lens.

These arguments around Australia's racialised and politicised approach to asylum must be understood through some key geopolitical framings; framings that are both particular to the Australian state and common to international responses. Australia is a settler-colonial institution predicated on the forced removal of land from First Nations peoples and the ongoing colonial project of asserting power through denial, oppression and the subjugation of black bodies. This colonial mindset permeates the practices of the modern nation-state – namely ownership over land, nation and identity – and a punitive response to those who threaten the white parameters of this construct. For First Nations peoples, this mindset constantly emerges in differing manifestations, the most recent in 2023 being the opposition to constitutional reform and a Voice to Parliament, signifying a form of internal bordering in the nation-building identity blueprint.

Another key geopolitical framing is that Australia's borders are increasingly governed through a securitisation framework. Here, we see a heightened emphasis on border enforcement measures to protect Australia's sovereignty and national security from unwanted migrants. The recent release of the 2001 Cabinet Papers revealed how securitisation took hold in political discourse and public policy following two events that reset the political global landscape in 2001 – Tampa and September 11 (Wallace, 2022). Racialised assumptions dominated the commentary around both these events, the former framed as 'not the type' of person Australia wanted and the latter linking Muslims with terrorism, creating a perceived security threat to Australian lives and therefore also not the kind of person Australian wanted. It is now almost universally acknowledged that these two events brought a heightened security response to securing Australia's borders and repelling the unwanted. Aileen Moreton-Robinson (2015) links this securitisation mindset with the enforcement of patriarchal white sovereignty: 'These two events served to position the Muslim as the invading "other", thus enabling Howard to demarcate, secure, and protect the territorial integrity of patriarchal white sovereignty within Australian and international law' (p. 148).

Finally, certain practices of the neoliberal state have enabled the dominance of Australia's offshore detention policy. In this chapter, we look at neoliberalism both as an ideology and as a practice, the former in its prioritisation of profit and capital accumulation over the rights of individuals who supposedly 'do not add value' to the system of neoliberalism and the latter as it involves the privatisation of immigration detention and the outsourcing of government services and responsibilities and the co-option of those who deliver the services such as health workers. Even more unscrupulous is the uptake by hotel proprietors of their facilities for detention purposes (Jerrems et al., 2023), a practice that escalated during COVID-19 as a means to offset tourism losses. We further argue that at the juncture of neoliberal ideology and practice sits the racialised refugee; a construct of the twinned manufactured crises of race and immigration (Stratton, 2009, p. 685).

That 'manufactured crisis', as Stratton has so eloquently put it, serves the purpose of optimising the neoliberal market at the expense of any moral concerns that might be attached to the plight of refugees and asylum seekers.

The settler-colonial framework is foundational to the development of the nation-state and the assumption of patriarchal white sovereignty. It set in motion repeated anxieties around dispossession which rise to the surface when 'the nation as a white possession is perceived to be under threat' (Moreton-Robinson, 2015, p. 138) – and here we can insert the perceived threats of irregular migration or multiculturalism or the other, to name a few. The neoliberal and securitisation frameworks are of course inter-connected, they are mutually beneficial in their operationalisation as an ordering mechanism, but both are also predicated on a system of belonging that centres wealth (or capitalism), whiteness and privilege. Over the remainder of this chapter, we look at some of the key characteristics of how seeking asylum has been politicised in the Australian context and the racialised practices that underpin this.

Buying Votes

In Australia, we're led to believe that detaining people seeking asylum is an electoral vote winner, a political green card. Asylum seekers have dominated a number of Australian federal elections over the last two decades, particularly positioned through a securitisation lens of posing a risk and threat. While public sentiment has certainly aligned with the Australian Government's harsher border policies to stop people seeking asylum (Sharples et al., 2023), it is less clear whether a political party's position on asylum seekers is indeed a vote winner. Can it change or influence peoples' voting behaviours?

Politicians certainly act as if it does. On the morning of the 2022 Federal Election, Prime Minister Scott Morrison emerged from casting his vote to announce that his government had intercepted a boat carrying people seeking asylum from Sri Lanka. In a blatant, highly politicised move, he said: 'I can simply say this. I have been here to stop this boat, but in order for me to be there to stop those that may come from here, you need to vote Liberal and Nationals today' (Karp, 2022). The statement was extraordinary, in that Morrison went against his own government's edict not to comment on 'on-water matters' to desperately appeal to the Australian public, using asylum seekers as a political wedge to sway voter intent. Shortly after his announcement, the Liberal Party sent out robo-text messages to voters, particularly in marginal seats. The text read: 'BREAKING: Australian Border Force has intercepted an illegal boat trying to reach Australia. Keep our border secure by voting Liberal today. https://vote.liberal.org.au' (Worthington & Bogle, 2022).

Morrison's intervention, while blatant, is not unusual. Politicians have often stood before the Australian public to profess the dangers of allowing people seeking asylum to arrive on our shore. These statements are often cached as humanitarian concerns (e.g. we need to save lives lost at sea) or political necessity (only we can provide tough border policies) or a sovereign right (we have the right to decide who enters our country) or as a threat to our national security (this will allow terrorists in) or bravado posturing (we're not going to be intimidated) or simply racism (we do not want people like that). Rarely are they empathetic to the plight of refugees and asylum seekers, or cognisant of their humanitarian obligations.

In the aftermath of many of these incidents, the claims made by the politicians were found to be largely manufactured and spoken to serve a political purpose. For example, asylum seekers had not thrown their children overboard in order to secure rescue and passage to the Australian mainland as was claimed by Howard Government ministers in the lead-up to the 2001 election (Briskman et al., 2008; Marr & Wilkinson, 2003) and the Government's announcement about a boat carrying asylum seekers from Sri Lanka on the day of the 2022 election was under investigation for possible breaches of national security (Noble, 2022). But one could argue that the damage was already done, the political objective of 'othering' asylum seekers in order to show a strong border security position had been achieved.

It would be easy to think these are the manoeuvrings of political elections, a tried and tested successful formula to sway public opinion. But this would be superfluous as politicians and the media are developing the groundwork between elections to ensure the story of asylum seekers retains currency. Valentino et al. (2002) have called this 'priming' an issue – ideas and considerations that are activated recently and often – in order to make some information more accessible in the memory than others. In other words, if we are told often enough that people seeking asylum are bad and that we need to protect ourselves from them, then we will automatically activate that information when needed, like at an election. The question becomes, to what purpose?

As we have discussed elsewhere (Sharples et al., 2023), research by Kathleen Blair on the 2013 Federal Election found that while people seeking asylum has been used as a political wedge across a number of elections, on its own, it was unlikely to change partisan alignment, and for non-partisan voters, the issue wasn't of concern and therefore unlikely to influence their vote. Blair (2018) did find some variation across partisan political affiliation with Liberal/National voters expressing the most negative attitudes towards asylum seekers and rating the issues of refugees and asylum seekers as very important when making their voting choices. This suggests some currency to the argument that the Liberal Party used the issue to shore up its conservative base and that priming the issue was especially effective with this base. However, voters are more likely to vote based on economic concerns – education, health, workplace and employment, and public infrastructure, than on a single-issue topic like asylum seekers.

While there is certainly volatility in the community when it comes to attitudes towards those seeking asylum and their willingness to support political and policy initiatives, Blair's research suggests it is worthy to question the salience of political party positions on asylum seekers, voting behaviours and electoral campaigns. If government policy on asylum seekers has, at best, an unstable influence on voting behaviours then it places a question mark around its usefulness as a tool for re-election. It is worth asking then what some of the other reasons behind the politicisation of this issue could be. One way may be to look at the problem through the key tenet of this chapter: that seeking asylum has become politicised through a mechanism of racialising those who seek it. In other words, Australia's excessive border securitisation operation, a now normalised political and policy tool, is a means for a racialised approach to immigration. This is not a new idea. Racialised practices of determining who can and cannot enter Australia have long underpinned our immigration programmes, but the scale of systemic abuse and public acquiescence seems to be different now.

Asylum seekers and refugees threaten the global order of nation-states and the race-based order of belonging. They defy the sacredness of territorial boundaries through their irregular movement across national borders. States fear this mobility, especially when they do not have control over it. For nation-states like Australia, built on the back of the ultimate territorial acquisition of another's land, this triggers a survival response. The manufactured crisis around people seeking asylum taps into Australians' fears and anxieties around race and immigration (Stratton, 2009, p. 679). The source of these fears and moral panics is foundational to the Australian state. First, there is the settler-colonial experience of eradicating Indigenous peoples deemed to be a threat. This was particularly enacted in resistance to the granting of Aboriginal land rights with campaigns to convince farmers and pastoralists that they would lose their property rights. As McMaster (2001) has argued: 'Indigenous peoples were colonised and subjugated until they were not perceived as a threat to the white settlers' (p. 128) – setting in place the state's preferred response to those deemed a threat. Second, the fledgling Australian state, defenceless and insecure, which needed to be protected both from invasion (typically billed as Asians from the North and more recently attached to the cultural change that asylum seekers and refugees bring) and the associated threat to the established order of the nation-state that is caught up in their irregular movement. As Mansouri (2023) states, 'treatment of asylum seekers in contemporary Australia is neither divorced from its historical context nor detached from an increasingly uncertain international environment' (p. 61).

Jon Stratton (2009) puts it this way:

> These people [asylum seekers] are placed outside the state, an empty category containing the anxieties of those who live their everyday lives in the neoliberal order, provoking the dread that they might cross the border and bring anarchy, the state of nature, out there, in here, into, in this case, the Australian nation-state. (p. 690)

Sometimes, the Australian Government's responses have racial motivations, often attached to contemporary geopolitical aberrations to which Australia has been a party. In such cases, the anarchy 'out there', could be seen as the creation of, or at the very least, sustained by, political and military decisions made 'in here'. For example, in 2010, the two largest source countries of asylum claims in Australia were Sri Lanka and Afghanistan. The government announced it would stop processing claims from Sri Lankan nationals for three months and Afghan nationals for six months as a way to deter further arrivals from these countries. Arrivals, at least in the case of Afghanistan, are largely driven by the military actions of key Western nations, including Australia. This plainly racialised response was also evident in 2022 when Australia announced increased humanitarian places for Ukrainians fleeing Russian military attacks, as well as a commitment to expediting Ukrainian refugee processing claims (Department of Foreign Affairs and Trade, 2022) and the allocation of three-year Temporary Humanitarian Concern visas to Ukrainians (Refugee Council of Australia, 2022). At the same time, Afghans were fleeing in droves due to the Taliban takeover of their country. An increase in the refugee intake was initially denied and financial support was directed towards supporting refugees to stay in host countries. Finally, in the 2022–2023 Federal Budget the government increased its humanitarian places for Afghans to 16,500 over four years 'in recognition of our sustained commitment following two decades of operations in Afghanistan' (RCOA, 2022). This delayed and frankly under-resourced response has led many to criticise Australia's double standards and racialised priorities when it comes to responding to conflicts and supporting refugees (see Asylum Seeker Resource Centre, 2021; RCOA, 2022).

At the very least we should consider these arguments as offering some explanation towards why asylum seekers have remained a dominant thread woven through Australian politics over the last two decades. While politicians have used these anxieties to shape election campaigns, this is not really about winning elections, though it is certainly a useful tool for mobilising certain cohorts, it is about establishing a rules-based white national order, and this has a racialised underpinning to it.

Dehumanising Asylum Through Racialisation: Twinning Human Rights Abuses

Behrouz Boochani speaks from lived experience as a racialised asylum seeker. For Boochani (2023), the legacy of White Australia remains:

> [...] the xenophobic impact of the White Australia policy had a significant impact on the trajectory of my life and choked the lives of thousands of asylum seekers and migrants who were held by Australia in offshore detention centers in its former colony Papua New Guinea and on the island of Nauru, a former protectorate. (p. 238)

If we see the legacy of the White Australia policy as embedding the structures for racialisation, then criminalising asylum predictably follows with minimal challenge outside the coterie of human rights activists. Unquestioned is the assumption that Australia is a harmonious multicultural nation with a proud history of protecting human rights. Discourses, policies and practices expose the cunning of Australia in the dehumanisation that allows criminalisation of asylum based on racialised constructs, revealing collusion between government and powerful media outlets that convinces the community writ large that asylum seekers are an enemy to be defeated. Deprivation of liberty without cause is an insidious sanction for those who have committed no crime and is directed at non-citizens; it is a racialised measure that would not be tolerated in the treatment of citizens (Briskman et al., 2008). The racialisation of offshore detention has a covert colonial layer as in the case of Nauru, where offshoring of people seeking asylum parallels with the island's colonial industry of phosphate extraction (Morris, 2023), and where denuding of the environment and subsequent economic collapse provided incentive for an economically desperate nation to house detention camps. Offshore detention continued to reinforce the lack of visibility associated with mainland detention, an out-of-site out-of-mind ideology which was somewhat disrupted through such incidents as the Woomera detention breakout in 2002 and the Christmas Island boat crash in 2010 which were highly publicised in the media. Twyford-Moore (2023) argues that by moving acts of barbarism offshore 'the iconography of degradation that rose from our border policies could not be immediately associated with the Australian landscape, and that access to these images could be more easily obstructed by the state' (p. 20).

Yet, it is more than that. Practices of containment have been a constant presence within Australia and the cumulation of the past suggests an interface with the present. The colonial project was premised on removal from the mainstream and isolation of Indigenous peoples on missions, reserves and in children's homes. Overt criminalisation practices exist today with excessive policing and subsequent imprisonment of First Nations people in juvenile (in)justice settings and adult prisons.

As noted above, dehumanisation is not only a political ideology, but also a practice that occurs most furtively through dividing people seeking asylum into two categories – the 'good' and the 'bad', the perilous and the grateful. The narrative argues that the good refugee languishes for many years in sub-standard camps abroad, patiently waiting for an invitation to Australia where they are chosen for their 'character' and contribution, unstated but underpinned by discredited notions of assimilation. In exercising control, a dominant Australian narrative is that its meagre quota contributes to the ever-increasing number of displaced people throughout the world that becomes dislodged by those seeking asylum by 'border invasion'. Building on Australia's multicultural story, the welcome mat is laid out for the invited refugee, permanent residence is granted, services are provided and good news stories of settlement are portrayed in the media.

By way of contrast, bad refugees arrive without invitation, usually by boat, and are pejoratively labelled as queue jumpers, bogus refugees and economic migrants. One Government Minister, Peter Reith, once infamously stated that boats could be a pipeline for terrorists (Khan, 2003). For boat arrivals, once racialisation kicks in, successive governments have been able to illegalise innocents by transporting people to detention sites within and outside Australia, where they are stripped of rights, including in many cases the right to life, for example, preventable deaths occurring in offshore immigration detention facilities, including suicide. Media colludes in dehumanisation discourses that garner headlines that 'confirm' criminalisation such as reporting on riots or fires in detention, even though protest is one of the few forms of resistance open to illegalised asylum seekers in order to assert their rights to be treated as human (Fiske, 2016). In his graphic novel *Still Alive*, Safdar Ahmed (2021), a visitor to Villawood Immigration Detention Centre in Sydney, depicts an anguished man who states: 'And I too sometimes feel judged and isolated by the bulk of humanity' (p. 19). In erasing their humanness, those detained are depicted as criminals, and their behaviour is attributed to their backgrounds with 'middle-eastern Muslim' at the top of the list through an unfounded association with terrorism. With Australia introducing an astonishing array of rushed anti-terrorism legislation (Williams, 2011) since the attacks in the USA in 2001; the conflation of asylum-seeking and terrorism is enabled through the national security refrain.

It is not only adults who are positioned as a threat. The cruelty inflicted on children in closed spaces as collective punishment and criminalisation amounts to what two social workers describe as organised and ritualised abuse (Goddard & Briskman, 2004), with transportation to Nauru (Briskman & Goddard, 2014) amounting to trafficking in children, consistent with the UN definition. Selective and uncommon compassion masks the cruelty, serves to placate high-profile advocates and reaps community and media support through feel-good stories. To appear sympathetic and compassionate the designation of illegality transmutes into a discourse of the benevolent state. Rather than being rights-based, a rescue/saviour mentality enters the national story. A high-profile example took place in 2022, when the newly elected Labor government permitted a Sri Lankan family of four – Nades Murugappan and Priya Nadesalingam and their two Australian-born daughters – to return to their home in Biloela in Queensland. The family had been seized from their home in 2018 and sent to immigration detention where they awaited deportation, a move that was thwarted at the last minute through legal processes (The Guardian, 2022). Although their return to the community as permanent residents is cause for celebration, as is the advocacy of the Biloela community who helped make this happen, the untold story is about those who still remain in a precarious state and how border security remains the dominant paradigm. Selective compassion is little consolation to the children whose situations in detention in Nauru became known in 2016 following leaked reports that were published by *The Guardian*. Documented were more than 1,000 incidents pertaining to children that revealed trauma and despair (Cassidy & Cordell, 2023). Even though there are few children now in closed detention, travesties of justice still remain. Through the Stop the Boats policies, asylum seekers who were transiting through Indonesia, in what we argue is another form of 'offshoring' are now immobilised there awaiting the slow process of re-settlement in other countries. These include families with children who are living a life in limbo, with impediments to rights and freedom of movement. In another example, the Australian outpost of Christmas Island, a devastating boat crash in 2010 took the lives of 50 women, men and children who were seeking the safety of asylum. Rather than the tragedy being a wake-up call to re-imagine Australia's border protection regime, the government narrative twisted into the need to save lives at sea, that was used to justify the re-opening of offshore detention sites. Once again, children were punished and traumatised in the quest for border securitisation and control.

The polarity, however, is slippery and there have been instances where 'good refugees' are also subjected to racialisation through political words and deeds. Belonging is contingent on the behaviour of the grouping with criminalisation never far from the surface. In 2018, Home Affairs Minister Peter Dutton pronounced that Victorians were scared to go out to restaurants because of African gang violence. More recently, during COVID-19 restrictions, migrant and refugee communities were targeted as a threat to the wellbeing of the state of Victoria through excessive and harmful lockdowns with criminality communicated by an active police presence at their social housing apartments (Robinson et al., 2021) and a significant police presence in Western Sydney that was not experienced in affluent suburbs. These examples further illustrate how governments use racialised constructs to imply hypothetical criminality, and to warn migrants and particularly refugees of their precarity of place in the suburbs of Australia. To break this ongoing cycle of abuse, it is necessary to look back in time to inform the present. This becomes increasingly difficult with the normalisation of neoliberalism in most domains of political endeavour.

Neoliberalism, Privatisation and Contracting: Financial Profiteering and Moral Costs

An advocate of open borders, Philippe Legrain (2006) writes of the benefits of migration for both the migrants and the receiving country. Legrain laments that the world is divided between those who are at liberty to move and others who are bound to one place. Instead of benefitting the economy through opportunities for those who wish to come, Australia uses the neoliberal turn to 'invest' in deterrence and confinement which not only benefits its ideological stance but fortifies the propaganda war on border securitisation. Grewcock (2013) calls for a rejection of border securitisation that focusses on 'politically manufactured imperatives of deterrence' (p. 12) and instead reminds us of the legitimacy of the refugee movement, and powerfully calls out the deviance of states that attempt to prevent this. One could argue that this deviance extends to the confinement of asylum seekers in offshore detention facilities, alleged in one legal class action as crimes against humanity (Davidson, 2018).

Detention is astronomically expensive, costing almost AUD400,000 per person per year compared to less than AUD50,000 for housing a person in the community (Global Detention Project, 2022). With irregular migrants denied rights that would be expected within the jurisdiction of the state (Carens, 2013), neoliberalism that devolved a multitude of activities to the private sector has not only infiltrated carceral environments but has done so in a way that causes suffering to the incarcerated and profit for the beneficiaries. Transparency diminishes, with secrecy a way of maintaining hold. Neoliberal ideology combines withholding information and presenting disinformation, enabling offshore detention to open and close with ease, beginning in 2001, closing in 2007 and re-opening in 2012, with the most recent opportunistically propagandised as saving lives at sea.

Cameron Smith (2019) draws on the concept of authoritarian neoliberalism to explain the securitisation and militarisation of the Australian border. As he notes:

> Having pursued the policy of mandatory detention of all undocumented migrants since 1992, the Australian government has also increasingly sought to outsource, privatize and offshore the construction and operation of its immigration detention facilities, while simultaneously engaging in increasingly authoritarian interventions via the militarization of border control. (Smith, 2019, p. 192)

Neoliberalism has also allowed private–public partnerships to flourish, bringing together what Tanya Golash-Boza (2009) has described as a confluence of public and private sector interests 'in criminalising undocumented workers and in immigration law enforcement', and the promotion of 'anti-illegal' rhetoric (p. 283). This web of privatisation has many guises. The most well-known are the hefty contracts that have been awarded to companies with international prison links, including Australian Correctional Management, Serco and in offshore detention to Transfield (later Broadspectrum) and now controversially on Nauru to the Management and Training Corporation (MTC). This contract is sealed despite the fact that MTC has been subject to scandals in the USA in its operation of private prisons (Doherty & Knaus, 2023). In 2023, allegations arose about foreign bribery related to offshore contractual arrangements with Radiance International (Karp, 2023), compounding the lack of transparency and ethical governance processes that have beset the privatisation of immigration detention from the outset.

Implementing marketisation approaches through neoliberalism, also means that 'benefit' to society rather than responsibility to humanity fosters acceptance. In a nine-country study, Graf et al. (2023) found that respondents were more satisfied if migrants rather than asylum seekers or refugees were their neighbours, friends or partners, with migrants perceived to bring more benefits to their societies. Racialisation becomes neutralised as another example of selective compassion and welcome, always conditional.

Despite the costs of immigration detention, the Australian Government has not budged. The latest contractual arrangement in Nauru is estimated to cost AUD485 million, even though there are few people held at the Regional Processing Centre at the time of writing. Compounding the shame of the entrenchment of gain for private providers, Australia refused to include offshore detention as a site for inspection under the Optional Protocol to the Convention Against Torture and Other Cruel, Inhuman or Degrading Treatment or Punishment. Australia argued that offshoring is outside its jurisdiction, despite paying for the facilities (Sadler, 2023). Such a view compounds the colonial project where, in relation to Nauru, Australia has 'suborned a poverty-stricken neighbour into doing whatever suits Australian policy' (Burnside, 2007, p. 61) with its underpinning of a racialised approach in exerting economic influence.

Although it is the major private providers that have been most criticised, the hard-to-track web of detention privatisation extends to health and the not-for-profit non-governmental organisation sector. Lucrative contracts for health service delivery by International Health and Medical Services have received significant criticism from human rights bodies, advocates and practitioners (e.g. Public Interest Advocacy Centre, 2018), with revelations of human rights abuses of significant magnitude reaching the public domain. This privatisation model is also a convenient means for the state to deny responsibility for what occurs in detention centres, or at the very least position asylum seekers as not deserving of, or having the right to, state protection. This creates the perfect storm in which human rights abuses can occur without sufficient pathways for legal redress or accountability for the perpetrators. Those 'othered' outside the borders of the state are therefore denied the rights and entitlements of those allowed within the borders.

It is difficult not to see this as a deliberate attempt by the state to apply treatment that degrades and dehumanises, and which supports the neoliberal border securitisation aims of deterrence and confinement. The opaque privatisation network has a moral dimension in its contribution to profiteering from the anguish of the dehumanised.

Not everyone uncritically accepts the privatisation thrust including the activist asylum seeker movement that speaks out about human rights abuses. Medical practitioners have been particularly vocal in pointing out the ethical dilemma of providing care, while working in environments that can amount to condoning torture (Isaacs, 2016) and contributing to harm despite good intentions (Winters et al., 2022), with the question of whether clinicians should boycott immigration sites frequently raised (Essex, 2019).

Social workers too are faced with ethical dilemmas to the degree that they might be seen as collaborators (Maylea & Hirsch, 2018), particularly those who worked offshore for The Salvation Army and Save the Children, both of which received pecuniary advantage and engaged in trickery to present their roles as ethical. The reality for those who worked for the organisations is that when witnessing human rights abuses they were denied the right to speak out and were barred from taking their concerns to the public domain. Their constraining is antithetical to the social work ethical imperatives which compel bringing attention to injustices.

The question remains as to how these arrangements have been able to take hold. Barnes (2022) argues that 'moral engagement' from the pain and suffering of those detained is justified through the humanitarian idea of saving lives at sea. The boat crash on Christmas Island that was witnessed through television screens that portrayed the horrendous final moments of 50 women, men and children about to lose their lives was convenient for the government to entrench offshore detention and torture and became known as the drownings, argument (Rothfield, 2014). There is a moral deficit at play here. In manufacturing a crisis – leaky boats resulting in lives lost at sea – the state provides an acceptable moral response to a political problem – the need to protect our borders. However, the moral concern is manufactured to mask the real intent, which is to integrate and normalise the neoliberal and racialised order. This is captured by Stratton (2009) when he states, '… that is the state whose purpose is to optimise the capitalist marker at the expense of moral criteria, and legal processes, in favour of profit and capital accumulation' (p. 685).

Exporting Trauma

In October 2015, former Prime Minister Tony Abbott delivered the second annual Margaret Thatcher Lecture.[1] He delivered this speech at the heart of British imperialism, the medieval Guildhall in London. He championed conservative politics and Thatcher's contributions to shaping the global order. Importantly, his key

---

[1]The full text of the speech can be found here: https://www.smh.com.au/politics/federal/transcript-tony-abbotts-controversial-speech-at-the-margaret-thatcher-lecture-20151028-gkkg6p.html.

message was on Australia's border security policies. If Thatcher were here, he said, she would be:

> [...] managing the nation changing, culture-shifting population transfers now impacting on Europe; winning the fight in Syria and Iraq which is helping to drive them; and asserting Western civilisation against the challenge of militant Islam. (Abbott, 2015)

Abbott thus drew on some classic tropes of racialised and nationalist right-wing rhetoric. He equated migration, and in particular the movement of refugees and asylum seekers, with negative impacts on nation and culture. He called the flows of asylum seekers and refugees into Europe 'a tide of humanity' that would quite possibly change it forever, and not in a good way. He noted the need to reassert the normative dominance of Western civilisation (meaning white, Christian, wealthy, democratic) against supposed threats. He targeted a single socio-cultural grouping, Muslims, and their faith, Islam, as the cause of this threat.

Abbott went on to highlight the success of Australia's border policies against those seeking asylum.

> The Australian experience proves that the only way to dissuade people seeking to come from afar is not to let them in. Working with other countries and with international agencies is important but the only way to stop people trying to gain entry is firmly and unambiguously to deny it – out of the moral duty to protect one's own people and to stamp out people smuggling. (Abbott, 2015)

Calling on European countries to follow Australia's lead in securing their borders against unwanted immigration, Abbot ended with a battle cry: 'But unlike you, we have at least solved one of the wicked problems now afflicting Europe: we have secured our own borders'. These might be dismissed as the musings of a recently ousted Prime Minister keen to cement his legacy, but it wasn't long before the UK and parts of Europe began implementing significant parts of Australia's border policies. In 2023, the UK and French governments signed a US576-million deal to combat irregular immigration across the English Channel. The deal included building a new detention centre and the deployment of French security agents to detect and stop attempted crossings (BBC, 2023). In 2022, the UK and Rwandan governments signed a memorandum of understanding to establish an asylum transfer scheme. Under the scheme, some people applying for asylum in the UK would be transported to Rwanda to have their claims processed there (Johnson, 2022) –an agreement that has been challenged in the courts, but regardless is a tactic taken straight from the Australian guidebook of offshoring asylum claims. In 2023, the UK Government introduced the Illegal Migration Bill to parliament. The rhetoric around the Bill was one of 'stopping the boats', 'ending illegal entry', 'stopping people smugglers from profiting from human misery' and 'taking back control of our borders' – the slogans that are a familiar refrain of Australia's border policies over the last two decades. Meanwhile,

Poland is constructing a Euro350-million wall along the border with Belarus to stop asylum seekers and refugees from entering the EU. Refugees and asylum seekers have become political pawns, pushed back and forth across the border by both Polish and Belarusian forces, both sides accused of human rights violations (Human Rights Watch, 2022). Greek and Italian authorities have reportedly been complicit in boat pushbacks, with reports asylum seekers have been cast adrift in inflatable dinghies and that both countries have forcibly returned boats to other countries' waters (see Giuffrida, 2023; Smith, 2023). These constitute key tactics of Australia's 'stop the boats' campaign and Operation Sovereign Borders policy.

To say that Australia wrote the rule book for human misery that is now being applied globally is not an overstatement. Others have become entangled in this political game. There was the speculative swap deal with New Zealand, at various points offering hope that asylum seekers might finally be removed from Manus and Nauru and re-settled in New Zealand, and then despair when the Australian Government on multiple occasions rejected New Zealand's offer. And then there was the US swap deal, first negotiated with President Obama and then left to be signed off by the new administration of President Trump, who famously called it 'the worst deal ever'. This was an agreement for the USA to take 1,250 asylum seekers residing on Manus and Nauru in exchange for Australia re-settling refugees from Central America. Turnbull's explanation of why Australia would 'not let in' people seeking asylum who arrived by boat was met with one of the few Trump truisms: 'You are worse than I am' (Jacobs, 2017).

A key doctrine of these swap deals is to move the 'problem' of asylum seekers offshore and as far from the Australian mainland as possible. By extension of that argument, that means shifting it to be someone else's problem or responsibility. Typically, this has involved Australia exploiting its regional and postcolonial relationships. It is no coincidence that Australia has, or has attempted, to make offshoring agreements with Timor-Leste, Malaysia, Cambodia, Papua New Guinea and Nauru. These agreements are often positioned as 'regional resettlement' but they clearly rely on Australia's financial power in the region; they are countries that depend on Australia's aid and development funding.

This expansion, or externalisation of the Australian border is an intended strategy. Josh Watkins (2017) has called this a 'layering' of borders that 'transforms domestic and foreign places in ways designed to immobilise asylum seekers at risk of irregularly travelling to Australia by boat' (p. 959). This process of externalisation is not just about offshoring the arriving asylum seeker cohort; Australia has pushed responsibility for refugees and asylum seekers back on countries of origin, countries of first asylum and poor countries it can buy off. Trauma is exported through every step of the process. It is embodied in the state of precarity and uncertainty this process of repelling reinforces. Asylum seekers are stuck in legal and administrative limbo. They experience long delays in their asylum claims. They are at greater risk of harmful and exploitative treatment. They have no recourse, because it is not always clear who they would seek recourse from. This state of exception and uncertainty, this control over time, is what Ruben Anderson (2014) has called a 'management technique' that is fully part of the state; 'an active usurpation of time for the purposes of migration control' (p. 796).

It is an ideology and a practice that now has global currency. Not only has Australia implemented practices that created or further embedded immense trauma in people seeking asylum, but they are also now exporting that praxis of trauma to other countries, pronouncing it as a success story, the only way to succeed in stopping the entry of the 'unwanted migrant', the 'racialised other'. This global uptake, worryingly on the increase, gives legitimacy to Australia's approach to securing its borders against refugees and asylum seekers. For years, Australia undertook this work alone and in the face of international outrage from human rights bodies and activists. But now they have secured buy-in from some of the world's biggest players.

It's the ultimate political manoeuvre. Create a problem. Provide a solution. Convince others to follow suit. Normalise the practice.

Conclusion

Our narrative decries the convergence of immigration, national identity, colonial practices, sovereignty and control over borders. The politicisation of this issue has given it legs and racialisation has consumed the Australian psyche to such an extent that it is vehemently denied and unwittingly accepted. It has been allowed to fester in the privatised offshore detention regime where successive Australian governments have removed all forms of checks and balances in order to ensure they can treat people seeking asylum with minimal oversight. It has been allowed to fester in the government's border securitisation apparatus that works to determine desirable migrants through a racialised lens of political, economic and electoral value. It festers in the political/policy and media rhetoric on this issue and in public attitudes that have tended to be hostile, punitive and exclusionary towards asylum seekers.

The tragedy of the Australian national drive for unity is a fiction of the necessity of pushing our borders outwards when it comes to asylum seekers, pushing the burden back on first receiving countries and source countries, and poor countries which we can buy off. The dominant exposition of whiteness, unheard and unspoken, is a pointer to what happens within Australia's official borders and the extension of its bordering to other nations that are racially othered in Australia's approach to buying off the Global South. Australia then exports these ideas to other Western nations that seek to enact similar offshore securitisation tactics. Although couched as equal partnerships, Global South nations become re-colonised with elements of deportation, detention and dehumanisation of non-whites.

We end by asking what it would take to reset the colonial racialised story of the Australian nation. To resolve the original crime of Aboriginal dispossession and all that follows, but also to dismantle the dominance of neoliberalism, to prioritise the rights of individuals over profit and capital accumulation, and to not allow politicians and leaders to manipulate this topic for their own agendas, where they exploit rather than placate existing fears and uncertainties. Part of the manipulation is a denial of the legitimacy of the powerful refugee social movement that calls out the deviance and criminality of the state as akin to crimes against humanity. This would mean overturning the dominant notion of crises and moral panic that is so ingrained in the Australian psyche. It would also require a reckoning with the nation's racist underpinnings; practices that continue to this day.

References

Abbott, T. (2015, October 28). Transcript: Tony Abbott's controversial speech at the Margaret Thatcher lecture. *The Sydney Morning Herald*. https://www.smh.com.au/politics/federal/transcript-tony-abbotts-controversial-speech-at-the-margaret-thatcher-lecture-20151028-gkkg6p.html

Ahmed, S. (2021). *Still alive: Notes from Australia's immigration detention system*. Twelve Panels Press.

Anderson, R. (2014). Time and the migrant other: European border controls and the temporal economics of illegality. *American Anthropologist*, *116*(4), 795–809.

Ang, I. (2003). From White Australia to Fortress Australia: The anxious nation in the new century. In J. Laksiri, D. Walker, & J. Gothard (Eds.), *Legacies of White Australia: Race, culture and nation* (pp. 51–69). UWA Press.

Asylum Seeker Resource Centre. (2021, October 22). *ASRC submission to the department of foreign affairs and trade on engagement in Afghanistan*. https://asrc.org.au/wp-content/uploads/2021/10/ASRC-Submission-Engagement-in-Afghanistan_22-October-2021_FINAL.pdf

BBC. (2023, August 15). *How is the UK stopping channel crossings and what are the legal routes to the UK?* BBC News. https://www.bbc.com/news/explainers-53734793

Barnes, J. (2022). Suffering to save lives: Torture, cruelty, and moral disengagement in Australia's offshore detention centres. *Journal of Refugee Studies*, *35*(4), 1508–1529.

Blair, K. (2018). *Boats, votes and political discourse: Anti-asylum seeker sentiment in the 2013 federal election* [Doctoral dissertation, Western Sydney University].

Boochani, B. (2023). "White Australia" lives on in immigration detention. In B. Boochani (Ed.), *Freedom, only freedom: The prison writings of Behrouz Boochani* (pp. 238–240). Bloomsbury.

Briskman, L., & Goddard, C. (2014, February 25). Australia trafficks and abuses asylum seeker children. *The Age*, 20.

Briskman, L., Latham, S., & Goddard, C. (2008). *Human rights overboard: Seeking asylum in Australia*. Scribe.

Burnside, J. (2007). *Watching brief: Reflections on human rights, law and justice*. Scribe.

Carens, J. H. (2013). *The ethics of immigration*. Oxford University Press.

Cassidy, C., & Cordell, M. (2023, May 11). How a leaked USB stick became the Nauru files – A tale of brutality and despair told in 160,000 words. *The Guardian*. https://www.theguardian.com/media/2023/may/10/how-a-leaked-usb-stick-became-the-nauru-files-a-tale-of-brutality-and-despair-told-in-160000-words

Davidson, H. (2018, December 10). Australia subjected refugees to crimes against humanity, class action allege. *The Guardian*. https://www.theguardian.com/australia-news/2018/dec/10/australia-subjected-refugees-to-crimes-against-humanity-class-actions-allege

Department of Foreign Affairs and Trade. (2022). *Russia's invasion of Ukraine*. https://www.dfat.gov.au/crisis-hub/russias-invasion-ukraine

Doherty, B., & Knaus, C. (2023, January 28). US operator accused of "gross negligence" wins $420 million contract to manage Australia's asylum processing on Nauru. *The Guardian*. https://www.theguardian.com/australia-news/2023/jan/28/us-operator-accused-of-gross-negligence-wins-420m-contract-to-manage-australias-asylum-processing-on-nauru

Essex, R. (2019). Should clinicians boycott Australian immigration detention? *Journal of Medical Ethics*, *45*(2), 79–83.

Fiske, L. (2016). *Human rights, refugee protest and immigration detention*. Palgrave Macmillan.

Giuffrida, L. G. (2023, September 28). *On Lampedusa, the lucky few who made it across the sea live in misery*. Al Jazeera. https://www.aljazeera.com/features/2023/9/28/on-lampedusa-the-lucky-few-who-made-it-across-the-med-live-in-misery

Global Detention Project. (2022). *Immigration detention in Australia: Turning arbitrary detention into a global brand*. https://www.globaldetentionproject.org/wp-content/uploads/2022/02/GDP-Australia-Detention-Report-2022-2.pdf

Goddard, C., & Briskman, L. (2004, February 18). By any measure, it's official child abuse. *Herald Sun*, 17.
Golash-Boza, T. (2009). The immigration industrial complex: Why we enforce immigration policies destined to fail. *Sociology Compass*, *3*(2), 301.
Graf, S., Rubin, M., Assilamehou-Kunz, Y., Bianchi, M., Carnaghi, A., Fasoli, F., Finell, E., Sendén, M. G., Shamloo, S. E., Tocik, J., Lacko, D., & Sczesny, S. (2023). Migrants, asylum seekers, and refugees: Different labels for immigrants influence attitudes through perceived benefits in nine countries. *European Journal of Social Psychology*, *53*(5), 1–14. https://doi.org/10.1002/ejsp.2947
Grewcock, M. (2013). Australia's ongoing border wars. *Race & Class*, *54*(3), 10–32.
Hurst, D. (2015, June 12). Tony Abbott refuses to rule out paying people smugglers to turn back boats. *The Guardian*. https://www.theguardian.com/australia-news/2015/jun/12/tony-abbott-refuses-to-rule-out-paying-people-smugglers-to-turn-back-boats
Huynh, K., & Neyland, S. (2020). Australian whiteness and refugee politics. *Australian Journal of Politics and History*, *66*(1), 111–129.
Human Rights Watch. (2022, June 7). *Violence and pushbacks at Poland–Belarus border*. https://www.hrw.org/news/2022/06/07/violence-and-pushbacks-poland-belarus-border
Isaacs, D. (2016). Are health professionals working in Australia's immigration centres condoning torture? *Journal of Medical Ethics*, *42*(7), 413–415.
Jacobs, B. (2017, August 4). 'You are worse than I am': Trump told Turnbull he admired offshore detention. *The Guardian*. https://www.theguardian.com/us-news/2017/aug/03/donald-trump-malcolm-turnbull-refugees-australia-phone-call
Jerrems, A., Barry, K., Burridge, A., & Ozguc, U. (2023). Border hotels: Spaces of detention and quarantine. *Environment and Planning C: Politics and Space*, *41*(6), 1049–1078. https://doi.org/10.1177/23996544231157254
Johnson, B. (2022). *PM speech on action to tackle illegal migration: 14 April 2022*. Prime Minister's Office. https://www.gov.uk/government/speeches/pm-speech-on-action-to-tackle-illegal-migration-14-april-2022
Karp, P. (2022, May 21). Scott Morrison breaks own rule against commenting on 'on-water matters' to confirm asylum boat intercepted. *The Guardian*. https://www.theguardian.com/australia-news/2022/may/21/scott-morrison-breaks-own-rule-against-commenting-on-on-water-matters-to-confirm-asylum-boat-intercepted
Karp, P. (2023, July 31). Labor launches inquiry into home affairs procurement after "serious issues" with home affairs. *The Guardian*. https://www.theguardian.com/australia-news/2023/jul/31/labor-nauru-contracts-inquiry-clare-o-neil
Khan, I. (2003). Trading in human misery: A human rights perspective on the Tampa incident. *Pacific Rim Law and Policy Journal*, *12*(1), 9–22.
Legrain, P. (2006). *Immigrants: Your country needs them*. Little Brown Book Group.
Mansouri, F. (2023). *The global politics of forced migration: An Australian perspective*. Springer Nature. https://doi.org/10.1007/978-3-031-26336-1
Marks, K. (2015, June 12). Australian government paid people smugglers $30,000 to take asylum seekers back. *Independent*. https://www.independent.co.uk/news/world/australasia/australian-government-paid-people-smugglers-30-000-to-take-asylumseekers-back-10317082.html
Marr, D., & Wilkinson, M. (2003). *Dark victory*. Allen & Unwin.
Maylea, C., & Hirsch, A. (2018). Social workers as collaborators? The ethics of working within Australia's asylum system, *Ethics and Social Welfare*, *12*(2), 160–178. https://doi.org/10.1080/17496535.2017.1310918
McMaster, D. (2001). *Asylum seekers: Australia's response to refugees*. Melbourne University Press.
Medhora, S. (2015, November 6). Julia Gilliard defends hardline asylum seeker policy in Al-Jazeera interview. *The Guardian*. https://www.theguardian.com/australia-news/2015/nov/06/julia-gillard-defends-hardline-asylum-seeker-policy-in-al-jazeera-interview

Moreton-Robinson, A. (2015). *The white possessive: Property, power, and indigenous sovereignty*. University of Minnesota Press.
Morris, J. (2023). *Asylum and extraction in the Republic of Nauru*. Cornell University Press.
Noble, F. (2022, May 27). *Deputy PM confirms government probing election day announcement about Sri Lankan asylum seeker boat*. 9 News. https://www.9news.com.au/national/federal-government-investigating-border-force-election-day-announcement-sri-lankan-asylum-seeker-boat-scott-morrison-richard-marles/c7234610-495a-44dd-808a-7b836cb6bc9e
Phillips, M., & Gottardo, C. (2023). Deconstructing the myth of the need for immigration detention. In J. Ravulo, K. Olcoń, T. Dune, A. Workman, & P. Liamputtong (Eds.), *Handbook of critical whiteness: Reconstructing with purpose and equity* (pp. 1–10). Springer. https://doi.org/10.1007/978-981-19-1612-0_49-1
PM Transcripts. (2001, November 2). *Transcript of the prime minister the Hon John Howard MP address at the launch of 'A Stronger Tasmania Policy'*, Launceston, Tasmania. https://pmtranscripts.pmc.gov.au/release/transcript-12332
Public Interest Advocacy Centre. (2018). *In poor health: Health care in Australian immigration detention*. https://www.piac.asn.au/wp-content/uploads/2018/06/18.06.14-Asylum-Seeker-Health-Rights-Report.pdf
Refugee Council of Australia. (2022, January 21). *Australia's Afghan resettlement response a bitter disappointment* [Press release]. https://www.refugeecouncil.org.au/australias_afghan_resettlement_response_a_bitter_disappointment/
Robinson, K., Briskman, L., & Mayar, R. (2021). Disrupting human rights: A social work response to the lockdown of social housing residents. *British Journal of Social Work*, *51*(5), 1700–1719. https://doi.org/10.1093/bjsw/bcab115
Rothfield, R. (Ed.). (2014). *The drownings' argument. Australia's inhumanity: Offshore processing of asylum seekers*. Labor for Refugees.
Sadler, D. (2023, May 20–26). Torture sights. *The Saturday Paper*, 8.
SBS News. (2013, July 19). *Aust will never accept boat people: Rudd*. https://www.sbs.com.au/news/article/aust-will-never-accept-boat-people-rudd/9hkvsh9kn
Sharples, R., Dunn, K. M., & Diallo, T. (2023). Categorising anti-asylum seeker sentiment through a regime of securitisaton. *Geopolitics*, *28*(4), 1535–1561.
Smith, C. (2019). "Authoritarian neoliberalism" and the Australian border-industrial complex. *Competition and Change*, *23*(2), 192–217.
Smith, H. (2023, May 20). Greek government under fire after video shows 'pushback' of asylum seekers. *The Guardian*. https://www.theguardian.com/world/2023/may/19/greek-government-under-fire-after-video-shows-pushback-of-asylum-seekers
Stratton, J. (2009). Uncertain lives: Migration, the border and neoliberalism in Australia. *Social Identities*, *15*(5), 677–692.
The Guardian. (2022, June 8). *After four years, Murugappan family begin journey home to Biloela*. https://www.theguardian.com/australia-news/2022/jun/08/after-four-years-murugappan-family-begin-journey-home-to-biloela
Twyford-Moore, S. (2023, August 12–18). Sold down the river. *The Saturday Paper*, 20.
Valentino, N., Hutchings, V., & White, I. (2002). Cues that matter: How political ads prime racial attitudes during campaigns. *American Political Science Review*, *96*, 75–90.
van Houte, M., Kaşlı, Z., & Leerkes, A. (2023). Introduction: Irregularized humanitarian migrants—policies, rationales, and the search for more durable solutions. *Journal of Refugee Studies*, *36*(3), 315–336. https://doi.org/10.1093/jrs/fead056
Wallace, C. (2022, January 1). *Cabinet papers 2001: How "securitisation" became the mindset to dominate Australian politics for a generation*. The Conversation. https://theconversation.com/cabinet-papers-2001-how-securitisation-became-a-mindset-to-dominate-australian-politics-for-a-generation-172056
Watkins, J. (2017). Bordering borderscapes: Australia's use of humanitarian aid and border security support to immoblise asylum seekers. *Geopolitics*, *22*(4), 958–983.

Winters, J. P., Owens, F., & Winters, E. (2022). Dirty work: Well-intentioned mental health workers cannot ameliorate harms in offshore detention. *Journal of Medical Ethics*, *49*(8), 563–568. https://doi.org/10.1136/jme-2022-108348

Williams, G. (2011). A decade of Australian anti-terror laws. *Melbourne University Law Review*, *35*(3), 1136.

Worthington, E., & Bogle, A. (2022, May 21). *Liberal Party text alert warns voters about illegal boat interception*. ABC News. https://www.abc.net.au/news/2022-05-21/liberal-text-alert-warns-of-illegal-boat-interception/101087650

Chapter 2

Torturable Subjects and Psychotic Pockets

Julie Macken

Western Sydney University, Australia

Abstract

This chapter explores the proposition that Australia's abusive treatment of refugees and asylum seekers can be traced back to a denial of the foundational violence of colonisation.

By adopting a psychoanalytic frame, the research explores three questions: is Australia engaging in cruel, degrading and humiliating treatment of asylum seekers, a treatment that devolves into torture? If so, how is this operationalised? And finally what does the abuse satisfy within the state?

The work uses Freud's paper, 'Mourning and Melancholia', and Melanie Klein's work on the paranoid/schizoid position to describe the psycho-affective terrain from which this abuse emanates.

The chapter takes this psycho-affective terrain as the foundation and then investigates the impact the privatised detention regime has had in enabling the known/unknowability of the abuse and mechanisms at work within media practice to create 'torturable subjects' (Mendiola, 2014, p. 13).

Keywords: Torture; psychoanalysis; neoliberalism; refugee; human rights; Australia

> This government will not indiscriminately 'make examples' of boat refugees by turning some of them back … we will not engage in risk taking action against genuine refugees just to get a message across. That would be an utterly inhuman course of action. (Peacock & Mackellar, 1977)

> A new UN report has found aspects of Australia's border protection policies have breached the international convention against

Deter, Detain, Dehumanise: The Politics of Seeking Asylum, 31–49

Published under exclusive licence by Emerald Publishing Limited
doi:10.1108/978-1-83753-224-720241004

> torture … Prime Minister Abbott responded saying, 'I really think Australians are sick of being lectured to by the United Nations, particularly given that we have stopped the boats'. (Kozaki, 2015)

Introduction

I have spent the last 25 years trying to understand why the state is abusing asylum seekers. As a journalist, I reported the abuse, expecting that if people knew what was happening, things would change. I was wrong. I wrote stories about the financial cost, as the spending grew to billions of dollars while incompetence and mismanagement became apparent. It made no difference. As a political consultant, I watched with my face pressed up against the window of power and I saw decent people paralysed and curiously unable to imagine that what was happening, was actually happening. Finally, as an activist and communicator, I experimented with different ways of discussing the trauma and reality, hoping that if I wrote with enough power, conviction and imagination, the truth of the abuse would cut through.

But whatever approach I took, it didn't seem to matter. Nothing stopped the abuse, degradation and humiliation of those who came to Australia seeking protection. And, despite a brief reprieve between 2008 and 2012, by 2013 the immigration camps were again filled, and the abuse continued.

Nor was I alone in my confusion and concern. Many people have borne witness to this crisis of statecraft and morality. The evidence proffered by those who have been subjected to this regime, such as Behrouz Boochani (2018) in *No friend but the mountains* and more recently the 'Writing Through Fences' group (Abdile et al., 2021) describe the abuse, the hopelessness and the torture with chilling personal detail. As do the witnesses who gave evidence published in *Human Rights Overboard: Seeking Asylum in Australia* (Briskman et al., 2008). Reports by human rights organisations including Amnesty International (2016) and the Human Rights and Equal Opportunity Commission (2004), a report I co-authored, *Protection Denied, Abuse Condoned* (Bacon et al., 2016), and finally a report by the United Nations Special Rapporteur on Torture and Other Cruel, Inhuman or Degrading Treatment or Punishment, Juan E. Méndez (2015), all describe different aspects of the abuse and torture. The literature detailing the damage done by this brutal policy is now vast.

But despite this and the commitment of thousands of clever, compassionate activists, academics, nurses, nuns, mums, grandmothers and lawyers, change has only ever occurred at the margins and has never been enduring. It is the substantial failure of this resistance over 25 years and the baffling lack of curiosity on the part of the electorate – the way the story so quickly slips from view – that has led me to dig deeper and ask: could the driver for this cruelty be unconscious? Is that why it evades detection and dissolution?

In this chapter I investigate how a nation can transition from being a capable, mature, defender of a person's right to seek asylum, to one that considers asylum seekers as 'torturable subjects' (Mendiola, 2014, p. 13). This term describes how the impact of dehumanising narratives creates the prospect for torture as inherent in the power relations; and how the transformation of a human being into the 'Other' enables the state to act with lethal intent. The dehumanised and disempowered person seeking Australia's protection provides the possibility of becoming a site for torture – a torturable subject. Finally, I outline how the abuse is operationalised and of equal importance, ask why the Australian state needs to treat those seeking its protection with abuse and violence.

Is It Possible to Put a Nation on the Couch?

To understand, or at least make sense of the state's practice and willingness to torture asylum seekers, Australia needs to be understood psychoanalytically as well as geopolitically, legally and ideologically. In this chapter, I focus on the psychoanalytic. Some may challenge the legitimacy of analysing a nation psychoanalytically in the same way an individual can be understood psychologically. But as Judith Butler (2004) suggests, 'Nations are not the same as individuals' psyches, but both can be described as "subjects", albeit of different orders' (p. 41). Just as an individual's psyche is revealed in large measure by what they do, the subjective nature of the Australian nation is revealed by its actions, by the stories it tells itself about itself, by how far those stories deviate from reality and by what it allows and accepts in the treatment of Others.

Evidence of the nation's dominant psychological condition can be seen in the construction of political campaigns, health campaigns, the regular use of terms such 'un-Australian' and 'Australian values'. It can be discerned in exhibitions like *Weird Melancholy: The Australian Gothic*. This was an exhibition of the University of Melbourne's 18th and 19th century painting and photograph collection. Curator Suzette Wearne sensed in these works the anxiety, claustrophobia and fear. This was 'a fear of retribution for the mistreatment of Aboriginal people … projected onto the landscape in the Australian gothic. Where Aboriginal presence is denied, or repressed, the landscape is embedded with this trauma – the ghosts of the brutal colonial encounter' (Power, 2015). It can be glimpsed in the ongoing motif and fear of being lost, disappeared or devoured by the bush as is explored in Peter Pierce's, *The Country of Lost Children: An Australian anxiety*. Using art, literature and the media, Pierce (1999) argues the 19th century Australian lost child represented, 'the apprehensions of [Anglo-European settlers] about having sought to settle in a place where they might never be at peace'. It can be seen in films like *Picnic at Hanging Rock* (Weir, 1975) *Wolf Creek* (McLean, 2005) in myths like the Anzac legend. It is seen in what the majority of Australians remember and what is forgotten, what is valorised and what is disdained.

Benedict Anderson (1983, pp. 6–7) defined the nation as an 'imagined political community'. This imaginative work of creating and stabilising the nation draws from shared unconscious assumptions and imaginings as much as the conscious construction of the idea of a nation. We need to reckon with the unconscious if we are to understand how subjects can become torturable at the same time as we hold onto our assumptions of goodness in our imagined Australia.

Mourning and Melancholia

There are three elements necessary in the formation of asylum seekers as torturable subjects. The first is a psycho-affective state that denies the abuse, even as it enacts it. This denial leads to the political and discursive developments that operationalise the abuse and torture of asylum seekers and refugees. It is important to acknowledge that this is a psychological process and therefore a messy one, and despite my attempts to explain the process, it remains one that surges and ebbs, stalls, and contracts. Nevertheless, I argue there is a discernible process within these different psychological states.

Using the work of psychoanalyst, Sigmund Freud's (1917/1957), 'Mourning and Melancholia' and Melanie Klein's (1946), 'Notes on Some Schizoid Mechanisms', I propose that the psychological states of mourning and conversely melancholia have driven the deep undercurrents of Australian formation since 1778 and continue to do so. I argue that melancholia is the unconscious driver of the current abuse of asylum seekers by the state. In 'Mourning and Melancholia', Freud (1917/1957) sought to understand and describe why some people who experienced great loss and death were able to go through a psychological and symbolic process, which he called mourning. Through this often-harrowing mourning process they were eventually restored back to life with a capacity to love and live fully in contact with reality. He contrasted that 'healthy' mourning with the pathological and narcissistic state of melancholia. The distinguishing psychological features of melancholia are 'a profoundly painful dejection, cessation of interest in the outside world, loss of the capacity to love' (Freud, 1917/1957, p. 244). The melancholic patients appeared to be locked in a repetitious cycle of denial and narcissism; it is a shallow and lifeless state because it has severed its connection to the vitality of reality through denial.

Melanie Klein's (1946) 'Notes on Some Schizoid Mechanisms' examines the process by which infants manage the terror of dissolution by splitting themselves and their world into all-good, all-bad bit parts and projecting the 'badness' into the all-bad (M)other and taking possession of the all-good for themselves. This work produced terms we now routinely use like projection, introjection – the unconscious adoption of the thoughts or personality traits of others – and splitting – the capacity to retain the all-good feelings and expel the all-bad feelings.

Applying these concepts, it is possible to see the colonisation of Australia – with its fatal fantasy of terra nullius – this was the myth that Australia was an 'empty land' waiting for the civilising touch of the British Empire – its subjugation of Aboriginal and Torres Strait Island people through musket, massacres, rape and poisonings – as the beginnings of White Australia's melancholic colonisation. This violent and ongoing colonisation ensured Aboriginal and Torres Strait Island people were thrown into an almost endless state of mourning and Sorry Business. Critically this state of melancholia on the part of White Australia was interrupted and it is possible to see the period from 1972 to 1996 as a phase in which Australia was offered the chance to mourn its contribution to Indigenous suffering.

This was a period when the nation began to come to grips with the reality of the colonisation. It was a national project of mourning that centred on the death of the nation's foundational myth of the good and peaceful settler. The reality of its violent origins as a British colony was exhumed in an enormous variety of ways. For many non-Indigenous Australians, it began with the image of then Prime Minister Gough Whitlam carefully pouring red sand into the weathered black hands of Gurindji man Vincent Lingiari (McKeon, 2016). Its most public performance of mourning can be seen in the Prime Minister Keating's Redfern Speech in December 1992 (Keating, 1992).

Mourning is difficult and disturbing psychological work; it is a betwixt and between state of being. It makes us feel bad as we contemplate the ways in which our actions or those of our forebears led to suffering. It is hard psychological work to metabolise our collective responsibility for harm done. So, when then Prime Minister John Howard told Australian Broadcasting Corporation (ABC) journalist, Liz Jackson, that his vision for Australia was, '... an Australia that was comfortable and relaxed... about their history, comfortable relaxed about their present and comfortable and relaxed about their future', it sounded curiously compelling for millions of Australians. He concluded by telling Jackson what this 'comfortable and relaxed' state depended on: 'that as a nation we don't spend our lives apologising for our past' (Jackson, 1996). Howard's promise of a 'comfortable and relaxed Australia' was contingent on an agreement to dismiss the violence of colonisation as nothing more than a 'blemish' of history. As he declared at the 1997 Reconciliation Conference, the founding story of Australia should never be repudiated, 'as little more than a disgraceful record of imperialism, exploitation and racism. Such a portrayal is a gross distortion and deliberately neglects the overall story of great Australian achievement that is there in our history to be told' (Howard, 1997). This was a siren song for the millions of Australians who felt irrelevant and no longer special in Paul Keating's Australia (Rutherford, 2000). For the millions of Australians who were tired and angry with destabilising questions around national identity that included the truth of colonisation, relaxed and comfortable sounded like a great plan.

In a recent essay, novelist Richard Flanagan has argued that this denial was a cornerstone in the creation of White Australia.

> We all became white because that was the way of denying the great truth at our heart: 60,000 years of Indigenous history and with that, the invasion and the genocidal wars that followed, lasting into living memory when, for example, Yunupingu's father, Mungurrawuy, was shot by a white man licensed by the government to do so during the massacres in far northern Australia in the 1920s and 1930s. (Flanagan, 2023)

With the denial of colonial violence, the project of national mourning – with its reconnection to reality – was stillborn. Reality – and mourning – were replaced with a growing denial of history and a descent into the half-life of melancholia.

This regressive psychological state gave rise to the third movement: a collapse into a defensive primitive stage of psychic development known as splitting. Psychoanalyst Melanie Klein (1946) used the term paranoid-schizoid to describe this psychic splitting. In this instance, it was the projection of the 'bad' onto the Other and the introjection of all the 'good' into the non-Indigenous Australian citizen. This is an infantilised psychological state from which the nation could demand, like a furious child, that you are 'with us or against us'.

Jamal Barnes (2022) argues moral disengagement is crucial in maintaining the practice of torture and cruel, degrading and inhumane treatment because it helps to remove uncomfortable moral dilemmas that can come from violating moral norms. As the UN Special Rapporteur on Torture argues:

> Where self-interested decisions contradict predominant moral values, for example when resorting to torture in an attempt to counter a perceived security threat, both perpetrators and bystanders tend to suppress the resulting moral dilemma through behavioural and perceptual strategies known as 'moral disengagement'. Given the universal, absolute and non-derogable prohibition of torture and ill-treatment, as well as the inability of the human psyche to sustain persistent moral dilemmas without harmful effects on mental health and emotional stability, it would be impossible for torture and ill-treatment to take place on any significant scale without the enabling effect of moral disengagement. (United Nations, 2020, p. 9)

The strategies used by the state did result in a form of moral disengagement. As Barnes goes on to explain, again quoting the UN, the self-deceptive strategies are critical to this moral disengagement, again quoting the UN Special Rapporteur on Torture:

> Moral disengagement always involves the self-deceptive denial of reality, which enables perpetrators and bystanders to engage in, participate in or acquiesce to morally wrongful conduct while at the same time denying either its occurrence (denial of fact), its wrongfulness (denial of wrongfulness) or personal or collective responsibility for its occurrence (denial of responsibility). (United Nations, 2020, p. 10)

This denial of reality is also a key feature of melancholia. The story of present-day melancholia began with the violence of Australia's colonisation and the denial of that violence by the colonising forces and subsequent generations of settlers. But this denial creates more than moral disengagement. It is the first step into a dangerous state of splitting that the Other – first Aboriginal and Torres Strait Islander people and then asylum seekers – are not only denied, but must also be Othered. They must carry the abject, disavowed material of the state out to sea and never return with this toxic cargo. They must be made as unlovable. Melancholia drains the nation's capacity to love (Freud, 1917/1957, p. 244). This loss of national love was made possible by 'a loss of imagination and empathy' deftly exploited by Howard and the five prime ministers that followed him. But the loss of love and the violence and abuse that followed were operationalised by two critical developments: the privatisation of immigration detention and the construction of torturable subjects through the mainstream media.

Creating Torturable Subjects

When it comes to creating torturable subjects from those seeking protection from the state, 'crimmigration' plays a critical role (Stumpf, 2006, p. 376). This is a term used to describe the fusion of migration law and criminal law; and which Monish Bhatia (2020) further described as 'a racialised system of control that is hostile, damaging and creates suffering' (foot note 1).

Victims of torture are made vulnerable by the system due to a lack of protection and neglect and by being framed as 'illegal' and therefore a threat. In a context of increased criminalisation of migration, violent acts by public officials in the enforcement of migratory policies are normalised and understood as a legitimate use of force in the protection of the state's sovereignty (Bigo, 2014).

How does the state stabilise its narrative of lawfulness with international treaty obligations while operating immigration camps that breach those same treaty obligations, and international norms and do so with impunity?

In 'Theorising Unknowability and Jane Crow', Black American feminist, Professor Kristie Dotson (2017) traces the steps that make it possible to disappear whole communities while holding them in plain sight either literally or metaphorically. Her work helps unpack how it has been possible to have asylum seekers and refugees provide such a powerful political presence as evidenced by their vilification in each federal election campaign, with the exception of the 2019 federal election, while being almost unknowable and invisible at the same time. In a sense, asylum seekers have been the dominating absence – the hole that makes the political doughnut.

Dotson (2017) presents three overlapping conditions that go to the creation of this public invisibility that makes asylum seekers unknowable, invisible and therefore suspect. In Australia's melancholic, paranoid-schizoid position being suspect is enough to be hated, feared and expelled. She describes these conditions as a person or population, 'firstly occupying negative socio-epistemic space, secondly persisting with reduced epistemic confidence, and thirdly, heightened epistemic backgrounding' (Dotson, 2017, p. 1).

It is not possible to know someone who has been disappeared or submerged by the lack of shared epistemic resources. This lack of resources can quickly make a population or group unknown and unknowable. Asylum seekers held in Australia's detention regime are among some of the most unknowable people on earth. They no longer have names but numbers. Even when trying to communicate their stories they cannot use their real names because their families may be targeted. They have no history as, often their documentation is destroyed at the outset of the voyage to Australia. They have no citizenship they can claim and no inherited resources – indeed almost no resources at all. They don't even have their face as a shared way of knowing who they are because access to them is close to impossible. With a few exceptions such as Behrouz Boochani, Priya Nadaraja, Nades

Murugappan and their daughters Kopika and Tharnicaa,[1] refugees become vague outlines of human, spectres waiting to be filled with the content of others more powerful, more detailed and embodied.

The second element is what Dotson calls, reduced epistemic confidence. Having reduced a person or community to a state of unknowability, the state and mainstream media's use of pejorative terms such as illegal and 'queue-jumper' makes them appear suspect and deceptive. Asylum seekers are rarely 'believed in'. An example of this can be seen in an interview given by then Immigration Minister, Peter Dutton in 2019 where he attempted to argue that young women raped in Nauru were lying.

> Some people are trying it on. Let's be serious about this. There are people who have claimed that they've been raped and came to Australia to seek an abortion because they couldn't get an abortion on Nauru. They arrived in Australia and then decided they were not going to have an abortion. They have the baby here and the moment they step off the plane their lawyers lodge papers in the federal court which injuncts us from sending them back. (Davidson, 2019)

Dotson (2017) introduces the final element of this process, saying, '... epistemic backgrounding refers to being relegated as a means of framing some other domain without ever becoming the "point" of inquiry' (section 4.3). Since 1999, those seeking Australia's protection have rarely been the point of the story in their own right. But rather they have collectively been put in harness to drive the political strategy of the state. Who they are, their stories, their needs have been submerged in the interests of the state's demand for control of its borders and the Australian electorate's demand for a bad Other uninterrupted by the facts of their humanity. The absence created by these interlocking dynamics has powered much of the state's authorisation of abuse.

Having been created as an unknowable, unbelievable, shadow population, it is extraordinary the story of any asylum seekers could be known as a singular issue of concern. Media revelations of the appalling treatment and conditions of Australia's detention regime have appeared at times over the last two decades like a lightning strike on a darkened landscape. Their stories are briefly illuminated before the darkness closes in and the whole population is again submerged under

[1]Known simply as the Biloela family, they are the Murugappan family, two Tamil asylum seekers and their two little, Australian born girls, who were living in the small country town of Biloela in Queensland, Australia having fled Sri Lanka in 2012. They had been living as integral members of the community for four years when they were woken by a dawn raid on their house by Border Force in 2018. So began four years of fighting to stay in Australia that took the family to Christmas Island, and in and out of the federal and supreme courts as the Biloela community fought to bring them back to 'Bilo'. Those doing the fighting were their friends within the Biloela community.

the unknowability, disbelief and marginal nature they occupy in Australia's epistemic landscape.

Having 'disappeared' asylum seekers through distance, denial and unknowability the next step was to frame some of the most powerless people in the world as a viable threat to the state. In this way, the state is not only able to act, it is compelled to act to defend its population.

Creating the Threat

This powerful absence, the inaccessibility of asylum seekers locked away in the detention camps, and the introduction of tactics such as 'on-water matters' gave the state unprecedented control of the narrative. Because of the invisibility, the state was able to co-opt the now-silenced asylum seekers to create entire federal election campaigns around the threat of their presence. The mainstream media played a vital role in all these developments.

It is important to note the Australian media market is one of the most concentrated markets in the world and the majority of journalists in the media are White. In 2020, a study of media diversity in television news by Media Diversity Australia (Arvanitakis et al., 2020) found that people from an Anglo-Celtic background made up almost 76% of the number of appearances on Australian live broadcast screens. The 6% were from an Indigenous or non-European background, despite the fact that these groups collectively account for about a quarter of the Australian population. The other 18% had a European background other than Anglo-Celtic.

This matters because the media, news gathering, news production, news reporting, what gets reported, what doesn't, are cultural constructs. Given the Whiteness of the Australian media and ownership, the news – what is and is not considered news – is viewed through a White lens, usually unconsciously so. Mainstream media organisations privilege the White world view of political, social, economic and cultural reality within Australia. This was a White worldview largely uninterrupted by any direct experience of immigration detention camps, let alone the wars and persecution many asylum seekers were fleeing.

The creation of asylum-seeker-as-threat hit the headlines when the Special Air Service (SAS) was called on to board a merchant ship, the *MV Tampa* in order to prevent the ship from carrying rescued asylum seekers to Australia in 2001. This was a critical political move on the part of the Howard government, a move that solidified the idea that an asylum seeker could pose a threat to the entire nation. Using a critical discursive methodology to analyse text from 42 print media articles covering the event, scholars O'Doherty and Augoustinos (2008) tracked the national discourse as it grew around the stand-off between the *Tampa* and the Howard government. They asked how military action was justified in public discourse against a group of civilians through the use of arguments relying on some form of nationhood and national identity. Their findings suggest three portentous outcomes:

> First, by emphasizing the (alleged) well-being of the nation above the individuals comprising that nation, a precedent is set for future infringements of individual freedom and rights ... Secondly, by

> emphasizing the autonomous rights of the nation, beyond the rights of individual human beings who are not Australian, a kind of siege mentality is evoked, which seems to reverse traditional notions of victims and perpetrators (Burke, 2001). That is, through anthropomorphizing the category 'nation', and portraying it as a vulnerable entity, refugees fleeing from violence and persecution are made to seem like aggressors. Thirdly, by drawing on the category of nation as a primary referent of association, differences between nations are foregrounded. (O'Doherty & Augoustinos, 2008, p. 578)

The work of O'Doherty and Augoustinos highlights the split between the reality of those seeking asylum and those denying such safety. On one side are the over 400 vulnerable people sitting on the deck of the cargo ship in the blistering sun having just escaped the sinking of their boat, surrounded by heavily armed soldiers. On the other, discussing their fate in the cool air conditioned offices, media conference rooms and political offices are the 'nationally empowered group' who determine the framework of the national interest.

Content analyses of media releases between 2001 and 2002 by Klocker and Dunn (2003, p. 71), sketch out the role played by mainstream media in reporting on issues concerning refugees to be of the type best described as propaganda. They reveal, 'the government's negative tenor was constant during the study period, the specific terms of reference altered, from "threat" through "other", to "illegality" and to "burden"'.

Klocker and Dunn (2003) also found Australia's media was captive to the negative narrative promulgated by the government: 'Analysis of newspaper reporting during the same period indicates that the media largely adopted the negativity and specific references of the government. The media dependence upon government statements and spokespersons in part explains this' (p. 71).

In an interview with *Guardian* journalist Ben Doherty, former immigration minister, Chris Evans, reveals how the language of government was profoundly influential on media reportage and consequently on public understanding of the issue.

> The media tend to use that language, journalists will use the lines out of a press release, young journos in particular are just trying to file their story, and if the government pushes the border security context, if the issue is presented in that way, you report it in that context. It's not just the particular words, it's the whole structure and context. The government can announce: 'as part of Operation Sovereign Borders, the minister for Border Protection announced the Border Force had caught 40 more illegals', or it can say, 'today, the Minister for Immigration and Citizenship reported customs had rescued 40 asylum seekers'. It's a different story. (Doherty, 2015, p. 12)

Doherty argues the government's rhetorical insistence that boat-borne asylum seekers had arrived improperly and were illegal was not an additional element to smooth the passage of a potentially controversial policy. Rather, the rhetorical campaign was a keystone to the policy outcomes being achieved. Asylum seekers were no longer refugees, but illegals. This construction did not simply allow the government to act against those people, it compelled it to do so as Ben Doherty explained in a Zoom interview:

> The government constructed the action of seeking asylum as something threatening and illegal and then said, I am the only one who can protect you. Because asylum seekers are now framed as illegal the government must act to protect the nation from such illegality .... By changing the language, you change people's understanding of what was going on and change the very nature of what seeking asylum is. And finally seeking asylum is presented as an injury to Australia's sovereignty. Even though obviously being able to grant someone asylum is an expression and demonstration of national sovereignty. By changing these words, the government was reconstructing what is meant by seeking asylum. These were structural changes. (Personal communication, 12 December 2020)

In 2015, Doherty interviewed Arja Keski-Nummi, an officer in the immigration department for 32 years from 1979 and First Assistant Secretary of the Refugee, Humanitarian and International Division between 2007 and 2010. Keski-Nummi argued the use of the word illegal to refer to asylum seekers was crucial to the government achieving its policy outcome. The government's rhetorical insistence that asylum seekers who arrived by boat were acting illegally – at the very least, behaving wrongly – enabled it to justify policies condemned as illegal. Implied by, and in alliance to, this argument was the government's converse position: that the government was acting to uphold the law and due process, to protect its sovereign mandate, and to defend the nation from a possibly malign external influence.

This faux inversion of power, where asylum seekers are framed as powerful criminals, illegals and the state is the plucky defender of its people, is in keeping with the narcissist world of the melancholic that sees itself as the victim of life and death.

Having successfully rendered those seeking asylum as illegals and a threat to national security, the final step was to silence asylum seekers altogether. There was the move to offshore detention camps, the directive to call people by numbers rather than names, an edict that no humanising images of asylum seekers were to be used by the Department of Immigration and finally, the creation of the bastard-child of the national security frames, 'on-water matters'.

When former Prime Minister Scott Morrison was Immigration Minister, he began using boat turnbacks to ensure no asylum seekers arrived in Australia by boat and he also introduced the idea of on-water matters. From 2013 onward, any media questions about the fate of those who attempted to come to Australia by boat were blocked by Morrison on the grounds that they happened on the water. By 2014, on-water matters included off-water matters such as what training navy personnel received, whether naval vessels had global positioning system devices and even the public statements of Morrison himself.

All of these incremental tactics worked to obscure the face of the asylum seeker, but without the creation of camps that became impenetrable, the level and duration of abuse may not have happened.

Privatising Abuse and Creating Psychotic Pockets

There is a slipperiness around these privatised camps that comes as no surprise if we imagine the camps themselves are an extension of the melancholic state with its denial and disavowal of reality. The camps become for the nation what psychotic pockets of trauma are for the individual; they are cut off from consciousness and external observation and contain the abject and terrorised contents that remain unspeakable and nameless. These psychotic fragments exist apart from the conscious life of the nation, and no one takes responsibility for them. This is true metaphorically and literally. From the state's perspective the privatisation of the immigration detention regime offered a number of political advantages. The first was legal and literal distance beginning with the whole question of whether the camps were even under Australia's control and therefore responsibility.

Italian philosopher Giorgio Agamben (1998) has described the notion of the camp as a 'piece of land placed outside the normal juridical order', a 'zone of indistinction between outside and inside, exception and rule, licit and illicit, in which the very concepts of subjective right and juridical protection no longer made any sense' (p. 97). These immigration camps on Manus Island and Nauru occupy such a liminal state that since 2001 the Australian Government has argued that it does not have any effective control over them. Consequently, the camps – and what went on within the camps – were not within Australia's jurisdiction – and the state could not be considered to have 'legal competence or regulatory authority' (Legal and Constitutional Affairs References Committee 2014, p. 131). This was not accepted by the United Nations and as the Director of Legal Advocacy at the Human Rights Law Centre told the Senate Committee in 2014 when asked about Manus Island:

> Australia designed the arrangements, Australia built and funds the detention centre, Australia contracts service providers to provide services at the centre and Australia is involved in the processing of claims within the centre. So not only is Australia a link in the causal chain, Australia built the chain and underwrites the chain and is involved very closely in every link of that chain. (Australian Senate, Legal and Constitutional Affairs References Committee. Commonwealth of Australia, 2014, p. 135)

The question of liability and responsibility was an ongoing struggle between the state, the courts and the companies that ran the immigration camps. Who was responsible for the abuse, the riots, and the destruction of two camps by fire? Who was responsible for ensuring the safety of babies born there and toddlers living there? Who could be held to account for the trauma inflicted on both those detained within and the young Australians employed by the various private companies that held various tenders over the last two decades? The lines of accountability blurred as neoliberalism not only ensured the transfer of what was once public into private ownership – and secured the details behind commercial-in-confidence contracts – but also played a critical role in determining what became thinkable and unthinkable.

John Howard understood what British Prime Minister Margaret Thatcher meant when she declared that within the neoliberal orthodoxy 'Economics are the method; the object is to change the heart and soul' (Butt, 1981). As economist Richard Denniss has argued, the real trick of neoliberalism is not the economic tools of outsourcing and privatising the provision of public services, but the cultural tools used to change our hearts and souls. 'Children in Australia die in the custody of our governments, but our public debate focuses on our fiscal deficits, not our moral deficits. That's quite a feat' (Denniss, 2018, p. 12). The immigration camps may offer the most powerful example of a nation whose heart and soul were transformed utterly.

While Howard may have been pursuing a change of our 'heart and soul', divestment of public goods was sold to the Australian public on the grounds that the private sector could deliver better value for money and greater efficiencies. The facts give lie to that. A Save the Children/UNICEF report, *At What Cost?* Button and Evans found the Australian Government's deterrence policies against refugees cost a total of AUD9.6 billion over four years between 2012 and 2016. Refugee Action Coalition reported that:

> Detaining a single asylum seeker on Manus or Nauru costs $400,000 per year, according to the National Commission of Audit in 2014. Amnesty put it at $570,000 per person in a 2016 report. Detention in Australia costs $239,000 per year. By contrast, allowing asylum seekers to live in the community while their claims are processed costs just $12,000 per year. (Button & Evans, 2016)

At What Cost? also found that as of December 2016, about AUD3.4 billion was going to private companies running the camps with contracts for security, cleaning, catering, recreational/education, and health in Papua New Guinea and Nauru. They estimated expenditure on boat turnbacks, onshore and offshore detention and other programmes amounted to more than AUD9.6 billion between 2013 and 2016. The bill for chartered flights alone to Manus and Nauru came to AUD45 million (Button & Evans, 2016).

Given the privatised camps are twelve times more expensive than community-based detention, and the camps have proven to be chaotic, controversial and cruel, why does each successive prime minister continue the practice?

Economist, Richard Denniss barely contains his frustration when the question of cost comes up in progressive political circles. In a conversation with me in 2021, he argued that the left is missing the point by railing against the economic contradiction at the heart of Australia's neoliberal practice of privatising immigration camps. He reiterates his observation that neoliberalism is not an economic project, it is about transforming the Australian community.

> And they will waste as much of your money on their project as they want. So stop saying they're ideologues. Stop saying they're into small governments. Stop saying they're free marketeers. Stop saying that it's head versus heart. All they are trying to do is reshape our entire community. (Personal communication, 16 December 2021)

The Australian Government is 'performing' economic rationality while pursuing distance and control. Saving money is not what privatising the detention regime is about or ever was about.

> You can't take seriously their stated objectives. Imagine if, when Scott Morrison was Immigration Minister he said to the electorate, 'Look privatising these camps is going to cost a shit ton, but that's okay because cruelty is the point, and the lack of accountability is the point, deniability is the point – saving money has never been the point of this privatisation'. But that construction of reality is impossible to share so he argues the private sector can do it better and cheaper. (Personal communication, 16 December 2021)

Denniss' logic underscores the lack of logic involved in this ongoing moral crisis. With a majority of the electorate in the grip of a melancholic denial of the violence, it is also unlikely the exorbitant costs of the immigration camps would prevent their operation.

Torture Prevention

Richard Carver and Lisa Handley (2016) published the first independent and global study of the impact of torture prevention measures, called simply, *Does Torture Prevention Work?* The reassuring answer is yes, torture prevention works. However, no single measure alone is sufficient to prevent torture because, as with every aspect of this ongoing abuse, prevention operates within an ecology of practices.

The global study found the most effective way to reduce incidences of torture was to put into practice a number of detention safeguards. These safeguards include abstaining from unofficial detention – in Australia's case, this would include the mandatory and arbitrary nature of immigration detention and the capricious and politically motivated changes to detention practice over the last two decades. Another safeguard is ensuring, within the first few hours of detention, relatives, lawyers and medical officers are notified and detainees are able to have contact with relatives, lawyers and medical officers. The report also highlights the positive impact of reducing reliance on confessions, which for obvious reasons often leads to coercion and torture. In Australia's detention regime, this would translate as not using abuse to 'send a message' to other people who would potentially claim asylum. Other important factors are disciplinary sanctions against perpetrators of abuse and the absence of amnesty laws for perpetrators – Australia has not prosecuted a single person in relation to the abuse, or even murder, of asylum seekers in detention.

Monitoring bodies (understood broadly to include National Preventive Mechanisms under OPCAT, the Optional Protocol to the Convention against Torture and other Cruel, Inhuman and Degrading Treatment or Punishment, but also civil society organisations and international bodies) have a direct effect in reducing torture. Other key elements include the ability to carry out unannounced visits and to interview detainees in private. None of those strategies are currently in place within Australia's privatised detention regime. Indeed, Australia has joined Rwanda as the only country where the United Nations Subcommittee on Prevention of Torture has been forced to terminate a visit due to a lack of access in 2023 (Karp, 2023).

Relocating the camps to the Australian mainland under public administration would not guarantee complete safety or humane treatment, as Australia's publicly administered jails attest. But it would change the culture of secrecy, and the lack of transparency and end the liminal, lawless nature of the camps. Anyone killed or who died in these camps would have a coronial inquiry into their deaths if the camp was in public administration. Finally, it would transform the camps from being sites of economic activity, to sites of political contest with some practical potential for public oversight through the various forms of media. And perhaps of equal importance, it would remove deniability from the state and her Ministers when people were killed, women raped, and children abused in the camps.

Why the Need to Harm?

If we take the accusation of torture, of cruel, degrading and inhumane treatment of asylum seekers seriously, we must consider whether this treatment is an accident, albeit an ongoing accident. That is, could it have arisen out of the state's inability to manage the immigration detention regime effectively and that a few 'bad apples' were employed and behaved badly; or that the state was unaware of this abuse and so took no action to prevent it? To ask the question in this way is to answer it. The abuse is no accident. It wasn't when it began in 2000 and it wasn't throughout the following two decades. So, what purpose does it serve? I propose the state is satisfying two needs through this abuse, one political, the other psychological.

Australia's treatment of asylum seekers has been compared to, 'a hanging in the public square' (Global Legal Action Network, 2017), designed to intimidate future asylum seekers and deter them from attempting the journey. Seen through this frame of intention and purpose – the intention being the infliction of pain and suffering and its purpose being to 'send a message' to deter people from seeking Australia's protection – its purpose is clearly one of deterrence. Torture is the outcome of this public policy.

But this was always about more than politics – that's why it has such bipartisan support – it was/is also about satisfying the need to harm on the part of the majority of the electorate. This is why it is so critical to bring a psychological lens to this crisis and to give the psyche its full and terrible weight.

Having embarked on the nation-building work of mourning the violence at the heart of this colonised nation, but then failing to complete that mourning, White Australia has been in search of an Other to carry the unwanted parts of the nation.

This is the psychological function provided by asylum seekers who arrive by boat seeking Australia's protection. They become the Other who can carry this split-off unwanted aspect of many Australians – they are put in harnesses to carry the unfinished work of mourning. Having been successfully split off from the Australian community, asylum seekers and refugees have been Othered and vilified, then loaded up with the Abject psychic material of Australia's stillborn mourning and pushed out to sea carrying this corrosive cargo. Here it must be noted that only those who arrive by boat are treated in this way. Those who arrive by plane confront difficult but less punitive treatment. There is something particular about arriving by boat that drives a deep fear within the state, perhaps an unspeakable anxiety that asylum seekers could treat the nation the way the nation treated Aboriginal and Torres Strait Islander people when they arrived.

This is no accident, nor is it simply clever politics. This is how an anxious nation like Australia manages its dread. Like a toddler, it splits people into all-good/all-bad groups and sends the all-bad people away thus apparently resolving the problem of badness.

The problem the infant/patient/nation is trying to solve is the dread that comes from the feeling of disintegration and being shattered. This fear of disintegration was roiling to the surface in the closing years of the Keating government. The questions around who and what constituted Australia and being Australian grew along with questions about the right national anthem, national day, flag, allegiances and history. I remember this as the time when many felt this as a shattering of national coherence.

Conclusion

Chillingly, melancholia also carries within it a sadism that seeks expression and outlet (Freud, 1917/1957, p. 244). The psychological path that has enabled the Australian Government to abuse and in some instances torture those who came to Australia seeking protection has been characterised by a growing indifference to the pain of the Other on the part of the electorate. This loss of love was made possible by the loss of imagination and empathy that began with the denial of violent colonisation.

Until the melancholic state has been transformed, and the reality of Australia's foundational violence acknowledged and mourned, the Australian state will continue to realise this abuse in one form or another because its psychology demands it and compulsive repetition is part of the melancholic state.

References

Abdile, H., Boochani, B., Galbraith, J., & Tofighian, O. (Eds.). (2021). Writing through fences: Archipelago of letters. In *Southerly* (Vol. 79, No. 2).

Agamben, G. (1998). *Homo sacer: Sovereign power and bare life* (D. Heller-Roazen, Trans.). Stanford University Press.

Arvanitakis J., Cage, C., Groutsis, D., Kaabel, A., Han, C., Hine, A., Hopkins, N., Lattouf, A., Liu, I. J., Lo, I., Lumby, C., Rodrigues, U., Soutphommasane, T., &

Weerakkody, U. (2020). *Who gets to tell Australian stories? Putting the spotlight on cultural and linguistic diversity in television news and current affairs*. Media Diversity Australia. https://doi.org/10.13140/RG.2.2.21683.04642
Amnesty International. (2016). *Island of despair: Australia's "processing" of refugees on Nauru*. https://www.amnesty.org/en/documents/asa12/4934/2016/en/
Anderson, B. (1983). *Imagined communities: Reflections on the origin and spread of nationalism*. Verso Books.
Australian Senate, Legal and Constitutional Affairs References Committee. Commonwealth of Australia. (2014). *Incident at the Manus Island detention centre from 16 February to 18 February 2014*. https://humanrights.gov.au/our-work/legal/submission/inquiry-incident-manus-island-detention-centre-16-february-18-february#:~:text=The%20Commission%20notes%20that%20the,of%2062%20other%20asylum%20seekers
Bacon, W., Curr, P., Lawrence, C., Macken, J., & O'Connor, C. (2016). *Protection denied, abuse condoned: Women on Nauru at risk*. Australian Women in Support of Women on Nauru. http://www.awswn.org/the-report
Bhatia, M. (2020). Crimmigration, imprisonment and racist violence: Narratives of people seeking asylum in Great Britain. *Journal of Sociology*, *56*(1), 36–52. https://doi.org/10.1177/1440783319882533
Barnes, J. (2022). Suffering to save lives: Torture, cruelty, and moral disengagement in Australia's offshore detention centres. *Journal of Refugee Studies*, *35*(4), 1508–1529. https://doi.org/10.1093/jrs/feac041
Bigo, D. (2014). The (in)securitization practices of the three universes of EU border control: Military/navy – border guards/police – database analysts. *Security Dialogue*, *45*(3), 209–225. https://doi.org/10.1177/0967010614530459
Boochani, B. (2018). *No friend but the mountains: Writing from Manus Prison* (O. Tofighian, Trans.). Picador, Pan Macmillan.
Briskman, L., Latham, S., & Goddard, C. (2008). *Human rights overboard: Seeking asylum in Australia*. Scribe.
Burke, A. (2001). *In fear of insecurity: Australia's invasion anxiety*. Pluto Press.
Butler, J. (2004). *Precarious life: The powers of mourning and violence*. Verso.
Butt, R. (1981). Mrs Thatcher: The first two years [Interview]. *Sunday Times*. https://www.margaretthatcher.org/document/104475
Button, L., & Evans, S. (2016). At what cost? The human, economic and strategic cost of Australia's asylum seeker policies and the alternatives. Save the Children Australia & UNICEF, United Nations Children's Fund. https://resourcecentre.savethechildren.net/document/what-cost-human-economic-and-strategic-cost-australias-asylum-seeker-policies-and/
Carver, R., & Handley, L. (Eds.). (2016). *Does torture prevention work?* Liverpool University Press.
Davidson, H. (2019, June 20). Peter Dutton says women using rape and abortion claims as ploy to get to Australia. *The Guardian*. https://www.theguardian.com/australia-news/2019/jun/20/peter-dutton-says-women-using-and-abortion-claims-as-ploy-to-get-to-australia
Denniss, R. (2018). *Quarterly essay 70. Dead right: How neoliberalism ate itself and what comes next*. Black Inc.
Doherty, B. (2015). Call me illegal: The semantic struggle over seeking asylum in Australia. Reuters Institute for the Study of Journalism, University of Oxford. https://reuters-institute.politics.ox.ac.uk/sites/default/files/2017-10/Call_me_illegal_The_semantic_struggle_over_seeking_asylum_in_Australia_0.pdf
Dotson, K. (2017). Theorising Jane Crow, theorising unknowability. *Social Epistemology*, *31*(5), 417–430. https://doi.org/10.1080/02691728.2017.1346721
Flanagan, R. (2023). The voice and our inauthentic heart. The Monthly. https://www.themonthly.com.au/issue/2023/july/richard-flanagan/voice-and-our-inauthentic-heart

Freud, S. (1957). Mourning and melancholia. In J. Strachey (Ed.), *The standard edition of the complete psychological works of Sigmund Freud* (Vol. 14, pp. 237–258). Hogarth Press (Original work published 1917).

Global Legal Action Network. (2017). *Communiqué to the Office of the Prosecutor of the International Criminal Court under Article 15 of the Rome Statute*. https://docs.wix-static.com/ugd/b743d9_e4413cb72e1646d8bd3e8a8c9a466950.pdf

Howard, J. (1997, May 26). *Opening address to the Australian Reconciliation Convention Melbourne* [PM Transcripts: Transcripts from the Prime Ministers of Australia]. Department of the Prime Minister and Cabinet. https://pmtranscripts.pmc.gov.au/release/transcript-10361

Human Rights and Equal Opportunity Commission. (2004). *A last resort? National inquiry into children in immigration detention*. https://humanrights.gov.au/our-work/asylum-seekers-and-refugees/publications/last-resort-national-inquiry-children-immigration

Jackson, L. (Reporter). (1996, February 19). An average Australian bloke [TV series episode]. In *Four corners*. ABC. https://trakt.tv/shows/four-corners/seasons/1996/episodes/2

Karp, P. (2023). UN torture prevention body cancels visit to Australia after access to facilities blocked. *The Guardian Online*. Retrieved November 11, 2023, from https://www.theguardian.com/australia-news/2023/feb/21/un-torture-prevention-body-cancels-visit-to-australia-after-access-to-facilities-blocked#:~:text=Australia%20has%20joined%20Rwanda%20as,of%20cooperation%20from%20two%20states

Keating, P. (1992, December 10). *Australian launch of the international year for the world's indigenous people, Redfern* [PM Transcripts: Transcripts from the Prime Ministers of Australia]. Department of the Prime Minister and Cabinet. https://pmtranscripts.pmc.gov.au/release/transcript-8765

Klein, M. (1946). Notes on some schizoid mechanisms. *The International Journal of Psycho-Analysis*, *27*, 99–110.

Klocker, N., & Dunn, K. M. (2003). Who's driving the asylum debate? Newspaper and government representations of asylum seekers. *Media International Australia*, *109*(1), 71–92. https://doi.org/10.1177/1329878X0310900109

Kozaki, D. (2015, March 9). Abbott says Australians 'sick of being lectured to by UN' after scathing report on asylum policies [Radio broadcast]. *Australian Broadcasting Corporation News*, *9*. https://www.abc.net.au/news/2015-03-09/tony-abbott-hits-out-united-nations-asylum-report/6289892

Legal and Constitutional Affairs References Committee. (2014, December). *Incident at Manus* (p. 131). https://www.aph.gov.au/parliamentary_business/committees/senate/legal_and_constitutional_affairs/manus_island/Report

Macken, J. (2020). The melancholic torturer: How Australia became a nation that tortures refugees. *Journal of Sociology*, *56*(1), 9–22.

McLean, G. (2005). *Wolf Creek* [Film]. Production Australian Film Finance Corporation & South Australian Film Corporation.

Méndez, J. E. (2015). *Report of the Special Rapporteur on Torture and Other Cruel, Inhuman or Degrading Treatment or Punishment. Addendum: observations on communications 146 transmitted to governments and replies received*. Office of the United Nations High Commissioner for Human Rights. https://ap.ohchr.org/documents/dpage_e.aspx?si=A/HRC/28/68/Add.1

Mendiola, I. (2014). *Habitar lo inhabitable: La práctica político-punitiva de la tortura [Inhabiting the uninhabitable: The political-punitive practice of torture]*. Edicions Bellaterra.

McKeon, N. (2016, March 2). *Vincent Lingiari & Gough Whitlam: The story behind the image*. NITV. https://www.sbs.com.au/nitv/article/vincent-lingiari-gough-whitlam-the-story-behind-theimage/t0m0ejh6i

O'Doherty, K., & Augoustinos, M. (2008). Protecting the nation: Nationalist rhetoric on asylum seekers and the Tampa. *Journal of Community and Applied Social Psychology*, *18*(6), 576–592.

Peacock, A., & Mackellar, M. (1977, November 29). *Refugees: Joint statement by minister for foreign affairs, Hon. Andrew Peacock, MP and minister for immigration and ethnic affairs, Hon. Michael Mackellar, MP* [Press release]. https://parlinfo.aph.gov.au/parlInfo/search/display/display.w3p;query=Id:%22media/pressrel/HPR08003062a%22

Pierce, P. (1999). *The country of lost children: An Australian anxiety*. Cambridge University Press.

Power, L. (2015). Weird melancholy: Exhibition probes fear at the heart of the Australian landscape. *The Sydney Morning Herald*. https://www.smh.com.au/entertainment/weird-melancholy-exhibition-probes-fear-at-the-heart-of-the-australian-landscape-20150328-1m9uk2.html

Rutherford, J. (2000). *The gauche intruder: Freud, Lacan and the white Australian fantasy*. Melbourne University Press.

Stumpf, J. P. (2006). The crimmigration crisis: Immigrants, crime, and sovereign power. *American University Law Review*, *56*, 367.

United Nations. (2020, July 20). *Torture and Other Cruel, Inhuman or Degrading Treatment or Punishment: Note by the Secretary-General* [Doc. No. A/75/179].

Weir, P. (1975). *Picnic at Hanging Rock* [Film].

Chapter 3

Examining the Politicisation of Asylum Through Public Information Campaigns: Deterrence Messaging for Whom?

Kate Coddington

University at Albany, State University of New York, USA

Abstract

Public information campaigns (PICs) have increasingly become part of global migration deterrence projects. Australia's *No Way* campaign has been widely publicised for its harsh messaging, declaring to would-be asylum seekers that 'you will not make Australia home'. In this chapter, the author argues that in addition to targeting potential asylum seekers throughout the Middle East and Southeast Asia, the *No Way* campaign is directed towards multiple audiences, including diaspora communities in Australia, the Australian voting public, and a wider network of anti-immigration political figures. The *No Way* campaign represented one of the largest and best-funded Australian deterrence campaigns to date, with the distribution of materials ranging from billboards and social media advertisements to street theatre performances and graphic novel storyboards between 2014 and 2016. In the sections that follow, the author situates this argument within the context of the rise of PICs throughout the globe, as well as their use within Australia. Through the lens of this campaign, the author considers the question: for whom is this deterrence messaging? How does it target multiple audiences? The author concludes by considering the future of information campaigns as deterrence projects around the world.

Keywords: Deterrence; public information campaign; *No Way*; target audience; Australia; advertising

Deter, Detain, Dehumanise: The Politics of Seeking Asylum, 51–64

Published under exclusive licence by Emerald Publishing Limited
doi:10.1108/978-1-83753-224-720241005

Introduction

Australian audiences had become accustomed to seeing PICs illustrating the dangers of seeking asylum since the early 2000s, with newspaper advertisements in mainstream Australian newspapers, radio and television spots, and social media advertising commonplace. Yet a wider international audience encountered Australia's PICs for the first time when then-US President Trump tweeted images of some of the campaigns that stated 'Australia's borders are closed to illegal migration' and 'You won't be settled in Australia' on 26 June 2019, saying 'These flyers depict Australia's policy on illegal immigration. Much can be learned!' (Henriques-Gomes, 2019). Trump's comments received over 67,000 'likes' on social media and a flurry of reporting that connected his hopes to build a wall between the USA and Mexico to Australia's hard-line policies communicated through these campaigns. Through this tweet and similar approval of right-wing politicians in other contexts, Australia's deterrence campaign was broadcast to a much wider audience than to would-be asylum seekers – but perhaps, this was always one of the intended strategies.

In this chapter, I describe how PICs are part of Australia's wider migrant deterrence projects. As a political project, however, these specific deterrence campaigns are aimed not only at would-be asylum seekers, but at different audiences as well, including communities in Australia, the Australian voting public and a wider network of anti-immigration political figures throughout the world. The chapter begins by introducing PICs as a tactic of border enforcement and then situates their use within the Australian context. Next, I focus on the specific campaign highlighted by President Trump in the tweet described above, detailing some of the products from the *No Way* campaign, the largest and best-funded information campaign as of 2023. Finally, I consider the questions: for whom is this deterrence messaging? How does it target multiple audiences? I conclude by considering the future of information campaigns as deterrence projects around the world.

What Are PICs?

PICs have been part of enforcement strategies in the Global North since the 1990s. Developed across national contexts, these public relations campaigns were designed to deter irregular migration, and often partnered with non-governmental organisations such as the International Organisation for Migration (IOM) in order to spread messages of deterrence. For instance, in the 1990s the IOM supported European campaigns advertising the risks of migration in Romania (1992–1996), Albania (1992–1995) and Ukraine (1998) (Musarò, 2019). In the USA, meanwhile, PICs initially appeared as responses to increasing fatalities along the USA–Mexico border in the 1990s (Williams, 2020). Across these national contexts, the use of PICs has emerged alongside increasingly harsh border enforcement tactics, such as walling, detention, and externalisation of enforcement into third countries. PICs, as Oeppen (2016, p. 66) notes, are popular as they 'allow governments to be seen to be doing something to control their borders whilst still maintaining a humanitarian image'.

Global Use of Campaigns

Since the 2000s, PICs have become a more frequent strategy of enforcement, particularly with the rise of social media. PICs operate across geographic contexts differently. Some campaigns, for instance, work in conjunction with messaging in countries of migrant origin to attempt to persuade migrants against travelling. Oeppen (2016) traces the development of PICs in Afghanistan, including a 2015 campaign funded by Germany titled *Rumors About Germany*. Billboards, social media, and radio and television advertisements funded by the German government were quickly joined by the Afghan Ministry of Refugees and Repatriation's own social media campaign discouraging Afghans from seeking asylum in Europe (Oeppen, 2016). Such campaigns are characterised by messages of deterrence, but may also have other functions, as Oeppen (2016, p. 57) concludes, noting that information campaigns 'serve a role of shifting responsibility for the risks of the journey onto Afghans themselves, rather than the restrictive border regimes of the EU'. In other campaigns, the target audience is purported to be migrants, but may also be residents in the destination country. For instance, Bajomi-Lázár (2019, p. 621) describes the rise of anti-migrant PICs in Hungary beginning in 2015, which focussed on migration from North Africa and the Middle East through advertisements that stated, 'If you come to Hungary, you must respect our laws'! However, the campaign materials were distributed throughout Hungary, written in Hungarian, and timed to coincide with national election periods, suggesting that the intended audience was Hungarian voters, rather than potential immigrants. Further campaigns accused Hungarian-born George Soros and the European Union (EU) of being behind the rise in immigration to Hungary (Bajomi-Lázár, 2019). Campaigns are also increasingly developed and distributed by non-state organisations such as the IOM. For instance, Musarò (2019) documents the emergence of the *Aware Migrants* campaign in 2016, funded by the Italian government and implemented by the IOM targeting migrants from Northern Africa and the Middle East attempting to reach Italy via the Mediterranean Sea. Messaging focusses on the dangers of travelling by sea and, as Musarò (2019, p. 631) concludes, work to 'normalize the extraterritorial border by negatively stereotyping migration, or even criminalizing it a priori'. While they have grown in popularity across the globe, the effectiveness of PICs is generally not well-studied. However, recent comparative studies of different PICs suggest that they tend to be judged on how well they reach an intended audience, rather than how much they impact potential migrants' decision-making. When the impact on decision-making is assessed, PICs generally have minimal effect (Ajzerle, 2016; Browne, 2015; Rodriguez, 2019; van Bemmel, 2020).

Australian Context

In Australia, PICs began with a TV and radio campaign which ran in Behai, China in 1994 to discourage asylum seekers from travelling to Australia (Watkins, 2017). Advertisements became more sophisticated with the rise of social media and targeted internet advertising in the early 2000s, with campaigns such as

By Boat, No Visa and *No Way: You Will Not Make Australia Home* becoming widely visible both domestically and abroad in the 2010s (Watkins, 2017). These campaigns have developed alongside Australia's use of harsh enforcement tactics to prevent asylum seekers arriving by boat. Mandatory detention of asylum seekers arriving by boat began in 1992, and after Prime Minister Howard refused to let over 400 asylum seekers rescued by the *M.V. Tampa* ashore in 2001, indefinite immigration detention became accompanied by offshore processing which eventually occurred both on the Pacific islands of Papua New Guinea and Nauru. Australia also conducted militarised patrols of national waters, interdiction of asylum seeker vessels, and the excision of parts of Australia from Australian territory for the purposes of making migration claims. Over the following two decades, PICs helped to communicate Australia's increasingly draconian asylum seeker policies. For instance, Australian campaigns frequently targeted the Indonesian fishing villages where asylum seekers would depart by boat. Detailing an Australian-funded counter-smuggling campaign implemented by the IOM titled *I know smuggling illegal immigrants is wrong* in Indonesia between 2009 and 2014, McNevin et al. (2016) describe how this campaign targeted members of small fishing communities and employed local religious leaders to craft negative messaging about the moral implications of assisting asylum seekers attempting to travel to Australia. Campaigns accompanied other types of externalised border enforcement, such as embedding Australian border enforcement into regional customs operations, surveilling Indonesian waters, and interdicting asylum seekers vessels which were in some cases forcibly towed back to Indonesian waters and abandoned offshore (Coddington, 2018).

Scholars of Australian immigration enforcement have drawn connections between enforcement tactics such as these and Australia's settler colonial status (Perera, 2002; Rajaram, 2003; Tedmanson, 2008). Australian history demonstrates a long-standing preoccupation with differentiating Australia from its Asian neighbours, from the Immigration Restriction Act in 1901, the first piece of legislation passed by the newly federated Australian government. The racialised criminalisation of asylum seekers occurs alongside the dispossession of and violence directed towards Aboriginal Australians, who continue to face the impacts of colonialisation from disproportionate imprisonment and child removal to income management and police violence. The widespread adoption of PICs in the period since 2001 must be situated within the wider context of settler colonialism and continued racialised violence in Australia.

Australian public information campaign scholars have argued that Australia has used PICs as a strategy of 'militarised deterrence' (Dehm & Silverstein, 2021, p. 19). The campaigns suggest that Australian has a humanitarian motive for preventing migrants from arriving, while also maintaining a sense of control over international borders (Dehm & Silverstein, 2021). Scholars' analyses of individual campaigns suggest that they are, in fact, not motivated by fairness or humanitarian concerns, but instead are tools used to promote government policies of deterrence (Schloenhardt & Philipson, 2013). Indeed, the messaging often contradicts Australia's international legal obligations towards asylum seekers (Schloenhardt & Philipson, 2013). The lack of useful information for asylum seekers is part of the point, argues Bishop (2020, p. 1092), noting that the promotion of 'strategic ignorance' is often part of the strategies of governments like Australia who produce these campaigns. While the overall vision and motive for Australian PICs has been a focus of much scholarship, so too are more detailed analyses of PIC content. Hightower (2013, p. 8), for instance, examines how Australian PICs employ the 'theatricalised encounter' to stand in for the actual complexities of asylum seekers' arrivals, and use emotional and affective messaging to contrast these invented encounters with asylum seekers who come the correct way. Emotional messaging employs particular constructions of gender and the family to target the relatives and communities of potential asylum seekers (Coddington & Williams, 2022; Williams & Coddington, 2023). Meanwhile, Watkins (2015) explores how an economic rationale underlies many Australian PICs, which try to emphasise the disastrous financial consequences of seeking asylum. Comics use emotional messaging to visually convey the dangers of seeking asylum, and use imagery that suggests danger rather than linking back to specific governmental policies or pieces of legislation (Humphrey, 2018).

Consistently, scholars of Australian border enforcement note that the increasing use of PICs has not resulted in changing migrant behaviours. Watkins (2017), for instance, writes that even as PICs show Australian attempts to shape potential migrant subject formation, migrants are not passive recipients of messaging. Indeed, migrants do not internalise these messages, nor do their actions change because of them (Watkins, 2017). Similarly, from the perspective of media and communication studies, Richardson (2010) explores the use of deterrence campaigns, arguing that the strategy of PICs relies on a misunderstanding of the audience – potential migrants are not as malleable as they are imagined to be. Ethnographic fieldwork backs up these conclusions: Fleay et al. (2016) conducted interviews with Hazara migrants who either attempted to reach Australia or were planning on doing so. Despite being on the receiving end of information campaigns, the migrants interviewed did not receive the majority of their information about migration from these efforts, nor were they deterred from migrating (Fleay et al., 2016). All of this scholarship points to a central question: if Australian PICs, by all accounts, are not effective in changing potential migrants' minds, what is their purpose? Why do they continue to be popular? For whom is deterrence messaging? In the remainder of this chapter, I address these important questions through the example of the *No Way* campaign from 2014 to 2016.

No Way: You Will Not Make Australia Home

Planning for the *No Way* campaign began in late 2013, after then Prime Minister Tony Abbott and the Liberal National Party won the Australian general election. *Stopping the Boats* had been a key campaign platform, and Abbott responded through the promotion of a new government initiative called *Operation Sovereign Borders*, which included uniting government departments responsible for border enforcement and policing, intercepting and push back of asylum seeker vessels – ultimately, between 2014 and 2020, Australia turned back 873 people, according to the Refugee Council of Australia (2023). PICs were a key component of *Operation Sovereign Borders*, conveying the message about the change of policy to potential migrants as well as becoming a deterrent in themselves, using emotional messaging and imagery to attempt to influence the decisions of migrants, their relatives, and their community members – as well as, perhaps, other audiences as well, as I will discuss below.

By February 2014, Australian media were reporting on a new series of advertisements targeting domestic and international audiences featuring this new messaging. Often, advertisements featured a small boat surrounded by rough ocean waters, featuring the words *No Way* in block letters across the top. A Sri Lankan billboard, for instance, stated:

> Never come to Australia without a visa! Never put your feet in Australia without a visa. In Australia there is a military that enforces this. People who come by boat without a visa will never be allowed to enter and boats that go to Australia without permission are returned to the deep sea. (Jesudason, 2015)

Image 1. No Way Campaign Poster in the Australian Embassy in Tehran, Iran 2014. Source: Linda Briskman.

No Way used various advertising mechanisms, including television, radio, press advertising, posters, billboards, internet advertisements on social media and blogs, an 18-page graphic novel storyboard, leaflets, stickers, community engagement meetings, transit advertising, street theatre, and a full-length film titled *Journey*. Image 1 shows the most widespread campaign imagery, with the text accompanied by a small boat in rough seas. Messaging targeted potential migrants from Afghanistan, Iraq, Iran, Pakistan, Somalia, Sudan, Vietnam as well as Tamil-speaking areas of Sri Lanka and India and Rohingya-speaking areas of Myanmar and Bangladesh. Messaging was also circulated in Australian domestic media, including full-page newspaper and social media advertisements. A spokesperson for the Immigration and Border Protection Department described the strategy as follows: 'The campaign is targeted at source and transit countries for people smuggling activity, as well as diaspora communities in Australia' and 'evaluation research consistently shows that family and friends are the primary information source for people in Australia and overseas (Dias, 2016, p. 1)'. *No Way* represented the largest spending on PICs to date, amounting to over AUD40 million over the course of the multi-year project.

Three examples demonstrate the breadth of the *No Way* campaign's reach and ambition. The first example was first reported in 2016, when newspapers across Australia broke the story of the full-length feature film funded by Australian taxpayers. Titled *Journey*, the film followed a group of would-be asylum seekers as they unsuccessfully attempted to reach Australia by boat. The film outlines the backstories of four key protagonists, one each from Afghanistan, Iran, Iraq and Pakistan, and describes their journey negotiating their way to Indonesia and finally onto a boat through their associations with people smugglers. The people smugglers are portrayed as greedy, threatening, and violent – and while most of the asylum seekers perish when the boat sinks, the people smugglers survive. The Australian government had contracted AUD4.3 million with a production firm to make the film, Put It Out There Pictures, a company that previously made films about Afghan women's empowerment and other topics funded by international development and aid organisations. The government paid another AUD1.6 million to an Afghan-based communications firm, Lapis Communications, to distribute the film to audiences in Afghanistan, Pakistan, Iraq and Iran. It eventually screened on local television in these countries in five different languages, Farsi, Dari, Arabic, Urdu and Pashto, and was accompanied by social media posts designed to facilitate audience engagement. As Dehm and Silverstein (2021) note, the film's release on YouTube with English-language subtitles did not occur until the Australian government had to respond to a freedom of information request. This was a campaign product clearly designed for an overseas audience, with little crossover to the domestic Australian audience until it was reported in Australian and global media.

The second example also made headlines in the Australian domestic media. In 2014, newspapers across Australia reported on the funding and distribution of an 18-page graphic novel storyboard that was released on the Department of Immigration and Border Protection as well as the Customs and Border Protection Services websites. The digital images feature the story of an Afghan man attempting to reach Australia by boat. In Afghanistan, the man is shown getting money from family members and paying a people smuggler, but when he reaches Indonesia his visions of a safe and comfortable trip are replaced with the reality of a small, overcrowded fishing boat. Rough seas and dangerous conditions are followed by a rescue by the Australian navy, after which the man is sent to immigration detention facilities on what is clearly the island of Nauru. The comic closes with pictures of the man, miserably waiting in detention, while his parents are left in limbo in Afghanistan, also waiting. Research into the creation of the digital storyboard shows that the author worked at the time for Statt Consulting, a Singapore-based media firm that eventually made over AUD17 million from the *No Way* campaign (xBorder, 2014). While it's unclear how and where the comic was distributed abroad, Australian media raised the profile of this campaign through frequent mention in media stories over the next two years, as well as using the illustrations in stories that documented the increasing reach of the *No Way* deterrence campaign.

The third example from the *No Way* campaign is less well-known. This audio clip was produced in Urdu and Dari, for distribution in radio spots abroad. This was likely released in 2014. Over the sound of the English-language speech given by Scott Morrison, the spot states:

> A message from Mr Scott Morrison, the Australian Government Minister for Immigration and Border Protection. My message to anyone considering getting on a boat illegally bound for Australia is simple, don't do it. Our government has implemented the toughest ever measures to stop people coming to Australia illegally by boat. You will be detected, you will be intercepted, you can be turned back, and if you do make it to Australia, you will not stay there and you will never ever live here. You will be quickly sent to PNG or Nauru where you will stay. You will not get what you are coming for, what you are taking the risk for, and I will make sure of that. (No Way, 2014)[1]

While the feature film and graphic novel storyboard received a great deal of media attention, less flashy products such as this radio spot were much more common within the *No Way* campaign. Billboards, leaflets, radio and television spots, and particularly targeted social media advertisements were ways that the campaign directly reached out to communities in potential source countries and addressed would-be asylum seekers and their relatives directly. Together, these three campaign products illustrate the diversity of deterrence messaging efforts and the breadth of this information campaign. With this better understanding of what deterrence messaging can look like, it is time to turn to the question of the potential audience.

---

[1]Note: this was an English translation provided by the Australian government on the *No Way* campaign website.

For Whom is Deterrence Messaging?

The *No Way* campaign operated both onshore and offshore, directed at multiple audiences. In this section, I detail the different audiences targeted by the *No Way* campaign in order to frame the wider question: if PICs are generally understood by scholars to be ineffective, then why are they deployed at the scale of *No Way*? For whom, then, is deterrence messaging?

The first and most obvious target of *No Way* messaging was potential migrants living offshore. For instance, a prominent billboard in English and Urdu was displayed at the Karachi Airport in Pakistan in 2014, with the *No Way* slogan plastered across the top in bright red letters (Sun, 2017). Clearly, this billboard, like the Urdu and Dari radio spot detailed above, was produced in the language of and distributed within regions from which asylum seekers had been travelling to Australia. According to Freedom of Information requests, detailed market research from firms such as McNair Ingenuity Research (Crows Nest, New South Wales) and Cubit Media Research Group (Melbourne, Victoria) provided overviews of target markets for the *No Way* campaign. Typically, these market research reports generate profiles of targeted groups broken down by ethnicity, location and gender, and consider which messages would be most meaningful to which audience. A previous campaign's market research report, released via freedom of information requests, details how Hazara men in Pakistan and Afghanistan, for instance, had different motivations for migrating to Australia: in Pakistan, economic opportunity was the primary motivation, whereas in Afghanistan, security was migrants' top concern. The range of distribution areas throughout the Middle East and South Asia and the diversity of types of advertising used in the *No Way* campaign demonstrate that potential migrants were indeed targeted by the campaign. For instance, the campaign conducted community outreach in Pakistan, Afghanistan and Iran; distributed over 100,000 graphic novel storyboards in Afghanistan and Pakistan; distributed leaflets in Malaysia, Indonesia, Thailand and Sri Lanka; advertised with posters in Indonesia; used motorcycle taxi advertising in Sri Lanka, Pakistan and Vietnam; and employed street theatre troupes to perform in India, Bangladesh and Vietnam (Hehir, 2016). The juxtaposition of motive and advertising medium was tragically displayed in photographs of a previous Australian deterrence campaign *You won't be settled without a visa*, where the campaign billboard could be seen in the background of pictures of a bombing in Quetta in 2010 which killed 73 people, mostly Hazara (Hazara.Net, 2016).

In addition to targeting potential migrants offshore, the *No Way* campaign also attempted to reach relatives, community members, and friends of potential migrants both on- and offshore. The attempt to reach potential migrants' Australian networks were part of a long-standing strategy, according to interviews with staff of departments who worked on migrant deterrence campaigns. Campaign producers asked: 'What were the ties between the expat and origin communities? We used our humanitarian resettlement teams and our multicultural teams and sat down with them to see what 'walking in their [the migrants'] shoes' might feel like (Pseudonym, 2023)'. This resulted in strategies that targeted what the Australian government classifies as the 'ethnic media' within Australia, including community newspapers, television and radio stations, to run deterrence advertising. Another interviewee noted, 'we created media for the diaspora and also used mainstream media [within Australia]'. For the *No Way* campaign, this occurred in various ways: for instance, records of the Australian government indicate that at least AUD200,000 was spent on 'ethnic media' radio spots targeting migrant communities within Australia between 2014 and 2015, with another AUD200,000 spent on 'ethnic media' digital advertisements targeting the same group (Department of Finance, Governance and Resource Management, Commonwealth of Australia, 2015). Some Australians who encountered these advertisements found them confusing: Aitak Salempour, an Australian citizen who migrated from Iran when she was one, encountered *No Way* materials in Farsi when she was browsing Facebook. She said,

> Maybe because I've put [on Facebook] my place of birth which is in Iran … I have no idea why they would have chosen me who is already an Australian citizen living here… I was confused and it was confronting, they've missed their target completely. (Dias, 2016, p. 1)

In addition to these two more obvious targets of deterrence advertising, it is clear that the Australian campaigns are also designed to persuade Australian voters. Considerable research shows that the 2001 use of the *M. V. Tampa* case to politicise the issue of asylum, connected to the fears of Muslim immigrants at the time of 9/11, helped win then-Prime Minister John Howard that year's general election, as well as the subsequent election. Border protection became the salient issue for key elections, McAllister (2003) notes. Voters were particularly swayed by Howard's use of language on border issues, which characterised 'boat people' as threats to Australian national identity (Clyne, 2005, p. 173). The line between information and election campaigning was so closely tied during the lead-up to the *No Way* campaign that the Auditor General had to review and justify the use of the *By Boat, No Visa* campaign in particular, which was deployed during the 'caretaker' period after the general election had been called. As the report states, 'the Australian general public was included as a secondary audience of the *By Boat, No Visa* campaign' because of the public's role as a 'friend and influencer of the target communities', though the government was accused of exaggerating this justification in order to publicise its anti-asylum policies to voters (Australian National Audit Office, Commonwealth of Australia, 2016, p. 60). Despite the over 20 years of government attempts to link border security with anti-asylum rhetoric, however, there still exists sympathy for refugees and asylum seekers, as Sharples et al. (2023) document. Summarising research conducted about the efficacy of anti-asylum messaging, Sharples et al. (2023, p. 1542) write that although asylum-seekers have been used as a political 'wedge' issue in general elections since the early 2000s, 'most voters do not care enough about the issue of people seeking asylum to let it influence their voting behavior' (also see Briskman & Sharples, 'Introducing the Politics of Deterrence, Detainment and Dehumanisation', this volume). Clearly, anti-asylum information campaigns – particularly the publication of products such as newspaper advertisements in mainstream

Australian media, the graphic novel storyboard on the *No Way* website or the production of English-language translations of campaign materials – are directly and indirectly targeting Australian voters, yet the efficacy of their messaging, similar to the migrants and relatives described above, remains questionable.

A wider group of right-wing anti-migrant politicians from around the globe formed a fourth potential audience for the *No Way* campaign, as President Trump's tweets introduced above demonstrate. Dutch politician Geert Wilders mimicked the slogans from the *No Way* campaign in his own anti-immigration videos in 2015, where pictured behind him reads: 'No Way. You will not make the Netherlands home' (Tovey, 2015). In 2019, US President Trump's tweets demonstrated the continued salience of the campaign for anti-migrant policymakers. Meanwhile, the UK's 2023 Illegal Migration Act was rolled out with messaging replicating 'No Way' slogans, with UK Prime Minister Rishi Sunak (2023) tweeting out messages stating: 'If you come to the UK illegally you will be BANNED from ever claiming asylum in the UK' as part of the government priority to *Stop the boats*. These politicians are not just mirroring the content of the messaging, but adopting aspects of Australia's harsh anti-asylum policies. For instance, Zirulia and Martinico (2022, p. 265) document how Italy has worked to close maritime borders while migrants' asylum claims are processed, describing these measures as 'resemble[ing] the Australian 'no way' approach'. President Trump's 2017 'Muslim Ban' was put into place days before his call with Australian Prime Minister Malcolm Turnbull, where he noted approvingly that Australia's policies towards asylum seekers were harsher than those of the USA, saying 'you are worse than I am' (Henriques-Gomes, 2019, p. 1). Meanwhile, Geibel et al. (2023) trace how the *No Way* message has resonated with far-right movements across Europe, including Germany and France. They link the racialised rhetoric of the *No Way* campaign in Australia to efforts to promote white supremacist, far-right ideologies in the European context. As a fourth audience of the *No Way* campaign messaging, the collection of right-wing, anti-migrant political figures who have adopted similar communications strategies is perhaps the most clearly influenced by the tenor of the messaging.

Conclusions

PICs are increasingly common forms of deterrence messaging across the globe – yet their efficacy, particularly in regard to their ability to change potential migrants' and asylum-seekers' decision-making processes, has remained in doubt. So why do these campaigns remain so popular? I argue here that these campaigns appeal to a wide variety of audiences, and messaging not only targets potential migrants, but also their relatives and community members, voters in countries such as Australia who have politicised issues of migration and asylum seeking, and crucially, have become important inflection points for right-wing politicians who adopt and amplify this messaging abroad. Why do these deterrence messages strike such a chord with right-wing politicians? Geibel et al. (2023, p. 2) note that the resonance of messages such as 'You will not make Australia home' is closely linked with racialised constructions of white national identities in the places where *No Way*'s message has become popularised. In Australia, the demonisation of 'boat people' has always been closely linked with the perceived threat of not just migration, but migration of black and brown asylum seekers: asylum seekers arriving by boat are on average poorer and racialised as browner than their counterparts who arrive by plane, and disadvantaged through their inability to fly to Australia with a legal visa (Bolger, 2016). Maintaining a sense of control over the whiteness of Australian national identity has motivated some of the intense Australian focus on 'boat people' over the past 20 years (Huynh & Neyland, 2020). Current efforts to deter asylum seekers arriving by boat echo colonial logics of containment that trapped Aboriginal Australians on reserves, confined migrants to quarantine stations, and detained residents in enemy alien internment camps during World War I and World War II (Nethery, 2021). The connections between deterrence efforts and work to maintain whiter national imaginaries are not unique to Australia. Bird and Schmid (2021, p. 6), for instance, write that migration deterrence is part of the 'racialised management of surplus populations within systems of global capital accumulation'. A focus on deterrence projects must necessarily consider the role of race, national identity, and the multiple audiences to which these deterrence efforts are targeted. As *No Way* demonstrates, corrosive anti-asylum messaging has a global audience, and migrants and asylum seekers continue to be impacted by the actions taken by those who adopt these messages.

References

Ajzerle, S. (2016). *The source of migrant information, the myth of the IOM's information campaigns and an examination of migrant decision-making processes*. Canadian Association for Refugee and Forced Migration Studies. https://carfms.org/research-and-papers/carfms-student-essay-contest/undergraduate/

Australian National Audit Office, Commonwealth of Australia. (2016). *Government advertising*: March 2013 to June 2015. Across Entities. https://www.anao.gov.au/work/performance-audit/government-advertising-march-2013-to-june-2015

Bajomi-Lázár, P. (2019). An anti-migration campaign and its impact on public opinion: The Hungarian case. *European Journal of Communication*, *34*(6), 619–628.

Bird, G., & Schmid, D. (2021). Humanitarianism and the 'migration fix': On the implication of NGOs in racial capitalism and the management of relative surplus populations. *Geopolitics*, *28*(3), 1235–1261.

Bishop, S. C. (2020). An international analysis of governmental media campaigns to deter asylum seekers. *International Journal of Communication*, *14*, 23.

Bolger, D. D. (2016). *Race politics: Australian Government responses to asylum seekers and refugees from White Australia to Tampa* [Doctoral dissertation, Western Sydney University]. https://researchdirect.westernsydney.edu.au/islandora/object/uws:37989/datastream/PDF/view

Browne, E. (2015). *Impact of communication campaigns to deter irregular migration* [GSDRC Helpdesk Research Report 1248, GSDRC]. https://gsdrc.org/publications/impact-of-communication-campaigns-to-deter-irregular-migration/

Clyne, M. (2005). The use of exclusionary language to manipulate opinion: John Howard, asylum seekers and the reemergence of political incorrectness in Australia. *Journal of Language and Politics*, *4*(2), 173–196.

Coddington, K. (2018). Boats: Settler colonial territorial imaginaries: Maritime mobilities and the 'tow-backs' of asylum seekers. In K. Peters, P. Steinberg, & E. Stratford (Eds.), *Territory beyond terra* (pp. 185–202). Rowman & Littlefield.

Coddington, K., & Williams, J. M. (2022). Relational enforcement: The family and the expanding scope of border enforcement. *Progress in Human Geography*, *46*(2), 590–604.

Department of Finance, Governance and Resource Management, Commonwealth of Australia. (2015). Campaign advertising by Australian government departments and agencies annual report 2014–2015.

Dehm, S., & Silverstein, J. (2021). Film as an anti-asylum technique: International law, borders and the gendering of refugee subjectivities. *Griffith Law Review*, *29*(3), 1–26.

Dias, A. (2016, November 7). *Government Facebook ads tell migrant Australians to deter family members from arriving illegally*. ABC News. https://www.abc.net.au/news/2016-11-07/facebook-ads-target-migrant-australians/8002818

Fleay, C., Cokley, J., Dodd, A., Briskman, L., & Schwarz, L. (2016). Missing the boat: Australia and asylum seeker deterrence messaging. *International Migration*, *54*(4), 60–73.

Geibel, M., Fozdar, F., & McGaughey, F. (2023). 'No way. You will not make [insert country here] home': Anti-asylum discursive transfer from Australia to Europe. *Current Sociology*. https://doi.org/10.1177/00113921231194093

Hazara.Net. (2016). *Refugees*. Retrieved on June 11, 2020, from https://www.hazara.net/refugees/

Hehir, G. (2016, October 19). Government advertising: March 2013 to June 2015 [ANAO Report 22 2016–2017, ANAO Performance Audit]. Australia National Audit Office.

Henriques-Gomes, L. (2019, June 27). Donald Trump says 'much can be learned' from Australia's hardline asylum seeker policies. *The Guardian*. https://www.theguardian.com/us-news/2019/jun/27/donald-trump-says-much-can-be-learned-from-australias-hardline-asylum-seeker-policies

Hightower, B. (2013) Australian hospitality: Overseas information campaigns and the 'theatricalised' encounter. Law, Text, *Culture*, *17*(3), 8–43.

Humphrey, A. (2018). Emotion and secrecy in Australian asylum-seeker comics: The politics of visual style. *International Journal of Cultural Studies*, *21*(5), 457–485.

Huynh, K., & Neyland, S. (2020). Australian whiteness and refugee politics. *Australian Journal of Politics & History*, *66*(1), 111–129.

Jesudason, T. (2015). *We asked Sri Lankans what they think of Australia's anti-refugee billboards*. https://www.vice.com/en/article/3bjq49/we-asked-sri-lankans-what-they-think-of-australias-anti-refugee-billboards

McAllister, I. (2003). Border protection, the 2001 Australian election and the coalition victory. *Australian Journal of Political Science*, *38*(3), 445–463.

McNevin, A., Missbach, A., & Mulyana, D. (2016). The rationalities of migration management: Control and subversion in an Indonesia-based counter-smuggling campaign. *International Political Sociology*, *10*(3), 223–240.

Musarò, P. (2019). Aware migrants: The role of information campaigns in the management of migration. *European Journal of Communication*, *34*(6), 629–640.

Nethery, A. (2021). Incarceration, classification and control: Administrative detention in settler colonial Australia. *Political Geography*, *89*, 102457.

No Way. (2014). *English transcript for radio advertisements: Urdu and Dari*. https://webarchive.nla.gov.au/awa/20140211193059/http://www.customs.gov.au/site/offshore-communication-campaign-people-smuggling.asp

Oeppen, C. (2016). 'Leaving Afghanistan! Are you sure?' European efforts to deter potential migrants through information campaigns. *Human Geography*, *9*(2), 57–68.

Perera, S. (2002). A line in the sea. *Race & Class*, *44*(2), 23–39.

Pseudonym. (2023, June 13). *Former government employee's experiences with public information campaigns* [Interview by Kate Coddington].

Rajaram, P. K. (2003). "Making place": The "Pacific Solution" and Australian emplacement in the Pacific and on refugee bodies. *Singapore Journal of Tropical Geography*, *24*(3), 290–306.

Refugee Council of Australia. (2023). *Statistics on boat arrivals and boat turnbacks*. https://www.refugeecouncil.org.au/asylum-boats-statistics/2/

Richardson, R. (2010). Sending a message? Refugees and Australia's deterrence campaign. *Media International Australia*, *135*(1), 7–18.

Rodriguez, A.-L. (2019). European attempts to govern African youths by raising awareness of the risks of migration: Ethnography of an encounter. *Journal of Ethnic and Migration Studies*, *45*(5), 735–751.

Schloenhardt, A., & Philipson, E. (2013). *'No to people smuggling': A review of Australia's anti-migrant smuggling awareness campaigns*. Migrant Smuggling Working Group, University of Queensland. https://law.uq.edu.au/files/6729/Schloenhardt-Philipson-SoM-Awareness-Campaigns-2013.pdf

Sharples, R., & Briskman, L. (Eds.). (2024). 'Create a Problem, Provide a Solution': The Racialisation and Politicisation of Seeking Asylum. In *Deter, Detain, Dehumanise: The Politics of Seeking Asylum* (pp. 11–30). Emerald Publishing.

Sharples, R., Dunn, K. M., & Diallo, T. M. O. (2023). Categorising anti-asylum seeker sentiment through a regime of securitisation. *Geopolitics*, *28*(4), 1535–1561.

Sun, K. (2017, April 19). *Australia is making covert propaganda videos to scare off asylum seekers*. Quartz. https://qz.com/960950/australia-is-making-covert-propaganda-videos-to-scare-off-asylum-seekers/

Sunak, R. (2023, March 7). [Twitter]. Retrieved January 9, 2023, from https://twitter.com/RishiSunak/status/1633158877473566752

Tedmanson, D. (2008). Isle of exception: Sovereign power and Palm Island. *Critical Perspectives on International Business*, *4*(2/3), 142–165.

Tovey, J. (2015, October 5). Anti-Islam campaigner Geert Wilders video replicates controversial 'No Way' campaign. *The Sydney Morning Herald*. https://www.smh.com.au/politics/federal/antiislam-campaigner-geert-wilders-video-replicates-controversial-no-way-campaign-20151002-gjzigx.html

van Bemmel, S. (2020). The perception of risk among unauthorized migrants in Ghana. *Journal of Risk Research*, *23*(1), 47–61.

Watkins, J. (2015). *Biopolitics and border externalization: Neoliberal securitization and subjugation in Australia's irregular migration information campaigns*. UC Davis Temporary Migration Cluster (Work in Progress). https://s.gifford.ucdavis.edu/uploads/filer_public/54/46/5446ce9d-f004-4e25-80e4-3e937f277fb8/watkinmanuscript.pdf

Watkins, J. (2017). Australia's irregular migration information campaigns: Border externalization, spatial imaginaries, and extraterritorial subjugation. *Territory, Politics, Governance*, *5*(3), 282–303.

Williams, J. M. (2020). Affecting migration: Public information campaigns and the intimate spatialities of border enforcement. *Environment and Planning C: Politics and Space*, *38*(7–8), 1198–1215.

Williams, J. M., & Coddington, K. (2023). Transnational affective circuitry: Public information campaigns, affective governmentality, and border enforcement. *Annals of the American Association of Geographers*, *113*(10), 2376–2391.

xBorder. (2014). *Mapping the deterrence supply chain: The Afghanistan storyboard*. https://xborderoperationalmatters.wordpress.com/2014/02/11/deterrence-supply-chain/

Zirulia, S., & Martinico, G. (2022). Criminalising migrants and securitising borders: The Italian "No Way" model in the age of populism. In V. Stoyanova & S. Smet (Eds.), *Migrants' rights, populism and legal resilience in Europe* (1st ed., pp. 259–279). Cambridge University Press.

Chapter 4

A Decolonial Critique of Kenya's Encampment and Asylum Policy

Bosco Opi

University of South Australia, Australia

Abstract

This chapter provides a decolonial critique of Kenya's encampment and asylum policy. By using a decolonial framework, the chapter examines how asylum, a supposedly humanitarian gesture, has become a political tool of deterrence, dehumanisation and detention in this country. In examining the camp through a decolonial lens, the author advances an Afrocentric perspective and foregrounds that asylum policy across the African continent, which is largely focussed on keeping asylum seekers on this continent, should be understood against the context of colonial relations in Africa. The author contrasts Kenya's refugee camp with Australia's offshore detention camp. Central to the author's critique is Australia's outsourcing of its offshore detention camps to Papua New Guinea and Nauru which epitomises a neo-colonial engagement with these post-colonies. Inspired by the author's personal experience as a former refugee, this chapter also challenges refugee literature which is dominated by voices either without lived experience of the camp or produce work that is inadequately attentive to such knowledge.

Keywords: Camp; borders; refugees; asylum seekers; decoloniality

Introduction

Historically, refugee studies have focussed on the geopolitics of borders, state sovereignty, security, and the camp. While the concept of refugee has a history which needs to be understood, the daily challenges and the life experiences of refugees like myself, which are central to this history, are being neglected.

Deter, Detain, Dehumanise: The Politics of Seeking Asylum, 65–80

Published under exclusive licence by Emerald Publishing Limited
doi:10.1108/978-1-83753-224-720241006

Cognisant of this deficit, I begin this chapter with my personal story, so it sits alongside my academic work. I also deploy decolonial and border theories to critique Kenya's encampment and asylum policy. In locating this chapter within decolonial theory, I also examine Australia's offshore detention camp policy and the European Union's (EU) externalisation attached to this project and the colonial legacy embedded within them. I foreground that refugees need to be afforded their fundamental human rights, the rights to the freedom of movement in a borderless Africa.

My Refugee Journey

I am a third-generation refugee and my journey started when I left my country of birth, South Sudan in 1992. I fled the devastating decades of civil war and sought asylum in Kenya. I became a refugee and lived in Kakuma refugee camp for about a decade. Kakuma camp is situated about 120 km from the Kenya–South Sudan border. I will never forget my sojourning, which included navigating armed personnel at numerous border checkpoints along the way. Although there was no official restriction to entry into Kenya, the right to entry was never guaranteed as the border was often closed during refugee mass exoduses.

I was among hundreds of other refugees who arrived at the refugee reception centre in a place called Lokichogio. The following day, we boarded a United Nations High Commissioner for Refugees' (UNHCR) truck en route to Kakuma camp. On my arrival, the immediate view of Kakuma camp was the large billboards pitched along the highway with the names of the donor countries such as the United States of America (USA), Canada, the United Kingdom (UK), the EU and their representative agencies: Catholic Relief Services, Lutheran World Federation, Cooperative for American Remittances Eveywhere – signifying who wields power in this camp. As I came to understand it, Kakuma camp is a site of neo-colonial power relations administered by multiple Western organisations. Having lived in an active armed conflict situation, a police post located at the entry of the camp drew my attention. The police patrolled the camp day and night sometimes with armoured vehicles; reminiscent of a colonial camp. Upon entry into the camp, I went through the usual registration process and was provided a refugee food ratio card. As numbers are essential for donor support, the UNHCR often took extreme measures during this exercise. The UNHCR conducts refugee census periodically. When it is time to be counted, the refugees are given very short notice, less than 12 hours. Whoever is not present in the camp without prior consent from the UNHCR, missed out and by default forfeit their refugee entitlements. The headcount is often carried out from midnight and by dawn it is over. The process involves herding refugees into an enclosed shelter, fenced with barbed wires and cordoned off by armed police and sometimes the army; an exercise predicated on colonial camps. This means, the UNHCR has to spend more time writing reports about the refugees' physical presence in the camp to donors to keep itself funded. The bureaucratisation of counting and documentation means that the UNHCR's staff are neither neutral nor innocent as they spend more time writing reports to please donors than the refugees. It is through the counting that the refugees become dehistoricised, dehumanised and become generalised victims.

Kakuma camp is demarcated into fenced blocks of about three hectares lined up in clusters, to allow free passage for the vehicles of the police and the healthcare workers. The policing of emergency, the 'here and now' of the camp, means that Kakuma assumes no past and no future, but is only a constant present. It is the UNHCR's policy to contain the refugees according to their ethnicity and country of origin. Each block strictly hosts specific ethnic groups with 150–200 refugees crammed into a shantytown-like setting. I was allocated a 15 square feet block of land in which I built my mud house. Kakuma camp became my home. I had access to the basic necessities of life such as water, healthcare and food. Idleness dominated my life in the camp. This idleness was directly related to my pre-exilic experience, the experience of war and abandonment throughout my refugee journey which affects every refugee. This experience kept me in a constant past without a future. Ghasan Hage (2003) explains that this quasi-complete absence of the future lends itself to a 'premature form of social ageing, even of social death' (Hage, 2003, p. 17). Although the UNHCR plays the role of a protector in this space, it is also fully informed that the very nature of prolonged encampment is precisely where violence flourishes. I see this as part of the neo-colonial project.

In terms of capacity, Kakuma camp is severely overcrowded with a population of sometimes over 100,000 refugees and asylum seekers. This was especially the case during the 1990s when a huge number of refugees from South Sudan, Sudan, Burundi, Rwanda, DR Congo, Somalia and Eritrea sought refuge in Kenya. Over the years, many of the refugees have returned home. As of February 2024 a UNHCR report indicated that the number of refugees in Kenya was 744,747 (UNHCR Kenya, 2024). It is in the camp space where refugees are counted, their movements monitored, mapped, their daily lives disciplined, and routinised by the institutional machinery of relief agencies overseeing the camp. Kakuma camp as I experienced it, is locked in a constant state of emergency. It is on this basis that I take a decolonial critique and argue that the UNHCR removes itself from the colonial legacy of the camp by portraying itself as a protector. It also insulates itself from culpability in reproducing this symbolic violence through exclusionary refugee law and policy and keeping refugees encamped for decades. It is this symbolic violence that demonstrates the ongoing refugee coloniality.

From the late 1990s, Australia expanded its refugee resettlement programme in Kenya. The refugees whose needs could not be met within the camp, were identified and recommended by the UNHCR for resettlement in Australia. My younger brother was one of those who came to Australia in 2001 through this programme. The vetting involved two-stage eligibility interview processes by Australian immigration officials which was preceded by a medical examination. A few years later, my family and I followed my brother's footstep and joined him. The journey from Kakuma camp to Australia took about seven years of waiting in limbo. Two years after our arrival, we took an oath and became Australian citizens. We now call Australia home. I had in mind to write my refugee story, but didn't know how and where to begin. I have always had a keen interest in refugee issues. So I studied refugee law at University. In 2009, I completed an internship with the UNHCR in Canberra. Thereafter, I worked for the Department of Home Affairs for about a decade. The journey from Kakuma camp to Canberra where I worked in the two main offices responsible for refugee policy in this country and globally, and then eventually into academia, was a big leap of faith. It is this experience and exposure that drove my zeal to write my story.

Although the institution of asylum in Kenya began to erode in the 1990s due to internal issues specific to the country, including its refugee non-integration policy, there were also external factors which played a key role in this decline. From the late 1980s, Western nations began to challenge the legal and ethical foundations of the 1951 Refugee Convention by claiming that it legitimises the entry of asylum seekers into their territories. They also introduced 'offshore asylum' legislation that undermines the principle of the international refugee regime. Policies such as 'regional solutions', 'protection in the regions of origin' and 'extra-territorial policy' or 'offshore processing', were also introduced to ensure that refugees and asylum seekers were returned and or are confined within the region of their origin, often in poorer and less stable nations. In addition, a number of travel measures were introduced, including visa restrictions, carrier sanctions, interdiction on the high seas, arbitrary detention, limitations on social welfare and the right to work, as well as restrictive interpretations of the 1951 Refugee Convention. As such, Kenya and many other African nations, especially those with far more pressing economic problems and much larger refugee populations, happily joined the party. In direct response to these developments, Kenya introduced a very strict encampment policy as a means of reducing refugees' visibility and discouraging their permanent settlement. This included objecting to local integration and refraining from *non-refoulement* obligations, but only if the needs of asylum seekers were fully met by the international community. *Non-refoulement* is a legal concept prescribed in international refugee law requiring that states refrain from returning refugees or asylum seekers to territories where their lives could be at risk. It was in this context that the UNHCR's role in Kenya was reduced from providing legal protection to care and maintenance of refugee camps.

The fact that the waning hospitality towards the refugees in Kenya has existed for several years is indisputable due to its persistent refugee non-integration policy. The shaping of this shift from hospitality to deterrence and containment from the 1990s has also underlined the plight of refugees in Kenya and Africa by extension. The virtually intractable containment of refugees is not temporary as it has dramatically changed every aspect of refugee policy in Kenya. This modern culture of describing refugees and asylum seekers as those who don't belong focusses increasingly on keeping them in the camp. Louise Holborn (1975) describes the effects of this semi-permanent apartheid of the world's refugees as 'engendering a new form of being-in-the-world, characterised by wandering and lasting destitution – or rather, a form of no longer being in the world, for a certain time or forever' (Holborn, 1975, p. 1436). As asylum policy is at least one part state interest and one part compassion, this has paved the way for the development of laws, policies and practices, but in ways that still retain their colonial origin.

Kenya's Refugee Encampment Policy

Prior to 1990, Kenya had neither a refugee camp nor domestic legislation dealing with refugees and asylum seekers. In late 1991, following large-scale arrivals of refugees from eight of its neighbouring countries, this nation established two of the largest refugee camps in Africa – Kakuma and Dadaab camps. In early 1991, the Kenyan government transferred refugee management to the UNHCR. This institutional change was significant as the UNHCR's responsibility shifted from overseeing a small number of urban refugees to the management of the two mega camps, which at the time of writing host about half a million refugees and asylum seekers. This encampment policy was intended as a temporary stopgap to allow for the Kenyan government to devise a long-term policy for dealing with mass influxes of refugees, but it ended up becoming a permanent feature of Kenya's asylum policy to date. These camps have turned their temporariness into a 'transient permanency', and over time, have evolved from their ghetto beginnings into a permanent state of limbo.

The camp as an enclosed structure, can take many shapes and forms: it can be a shackle, a mud house, a tent, or an enclosure constructed haphazardly and temporary to accommodate emergencies or for long-term purpose. Although the camp varies tremendously in terms of size and capacity, this space is always overcrowded. This enclosure is carefully designed whereby the refugees' movement is carefully monitored, regulated and mapped, they are regularly counted to ensure their constant presence. Unschooled in refugee issues, the French anthropologist Michel Agier, after visiting Dadaab refugee camp in Kenya, wrote in his book, *On the Margins of the World: Refugee Experience Today*, an emotional expression about the camp space, describing the people in it as those who are in the 'outer limit of life' (Agier, 2008). His analysis is a reflection of the fact that the camp space, a UNHCR de facto fourth durable solution, resembles uneven geographies of power and status, a political space in which the refugees live, but don't belong. Kakuma, one of the largest refugee camp in Africa, demonstrates that time is suspended in this space and it enters a state of irrevocable and infinite temporality.

Kakuma camp's 7 km^2 landscape is covered with makeshift plastic tents, punctuated with the UNHCR logo which is indicative of the most conspicuous element of refugee assistance on this continent. It also shapes Western image of the refugee phenomenon in Africa. The camp was constructed in a way that allows it to distinguish between the refugees and the Kenyan citizens. This makes Kakuma camp a border zone where refugee admission into Kenya is heavily policed. Although refugees are allowed to enter Kenya, their refugee status technically locates them outside of Kenya. This inclusion and exclusion, or inside and outside politics, meant that the refugees are unassimilable. Although the Kenyan government fulfils its international obligation by admitting refugees, Kakuma camp serves as a deterrent to prevent the refugees' onward migration.

In 2006, the Kenyan government passed into law, the Kenya Refugee Act 2006. This legislation prohibits refugee movement outside the camp unless authorised by the Kenyan government. As per this legislation, it is an offence for a refugee to reside outside the camp's thorny fence. This encampment policy removes the refugees' legitimacy and makes them illegitimate bodies. It is this exclusion that reinforces Kenya's non-integration policy. It is on this basis that Kenya's encampment policy initially attracted a significant amount of donor funding as the refugee agency's responsibility shifted from managing urban refugees to mega camp operations. However, after the emergency was declared over, the UNHCR still finds itself locked in a state of emergency as the camps have transitioned from temporality to permanency by default with significant human rights concerns.

Kakuma camp which is administered like a colonial enclave, has transformed the refugee landscape into a modern security architecture for controlling refugees and asylum seekers' movement. In Kakuma camp, the refugees live in the present time with no past and no future – a life of limbo, a life of nowhere. This regulative bordering practice or what Ana María Alonso (1994) calls the 'spatialisation of being' (Alonso, 1994, p. 382), is based on ontological and epistemological resolutions of the state. Here, the state in its surveillance and control of the refugee population, is indifferent to how it relates to its citizens. Although Kenya's encampment policy has gained a reputation for having attained two key protection elements – asylum and non-refoulement, it also encourages the indefinite containment of refugees and asylum seekers in this political space.

Turkana land on which Kakuma camp is established, has a unique history. According to human evolutionary scholars, Turkana is an archaeological site over three million years old (Harmand et al., 2015). Although considered the epicentre of human civilisation during pre-colonial Africa, to date, Turkana remains the most impoverished region in Kenya with both illiteracy and chronic poverty rates as high as 95%. Interestingly, it was in Turkana that colonial Britain set up a detention camp in the late 1950s and imprisoned Kenya's first President Jomo Kenyatta for eight years. Suffice it to state that the concentration and isolation of the civilian population as punishment was invented during the 19th century decolonisation wars. This colonial practice is heavily embedded within the social structure of Kakuma camp which demonstrates a new phase of 'othering' of refugees and asylum seekers (Krause, 2021). In essence, Kakuma camp continues to reproduce practices developed by colonisation.

This colonial practice has continued in the camp space as the refugees are routinised, segregated and isolated through the logic of humanitarianism. This space is carefully designed to disguise the violence of the crime of prolonged encampment being inflicted on its residents. Zygmunt Bauman (1989) argues that 'this crime … is easy to commit with every inch of social distancing', especially for Western donors who do not have a closer visibility of these internationally funded camps (Bauman, 1989, p. 22). The main concern here is not about the colonial camp, but that many Western nations have either instituted or legislated the phenomenon of the camp. Although framed in humanitarian language as a space of protection, the camp continues to operate with force as a tool of deterrence by creating a situation of power to justify the violence of prolonged encampment being inflicted on refugees and asylum seekers.

The Colonial Origin of 'Protection'

From the 16th century, several European nations participated in the Transatlantic Slave Trade. Subsequently, protection regimes were deployed throughout European colonial' empires in Africa and the Global South. In most cases, the colonialists entered into protectorate arrangements by forming alliances with the natives without claiming political sovereignty or making jurisdictional claims, but embedding within it the possibility of conquest. A protectorate is a system of indirect rule through which the British used pre-existing local chiefs to rule their colonies on their behalf (Opi, 2021b). In colonial terms, protection meant acquiring partial or full control over natives or their territory through invasion and laying claims over them in what the colonialists refer to as the 'civilising mission' (Elkins, 2005, p. 80). Gradually, the claim for alliance shifted to subjecthood which provided a clear inroad for imperial annexation. This was authorised by the Berlin Conference of 1885 which legitimatised European colonial administrations across Africa (Gathara, 2000).

When the UNHCR intervened in Africa in the 1950s, almost the entire continent of Africa was still under protectorate arrangements. Ever since, protection continues to be its most powerful colonial symbol. Just as the natives were considered unprotected in the colonies, lack of protection is a qualification threshold for refugeehood. It is in this context that this chapter foregrounds that the framework of protection continues to function as a neo-colonial project. Evidently, refugee camp as a space of protection, has continued to be a symbol of refugee coloniality. A refugee camp is one of the most controversial elements of refugee protection.

Historically, the camp was first introduced in Africa in the 18th century as a laboratory for testing punitive confinement to restrict the natives during carceral settler expansion. Currently, 33 of the 54 African countries have established some of the largest refugee camps in the world, some established over three decades ago. I argue that in its primordial form, refugee protection and the refugee camp have retained colonial heritage and use border externalisation to symbolise a return to the protectorate regime.

When International Refugee Law was being crafted by the United Nations between 1920 and 1935, asylum seekers were defined principally in relation to their vulnerability as individuals who did not enjoy state protection (Goodwin-Gill, 1983). The concept of 'protection' was later enshrined in the 1951 Refugee Convention, but the instrument of ratification was not extended to post-colonial territories due to the presence of powerful states such as France, Britain and Germany still holding claims over territories in Africa. When the UNHCR was founded in 1950 by European nations with a strong colonial presence in Africa and around the world, it adopted the doctrine of protection in all its humanitarian work. Just as it was in the colonies, refugees are depicted as unprotected persons and lack of protection is a qualification threshold for refugeehood. This perspective is significant in examining the political context in which the term protection continues to be used throughout the centuries, to ensure refugees and asylum seekers constantly remain in captive mode.

Although colonialism was present during the drafting of the 1951 Refugee Convention, Glen Peterson (2012) stated that, 'the colonial origin of the UNHCR might have escaped the attention of refugee scholars' (Peterson, 2012, p. 331). Over the years, the UNHCR has reformulated the term 'protection' to mean humanitarian assistance to refugees and asylum seekers. This reappraisal meant the refugee agency portrays a humanitarian image of protection to cleanse itself from Africa's colonial past.

Angela Woollacott raised the provocative question in reference to the protection of Indigenous people in colonial Australia. She asked, 'who is protecting whom and for what purpose?' (Woollacott, 2003, p. 316). Here, the term 'protection' was colonially structured, aimed at segregation, subordination, control and informed by racial hierarchy and privilege that was embedded within White Australia policy. This colonial perspective is significant in examining European colonial engagement in Africa. When Britain colonised Kenya, it used the same theme of protection as a template to control the natives as its colonial subjects.

The EU's Externalisation Policy

The EU and its member states introduced border externalisation policy in 2015. Externalisation refers to measures taken by states to extend their border policies to locations beyond their territorial borders (Crisp, 2019). In the same context, externalisation refers to the transfer of border protection responsibility from the rich countries in the Global North to poor countries in the Global South and the funding of asylum detention camps to prevent refugees from reaching their shores (Opi, 2021b). In other words, externalisation refers to the outsourcing of border management to distant countries through readmission agreements, interdiction agreements, or imposing border checkpoints and visa procedures in countries of departure. The intent of the policy is to allow the EU to extend its borders beyond the physical lines on the map. This allows the border to move forward or backward or sideway. This elasticity is designed such that refugees and asylum seekers arrested on the high seas are refouled to Africa and detained in camps built and funded by the EU. Through this policy, the EU seeks to deter and prevent refugees and asylum seekers from entering Europe. It is in this context that the EU 'search, detain, and deport' operations in the Mediterranean sea demonstrate a return to the Trans-Atlantic Slave Trade, but in a new form (Opi, 2021a, p. 17).

In 2015, the EU established what it terms 'cooperation' initiative with Africa in addition to opening the Africa Trust Fund aimed at contributing to safe, secure, legal and orderly migration (Polis180, 2021). Through this initiative, the EU invoked the framework of partnership with poor countries in the Global South bordering the Mediterranean sea by signing interdiction agreements. This allows the EU to refoul asylum seekers arrested on the high seas which should be interpreted as a pure violation of the principle of nonrefoulement which is the cornerstone of the 1951 Refugee Convention.

To complement its externationalisation policy, the EU also began outsourcing its border control by funding asylum detention camps in countries of the Global South to prevent refugees from migrating to Europe. The EU racialised externalisation policy aligns with immigration and domestic policies of other developed Western nations such as Australia, Canada and the USA. These countries have introduced a number of border policies, including building border walls and fences, boosting security personnel at the borders, and surveillance measures not only as a deterrence to people smugglers, but also closing legal migration pathways. By intercepting refugees on the high seas and refouling back to Africa through a 'turn back' policy, externalisation functions as a trailblazer of the overall EU refugee policy. This is because the border as mobile technology, can move forward or backward or sideways. This elasticity is designed to capture refugees, far away from where the physical border lies. While this policy seems to be working in the short run, it has only driven refugees to use dangerous routes.

Deterrence at the borders, xenophobia and anti-immigration slogans have become an enduring feature of contemporary politics across Europe. This was witnessed in Greece where the neo-Nazi organisation the 'Χρυσή Αυγή' (Golden Dawn) invoked racial purity under the slogan 'Greece belongs to Greeks'. Since the emergence of refugees and asylum seekers on the shores of Europe in the last decade, populist far-right movements surged in countries facing similar cultural and economic crises across Europe. These include the Spanish National Democracy, Alternative for Germany, Freedom Party in Austria, Northern League in Italy and National Renovator Party in Portugal. Although being the third largest party in the Hellenic Parliament, Golden Dawn still carries out far-right violence and racist vigilantism against refugees and asylum seekers.

By processing asylum claims in Africa, the EU insists that its externalisation policy does not amount to refoulement, but acts as a substitute for internal EU refugee policy (Betts & Milner, 2006). In contrast, about 86% of people displaced worldwide are hosted in developing countries, with no intent to migrate to Europe (UNHCR Kenya, 2023). This means Africa's humanitarianism plays a critical role in protecting the institution of asylum. It is on this basis that I argue for Africa to adopt an indigenous policy to allow for the free movement of goods and people across the entire continent.

The neo-colonial intent of the EU externalisation policy was expressed by Anders Samuelsen, former Danish Minister of Foreign Affairs when referring to the refugee crisis in Europe, did joked that 'we will make a little piece of Denmark in Jordan, Lebanon or Israel' (Copenhagen Post, 2014). Samuelsen's claim is very much a postcolonial overboard, imperialistic and attitudinal. His claim is characterised by an irrational representation of refugees who are considered the most vulnerable people on earth. Edward Said critiqued that it is through such civilising language that the expansion of empires is couched. Said is concerned that such civilising language has created the very 'orient' that defined the colonial hegemony of the West (Said, 2003, p. 205).

By focussing on sending humanitarian assistance as a payback to countries that accepted to implement its externalisation policy in Africa, the EU uses a colonial lens and sees Africa as a welfare state in need of care, edification, disciplining, punishing and sometimes coercion (Van Beek, 2011). This colonial legacy aligns with Fredrick Lugard's observation that European brains, capital, energy have not been and never will be, expended in developing the resources of Africa from motives of pure philanthropy. This explains why the number of African refugees who have been granted refugee status in Europe is very insignificant. Needless to say that it would be difficult for African refugees to be granted asylum seeker status in Europe due to the polarised European asylum policy. As a former colonial administrator, the EU which inherited this colonial hegemony, is aware that colonialism created the failures of the post-colonial state.

As asylum seekers are technically produced through the technique of externalisation practices, it is evident that the camp will continue to be a significant security apparatus for some decades to come. It is in this context that externalisation or offshore bordering demonstrates a neo-colonial engagement with the post-colonial world, but in a way that is epistemologically untenable.

Australia's Offshore Detention Camps

While largely considered a third-world phenomenon in refugee literature, the camp space is also manifested in Australia in the form of mandatory detention camps, transit camps and offshore camps or what Suvendrini Perera (2002) calls neo-colonial outposts. In this context, a new 'juridico political' space, 'the camp' (Agamben, 1997), has been created inside, yet outside of the nation-state. Historically, the camp as a colonial outpost has contributed to the production of racial formation in Australia. As Giannacopoulos (2009) points out, Australia's migration law is not indigenous to this country as it arrived through an imperial force. In other words, this colonial law actively legitimatised white policy and delegitimised the presence of other races, including the Indigenous peoples. The reference to 'other races' is important because it suggests that white settlers have technically assumed the position of the natives. This colonial relation has not only shaped Australian immigration policy and political identity to date, but other colonisers have also assumed similar positions in their colonial empires around the world, including the UK.

Describing the historical camp in the context of white settlers aligns with what Arendt (1967) refers to as racial ordering that was associated with colonial histories. Although White policy in Australia was abolished by the Whitlam government in 1973, the 1958 Immigration Act is embedded exclusively within the Anglo-centric colonial system that established it. By and large, Australia as a colonial state, has retained its colonial legacy by reproducing the practice of encampment through its mandatory detention policy, hence making the camp a pathology of power. This colonial legacy of exclusion is derived from institutional forces rather than from a position of insecurity about Australia's sovereignty. Therefore, Australia's detention policy should be understood in the context of the ongoing colonial relations based primarily on Indigenous dispossession. This colonial continuity is maintained by perpetrating racial violence against refugees and asylum seekers who are regarded as illegals and assimilable only by white power (Giannacopoulos, 2009).

Giannacopoulos (2009) argues that the 'evolution of Australia's camps began from the moment 'the British law arriv[ed] through imperial force' (Giannacopoulos, 2009, p. 20). The camp was crucial for the dispossession of the Indigenous people and was the basic requirement of colonialism. Using the observation of Hannah Arendt (1967), the residents of the contemporary camp are refugees and asylum seekers who have lost the right to have a right. The Australian case demonstrates that the camp has become a form of social exclusion as it is linked to the political trilogy of citizenship, borders and sovereignty. As a product of both colonialism and modernity, the camp will continue to be a significant security apparatus to keep refugees and asylum seekers invisible, immobile and located outside of the nation-state. My central argument throughout this chapter is that the camp should not only be understood as a longstanding historico-geographical event, but as an ever-existing condition within our present juridico-political system where refugees and asylum seekers are stripped of their human rights.

In 2001, the Australia Parliament passed legislation to excise Australia's mainland from its migration zone, meaning that when asylum seekers arrived outside of Australia's migration zone, their asylum claims could be processed outside of Australia. The Parliament convened again in 2012 and further legislated that the Migration Act 1958 be amended so that arrival anywhere in Australia by irregular maritime means will not provide individuals with a different lawful status than those who arrive in an excised offshore place (Howard, 2001).

As the amended legislation was being exercised over the whole of Australia, it technically shifted Australia's borders so that asylum seekers who arrived in Australia by sea irrespective of the port of entry, whether in mainland Australia or the territorial seas, could not claim asylum in Australia. This border excision renders asylum seekers voiceless as they are cast into a life of oblivion in offshore camps in Nauru and Papua New Guinea (Barlow, 2013, p. 22). It is through such docility that the border expresses itself through those it excludes. This exclusion happens by expelling asylum seekers by merely articulating it. The shifting of borders and the territoriality of asylum in the Australian case is reflective of the colonial history of this country.

On 15 December 2010, 89 asylum seekers boarded Siev 221 and set sailed from Indonesia to Australia. 50 of them were killed when their wooden boat crashed against the rocks off Christmas Island. When the relatives of the passengers sued the Australian government for failure to provide a duty of care, the New South Wales Supreme Court ruled that the government did not have a duty of care to asylum seekers because it had no control over the primitive nature of the vessel or of those controlling it (Boochani, 2018). As this judgement demonstrates, when law and violence amalgamate, they draw the line in the sea to separate those inside and outside so that asylum seekers are excluded through legal mechanisms. This aligns with what former Prime Minister John Howard said, 'We will take whatever action is needed within the law of course to prevent the landing occurring'

(Howard, 2001, p. 2). This sovereign discourse of portraying Australia as the victim, allows this country to police its borders through violence. The critical point is, when refugees and asylum seekers are sighted along the borders, they invoke insecurity prompting the state to react with violence.

Over the years, the term asylum has undergone a paradigm shift and is now increasingly being interpreted as the right of the state to grant protection to asylum seekers. In the current environment where there has been an increase in the restrictive state practice in the asylum space, there is a need to hold states to the highest standard necessary over their protection obligation to asylum-seekers. In contrast, most countries spend large sums of money in attempting to prevent asylum seekers from entering their shores or outsource the processing of their asylum claims to poorer countries (Opi, 2021b). For example, Australia spent more than AU$4 million of taxpayers' money per year to hold a single refugee or asylum seeker on Nauru, or nearly $12,000 a day, money spent that was not cost-effective or humane (Catholic Social Services Australia, 2022). The Australian Government claims that this policy is intended to prevent unnecessary deaths at sea caused by reckless people smugglers (University of New South Wales, 2019). This political rhetoric serves to justify the astronomical amount of money being spent to exert punitive measures against asylum seekers fleeing persecution. Successive Australian governments have prioritised offshore detention to deny asylum seekers entering Australia. This offshore bordering should be understood through the concept of Manus Prison Theory which is intended to oppress and dehumanise the detainees (Boochani, 2018). Although Australia removes itself from any responsibility for what occurs in those offshore detention camps, its militarised border policy aligns with the EU externalisation policy, both of which reinforce neo-colonial engagement with the post-colonial world.

Article 1A of the 1951 Refugee Convention recognises the pre-emptory rights of the state to grant asylum to an individual where the fear of persecution is clearly identified. This means that it is within the purview of the state to deny or grant asylum. The state's pre-emptory rights to exclude aliens from its territory is illustrated below in the case of Victorian Council for Civil Liberties Inc. v Minister for Immigration and Multicultural Affairs (2002):

> The power to exclude or expel even a friendly alien is recognised by international law as an incident of sovereignty over territory. As Lord Atkinson speaking for a strong Judicial Committee of the Privy Council, said in Attorney General (Canada) vs Cain and Gilhula: one of the rights possessed by the supreme power in every state is the right to refuse to permit an alien to enter that state, to annex what conditions it pleases to the permission to enter it.

The state's supreme power to expel asylum seekers has already been legislated by and through the institution of the court. As this court case demonstrates, the right of the sovereign to protect itself by violence against rightless people is anchored in the corridors of the law. This means sovereignty is synonymous with the law itself. The state's power to exclude shows that asylum seekers are not the only ones constantly on the move. The state too is on the move, violently targeting any movement across its borders. Whether asylum seekers enter Australia's immigration zone or not, whether they are inside or outside, the law can still devour them without mercy.

In this age of *borderphobia*, borders have been expanded beyond the physical boundaries of the state and/or de-territorialised to control immigration (Burke, 2002, p. 1). As an asylum seeker fits well into the statist assumption of not belonging to a territory, their presence creates a fear factor that moulds comfortably to the citizen/non-citizen dichotomy. In essence, border security is intended to create *phobia* and to inflict violence by way of deportation, detention, quarantine or control of those considered aliens. In so doing, *phobia* continues to embody the structural imperial violence embedded within the encampment paradigm because refugees and asylum seekers are regarded as foreign bodies and a threat to the state (Opi, 2021a). Subsequently, post 11 September, when refugees and asylum seekers are sighted across international borders, this is interpreted as a direct challenge to state sovereignty. As such, they have to be exclusively confined in onshore and offshore camps which denies them their fundamental human rights. This is to ensure that refugees are either prevented from entering or are immediately directed to the camps upon entry into another state. In fact, what we are now dealing with is the permanent temporality of the camp. This policy of containment has transformed refugee policy across the world.

Conclusion

This chapter presents a decolonial critique of Kenya's encampment policy dating back to the 1990s. This historical and institutional approach to refugee management makes the camp a space where refugees are deprived of their human rights. It is in this context that the camp should not only be understood as a neo-colonial project, but also as a modern technology for the containment of millions of people. By keeping refugees in indefinite encampments, this humanitarian logic often silences and makes this population group become generalised documented victims who need to be locked up in limbo.

Funded by the West, these camps position Africa as a 'major' site for the reproduction of race and identity politics. This is indicative of the fact that some of the core features of confinement, including borders, detention camps and refugee camps were pioneered in the colonies. As a conduit of state violence, the camp continues to represent racialised geographies of the post-colonial world. It is this topological elasticity which has made the camp representative of permanent crisis across Africa and globally. Understanding this historical evolution is important as it provides both the foundation and the long view which are essential to understanding the paradigm shift in the way states continue to engage with refugees and asylum seekers. In this age of border phobia, it is the states that are in need of protection and not the refugees. Over the years, refugee camps and offshore detention camps have become an acceptable norm because donor states present this space as a safe haven for refugees and asylum seekers. Although states play the role of a patriarch in this space, by providing supposedly humanitarian assistance, they are also fully aware that the very nature of humanitarianism is precisely where violence flourishes as an imperial project. This humanitarian project is what Michael Agier (2002) refers to as 'the left hand of empire' (Agier, 2002, p. 320). For him, humanitarianism forms part of the 'global police' which exercises control over the Global South as part of the imperial politics of containment. It is this exercise of containment of refugees and asylum seekers that invokes images of Foucault's governmentality. It is in this context that this chapter foregrounds that by keeping refugees and asylum seekers in indefinite encampments, states do not only remove themselves from the narrative of violence, but also insulate themselves from culpability in producing this symbolic violence. Bourdieu (1977) advances the argument that:

> symbolic violence is the coercion which is set up only through consent that the dominated cannot fail to give to the dominator (and therefore to the domination) … which, being merely the incorporated form of the structure of the relation of domination, makes this relation appear as natural. (Bourdieu, 1977, p. 170)

In the context of colonialism, symbolic violence was often orchestrated by the colonialists as a critical mechanism for asserting colonial order. This violence was visible, but immutable to the colonised.

The technologies, practices and ideas of modern mass incarceration originated from the 18th century colonial camp and have become a permanent feature of asylum management. It is in this context that the EU's externalisation policy in Africa and Australia's offshoring detention camp has become a way of shifting responsibilities towards asylum seekers to poorer nations. I extend the argument that externalisation practice is associated with neo-imperial politics of difference. Although refugee camps or asylum detention camps and colonial camps are not identical in any shape or form, they are built using the same colonial lens. As such, the camp continues to reproduce colonial structures through epistemic hierarchies of exclusion and deterrence.

There is, a need for a new political thinking that recognises the inalienable right to seek asylum. Given that carceral detention has become widely acceptable in society, the chapter's abolitionist approach not only aims at ending carceral infrastructures, but also decolonising the endemic racialised logic embedded within them. We should not only be concerned about the historical and colonial camp, but also the global portability and permanency of the current institution of the camp.

References

Agamben, G. (1997). The camp as the nomos of the modern. In de Vries & S. Weber (Eds.), D. Heller-Roazen (Trans.), *Violence identity and self-determination* (pp. 106–119) Stanford University Press.

Agier, M. (2002). Between war and city: Towards an urban anthropology of refugee camp. *Ethnography*, 3(3), 317–341. https://doi.org/10.1177/146613802401092779

Agier, M. (2008). *On the margins of the world: The refugee experience today*. Polity Press.

Alonso, A. M. (1994). The politics of space, time, and substances: State formation, nationalism and ethnicity. *Annual Review of Anthropology*, *22*, 379–405.

Arendt, H. (1967). *The origins of totalitarianism* (3rd ed.). Harcourt, Brace & World, Inc.

Barlow, K. (2013). *Parliament excises mainland from migration zone*. Australian Broadcasting Corporation. https://www.abc.net.au/news/2013-05-16/parliament-excises-mainland-from-migration-zone/4693940

Bauman, Z. (1989). *Modernity and the Holocaust*. Polity Press.

Betts, S., & Milner, J. (2006). *The externalisation of EU asylum policy: The position of the African states* [Working paper no. 36, Centre for Migration Policy, Oxford University].

Boochani, B. (2018). Manus Island and the book written one text at a time. *The Guardian*, https://www.theguardian.com/australia-news/2018/aug/02/behrouz-boochani-manus-island-and-the-book-written-one-text-at-a-time

Bourdieu, P. (1977). *Outline of a theory of practice*. Cambridge University Press.

Burke, A. D. (2002). Borderphobia: The politics of insecurity post-9/11. Borderlands – new spaces in humanities, *1*(1). https://hdl.handle.net/2440/15854

Catholic Social Services Australia. (2022). *Nauru offshore detention company making $500,000 profit a year for each detainee*. https://cssa.org.au/news/nauru-offshore-detention-company-making-500000-profit-a-year-for-each-detainee.pdf

Copenhagen Post. (2014). *DF and Liberal Alliance propose sending refugees back to countries neighbouring conflict zones*. https://cphpost.dk/2014-10-09/general/df-and-liberal-alliance-propose-sending-refugees-back-to-countries-neighbouring-conflict-zones/

Crisp, J. (2019). *Externalisation and the erosion of refugee protection: An initial enquiry*. https://arts.unimelb.edu.au/school-of-social-and-political-sciences/our-research/comparative-network-on-refugee-externalisation-policies/blog/externalisationand-the-erosion-of-refugee-protection

Elkins, C. (2005). *Imperial reckoning: The untold story of Britain's Gulag in Kenya* (pp. 1–475). Henry Holt.

Gathara, P. (2000). *The problem is not negative Western media coverage of Africa*. https://www.aljazeera.com/indepth/opinion/problem-negative-western-media-coverage-africa-190708100429209.html

Giannacopoulos, M. (2009). *The non-justiciability of justice: Mabo, Tampa, and the violence of law* [PhD thesis, Macquarie University].

Goodwin-Gill, G. S. (1983). *International law and the movement of persons between states* (pp. 138–39). California Clarendon Press.

Goodwin-Gill, G. S., & McAdam, J. (2021). *The refugee in international law* (4th ed.). Oxford University Press.

Hage, G. (2003). *Against paranoid nationalism: Searching for hope in a shrinking society* Pluto Press.

Harmand, S., Lewis, J. E., Feibel, C. S., Lepre, C. J., Prat, S., Lenoble, A., Boës, X., Quinn, R. L., Brenet, M., Arroyo, A., Taylor, N., Clément, S., Daver, G., Brugal, J-P., Leakey, L., Mortlock, R. A., Wright, J. D., Lokorodi, S., Kirwa, C., & Roche, H. (2015) 3.3-million-year-old stone tools from Lomekwi 3, West Turkana, Kenya. *Nature*, *521*, 310–315. https://www.nature.com/articles/nature14464

Holborn, L. W. (1975). *Refugees: A problem of our time. The work of the UNHCR, 1951–1972, vol. 1 and 2*. Scarecrow Press.

Howard, J. (2001). *Transcript of the Prime Minister* [The Hon John Howard MP doorstop interview, Sydney Airport]. https://pmtranscripts.pmc.gov.au/sites/default/files/original/00010545.pdf

Krause, U. (2021). Colonial roots of the 1951 refugee convention and its effects on the global refugee regime. *Journal of International Relations and Development*, *24*, 599–626.

Opi, B. (2021a). Borders recolonised – the impacts of the EU externalisation policy in Africa. *Journal of Decolonising Disciplines*, *3*(1–23).
Opi, B. (2021b). *Refugee coloniality: An Afrocentric analysis of prolonged encampment in Kenya* Flinders University Theses Collections.
Perera, S. (2002). *What is a camp?* http://www.mcrg.ac.in/RLS_Migration_2020/Reading_List_2020/Module_E/Perera_what%20is%20a%20camp.pdf
Peterson, G. (2012). The uneven development of international refugee law regime in post-war Asia: Evidence from China, Hong Kong and Indonesia. *Journal of Refugee Studies*, *25*(3), 326–343.
Polis180. (2021). *Where are Europe's borders? The EU border externalisation policies discussed.* https://polis180.org/polisblog/2021/06/03/where-are-europes-borders-the-eu-border-externalisation-policies-discussed/
University of New South Wales. (2019). *What is Australia's policy on turning back boats?* https://www.kaldorcentre.unsw.edu.au/publication/turning-back-boats-0
UNHCR Kenya. (2024). *Operation update 2024*. https://www.unhcr.org/ke/wp-content/uploads/sites/2/2024/04/UNHCR-Kenya-Operational-Update-February-2024.pdf
Van Beek, W. (2011). Cultural models of power in Africa. In J. Abbink & M. de Bruijn (Eds.), *Land, law, and politics in Africa: Mediating conflict and reshaping the state* (pp. 25–48). James Currey & Heinemann.
Victorian Council for Civil Liberties Inc. v Minister for Immigration and Multicultural Affairs. (2002). 182 A. L. R. 617, 2001, FCA 1297 at para. 199.
Woollacott, A. (2003). The meanings of protection: Women in colonial and colonising Australia. *Journal of Women's History*, *14*(4), 213–221.

Chapter 5

Anonymous Lives: The Counted and Uncounted

Claire Loughnan

The University of Melbourne, Australia

Abstract

In this chapter, the author dwells on the effects of documenting and the failure to document, border lives and deaths. Despite their apparent differences, both practices function as forms of erasure. While the Australian government has historically been keen to document the number of asylum seeker arrivals in this country, it has shown no interest in the numbers and names of those who have died in attempting to arrive here. In contrast, those who manage to cross the border, are subject to intense classificatory and numbering regimes. The latter manifests in bureaucratic control and excessive intervention, while the former reveals governmental denial of complicity in these deaths by not acknowledging them. Both practices share a refusal to encounter the other on ethical terms, reflecting the politics of numbers (Andreas & Greenhill, 2010) at and within the border. This also reveals a paradox, between being represented and not being represented. In the lacuna of details about border deaths, human rights organisations, researchers and advocacy groups have sought both to honour these deaths and to ensure that the scale of border violence is marked by statistical records on the numbers of border deaths. While it might seem that being 'counted' – or in Butler's (2003, p. 41) terms – 'represented' is better than not being counted/represented at all, representation is never straightforward (Szörényi, 2009b, p. 185): being counted is often barely a form of representation, with such 'numbering' practices contributing to the effacement, rather than the recognition of refugees' humanity.

Keywords: Border deaths; refugees; Deathscapes; SEIV-X; Operation Relex; Manus Island; dehumanisation; borderlands

Deter, Detain, Dehumanise: The Politics of Seeking Asylum, 81–98

Published under exclusive licence by Emerald Publishing Limited
doi:10.1108/978-1-83753-224-720241007

Introduction

On 19 October 2001, a boat – classified by the Australian government as a 'Suspected, Illegal Entry Vessel' (the SIEV X) – capsized in international waters between Indonesian and Australian territory. Although 41 adults and 3 children survived, 352 people drowned. Their bodies were never recovered (Australia Senate, Commonwealth of Australia, 2002a, p. 195). The boat was given the designation 'X', as the marker used by the Australian government when a SIEV has not yet been assigned a 'tracking number' (Armbruster, 2021). As it was later reported: '"SIEV" stood for "suspected illegal entry vessel" and it was given the "X" designation because unlike other boats that were given a number as they were intercepted and returned by Australia, this ill-fated one … was not' (Armbruster, 2021).

There was considerable secrecy surrounding the circumstances. Survivors recounted that after the boat sank, there were several – presumed Australian – military boats that approached with lights, but that did not attempt to rescue them (Australia Senate, Commonwealth of Australia, 2002a). Instead, a passing Indonesian fishing boat took on board those who were still alive (Armbruster, 2021). It took three days after the event for this news to be made public by the Australian government. This is the worst *known* tragedy of deaths at sea in the region. Those on board had sought to come to Australia to seek refuge under the terms of the Convention relating to the Protection of Refugees. Former Australian Diplomat, Tony Kevin, later reflected on the intentions underlying the failure to rescue those on board. He pointed to evidence suggesting the boat was never intended to arrive safely (Australia Senate, Commonwealth of Australia, 2002b) as part of the performance indicators associated with the maritime interception programme *Operation Relex* and in light of an imminent Federal election (Australia Senate, Commonwealth of Australia, 2002b, pp. 7–8). Mirroring these concerns, a former senior official in Australia's Defence Department, Allan Behm, also observed that:

> The key performance indicator, if you like, for the success of Operation Relex is the exclusion of these people from Australia. What you might describe as humanitarian issues, or compassion issues, seem completely to have been lost sight of and I don't think that they are mutually exclusive. (Parish, 2002)

It is unsurprising then that Kevin later described the SIEV X as a 'coffin ship'. As one of the survivors, Amal Basry also reflected, 'it was like the doors of hell opening on to us' (Armbruster, 2021).

Almost a decade later, another boat carrying what is thought to have been 90 asylum seekers – the SIEV 221 – crashed into the rocks off Christmas Island, an Australian territory located northwest of the mainland.[1] Approximately 50 people died. Whereas the deaths at sea of people on the SIEV X occurred far from the eyes

[1]Christmas Island is closer to Indonesia – 350 kilometres south of Indonesian territory – than it is to mainland Australia. It is located 1,500 kilometres west of nearest Australian landfall, and 2,600 kilometres from Perth, the closest capital city in Australia.

of the Australian community, those who drowned and struggled to be rescued, were in plain view of local residents at Rocky Point, located 'directly in front of the Christmas Island township' (O'Connor, 2010). Images of the floundering vessel and its desperate passengers were plastered across media outlets. Many within the local community who witnessed the horror of this scene remain traumatised by it (O'Connor, 2010). Tears were also shed in the Australian Parliament. But the grief was hollow. As Weber and Pickering (2011) observed: 'the Prime Minister herself does not grieve; her acts do not remember. Rather, recognition, grief and mourning for lives lost are proximate to the incident: borne by the survivors and the local residents' (p. 76).

These two incidents are perhaps the most notable in the Australian public imagination regarding deaths at sea of asylum seekers, attracting public outrage at the tragedy of lives lost. Yet paradoxically, those who are governed *within* the immigration detention system, are subject to other practices of erasure through numbering processes. There is a clear pattern of those detained being referred to and called upon, by their ID number, rather than their names. The testimony of 'Osman', who was detained under Australian immigration law, attests to the dehumanisation associated with the use of these ID numbers: 'When officer call me "0276", I said "Oh God! I've got name. Your donkey, er your dog and your cat has name. I'm a human like you. Don't call me by number"' (Fiske, 2015, p. 20).

However, in interrogating the violence of the border, one must also acknowledge that this is the violence of particular bordering structures, that of *colonial borders* (Giannacopoulos, 2006; McKinnon, 2020; Weber et al., 2023). Nation state borders, as argued by Weber et al. (2023) are colonial structures that have been externally imposed upon the lands of Indigenous peoples. Functioning as a necessary violence for the extension of colonial rule, their consolidation has been 'achieved through settler claims to lawful authority' (Weber et al., 2023, p. 72). At the same time, First Nations peoples have been erroneously positioned under colonial, settler law as those who have no law, who have no land. The dominance of the nation state border and the associated assumption that this is the normal order of things (Weber et al., 2023, p. 205) renders as 'naturalised' the border harms that are endured by the racialised other. Acknowledging borders as places of death and mourning is one attempt to resist the normalisation of this suffering. It contests the framing of these harms as merely the collateral damage of people's 'poor' choices in seeking to cross the border without prior authorisation, especially since these borders were imposed without the consent of Indigenous communities who hold prior authority over this land.

Here I dwell on the effects of documenting *and* the failure to document, border lives and deaths. Despite their apparent differences, both practices function as forms of erasure. While the Australian government has historically been keen to document the number of asylum seeker arrivals in this country, it has shown no interest in the numbers and names of those who have died in attempting to arrive here. In contrast, those who manage to cross the border, are subject to intense classificatory and numbering regimes. The latter manifests in bureaucratic control and excessive intervention, while the former reveals governmental denial of complicity in these deaths by *not* acknowledging them. Both practices share a refusal to encounter the other on ethical terms, reflecting the 'politics of numbers' (Andreas & Greenhill, 2010) at and within the border. This also reveals a paradox, between being represented and *not* being represented. In the lacuna of details about border deaths, human rights organisations, researchers and advocacy groups have sought both to honour these deaths and to ensure that the scale of border violence is marked by statistical records on the numbers of border deaths. While it might seem that being 'counted' – or in Butler's (2003, p. 41) terms –'represented' is better than not being counted/represented at all, representation is never straightforward (Szörényi, 2009b, p. 185): being counted is often barely a form of representation, with such 'numbering' practices contributing to the effacement, rather than the recognition of refugees' humanity. Ironically the Australian government is willing to honour those in the military who have died as a result of 'Operation Sovereign Borders'[2] while those who have been the fatal targets of this maritime surveillance programme, simply do not appear.

Border Deaths/Border Lives: Who Counts?

The discussion that follows focusses on the Australian context, although it is clear that such border violences and the counting/uncounting practices accompanying them, are global in scope. In their book *Deaths at the Global Frontier*, a remarkable account and analysis of border deaths, Weber and Pickering (2011) observe that 'for every dead body washed up on the shores of the developed world experts estimate there are at least two others that are never recovered' with approximately '14,000 people known to have died between 1993 and 2010' (p. 1). In some contexts, the amount of material gathered and recorded about border deaths is extensive and in others, remarkably absent. Many 'counts' of border deaths are disputed and often, there is 'no count' at all. It is extremely hard to get any information about the deaths at the border and caused *by* the border, especially where there is no body, no witnesses, or the testimony of witnesses is neither sought, nor heard. In the US context, border patrols often result in individuals seeking alternate routes, for example, across the dangerous waterways of the Rio Grande and into the Arizona desert (Weber & Pickering, 2011) in order to circumvent these patrols. Borderland deaths then, are the direct product of highly militarised and intensively policed bordering practices in the region, accompanied by high border walls and fences across the United States (USA)/Mexico border (Weber & Pickering, 2011). Such locations also make the bodies hard to find or identify. Accordingly, many deaths remain invisible (Border Crossing Observatory, n.d.). Although estimates suggest an average of about 500 deaths each year at the USA/Mexico border, it is commonly acknowledged that such deaths are significantly under-reported (National Immigration Forum, 2022). To report a death, someone or some organisation must not only know that it occurred, but must wish to make this known.

In the absence of government attention to 'who counts' in relation to border migrant deaths, sites like *Deathscapes*, and the *Border Crossing Observatory* as well as numerous civil society organisations, in Australia, southern Europe, the USA and

[2]The Australian war memorial has a plaque dedicated to a soldier who died while on military service as part of 'Operation Sovereign Borders'.

beyond, are dedicated to mapping and documenting deaths at the border. The key aims are two-fold: to honour the memories of those who died and to draw attention to the lethal effects of border violence (Weber & Pickering, 2011).[3] Many of these sites push for the collation of statistics on border deaths and scrutiny over border policing so that such evidence will 'enable research and provoke public awareness and discussion leading to 'concrete recommendations and policy changes' (Border Crossing Observatory, n.d.). Each shares a motivation to uncover the violence of the border for those who are unable to cross it safely, or who are deemed border transgressors (Border Crossing Observatory, n.d.; Deathscapes, n.d.; Missing Migrants Project, n.d.; Weber & Pickering, 2011). For Weber and Pickering (2011), this is an important step in holding governments to account, simply because bordering technologies and infrastructures have been 'instrumental in those deaths': such documentation is a first step in enabling 'responsibility to be correctly attributed' (Fekete cited in Weber & Pickering, 2011, p. 37). The Observatory also records deaths of asylum seekers and refugees that have occurred after their release from detention: many of these deaths are arguably the effect of the persistent health-related harms of immigration detention (Hartley & Fleay, 2012). This is significant given that there are no coronial inquests for deaths that occur in places of offshore detention or once released from detention: such deaths fall outside the jurisdiction of state coroners and the requirement to report deaths in custody.[4] Attempts to measure and to chronicle lives lost as an effect of border violence are thus critical in revealing the loss and harms that contemporary borders produce.

If data are the means by which contemporary governance makes knowledge claims and renders society 'legible' (Andreas & Greenhill, 2010, p. 11) then the counting/uncounting practices at the border by states that seek to prevent 'illegal' arrivals, marks a determination to make unknown and unseen the ways that border violence is experienced. While counting practices are a political exercise (Weber & Pickering, 2011) so too is the failure to count. In the case of border deaths, the refusal to count, is to take the problem out of the view of the public, to assert that there is *no* problem and at the same time – and paradoxically – managing this problem by the refusal to document border deaths. This points to the ways that governance, through the management and communication of statistics, is always

---

[3]See for example: Migrants at Sea; Deaths at Borders Database; Border Crossing Observatory; Missing Migrants Project; Deathscapes Project; Remembering the Dead; Recovered Bodies Project; SIEV X Memorial, International Organisation for Migration. See also a recent report on deaths in Southern Europe, from the International Committee of the Red Cross (2022) *Counting the Dead: How registered deaths of Migrants in the Southern European Sea Border provide only a glimpse of the issue*, and blog posts on the Oxford Border Criminologies website, on border deaths. A recent example can be found here https://blogs.law.ox.ac.uk/border-criminologies-blog/blog-post/2023/06/normalisation-migrant-deaths-and-its-implications.

[4]This is a requirement that was instituted following Australia's 1991 Royal Commission into Aboriginal Deaths in Custody. https://www.naa.gov.au/explore-collection/first-australians/royal-commission-aboriginal-deaths-custody#:~:text=The%20Royal%20Commission%20was%20established,General%20on%2016%20October%201987.

subject to manipulation through the non-disclosure of information. In their analysis of how policy problems are represented politically, Bacchi and Goodwin (2016) argue for an appreciation of how government representations of policy 'problems' are designed and produced to serve political interests and preferences. In relation to illicit drug use, for example, the problem is usually framed as a criminal problem and not a health problem, reflecting a 'governing through crime' preference. However, the practices of uncounting I have described go beyond government actions in 'framing' the problem in a particular way. When the figures do not even appear, when deaths are not even registered, then something more is happening. This exemplifies the observation that it behoves us to take note of what is also rendered invisible (Bacchi & Goodwin, 2016, p. 22). The absence of details about border deaths reveals an excess of data manipulation, as a form of silencing. Stanley Cohen (2001, p. xi) has described such practices as techniques in denial enabled by a 'collusion to ignore (or pretend to ignore?)' the actuality of violence and suffering around us. In this way, the problem is made to disappear, as if border deaths are simply unintelligible as a problem that demands attention and action.

In contrast, as Nikolas Rose (1999) has observed: 'To count a problem is to define it and make it amendable to government. To govern a problem requires that it be counted' (p. 221). Even when governments do gather data that reveals institutional harms (Rose, 1999, p. 197) that would otherwise not be appreciated as significant (Weber & Pickering, 2011), publishing such data is no assurance that such harms will be addressed. Publishing such figures is no assurance that they will be acted upon, as we have seen in the case of border deaths. States are reluctant to draw attention to anything that might point the finger at their complicity in these deaths. Moreover, such deaths are typically not seen as grievable deaths to begin with, by the media, the public and their political representatives (Szörényi, 2009a, p. 184).[5] They become, following Daulatzai and Ghumkor (2023, p. 205) 'naturalised deaths', deaths that are simply the remains of the constructed illegality of the racialised other.

Surveillance and an Excess of 'Counting'

As with contemporary governance and research more generally, such a focus on numbers and with *measuring* life (and death) and gathering data about both, is assumed necessary to identify a problem and to act upon it: they enable 'modern modes of governance' (Andreas & Greenhill, 2010, p. 2). This is as much the case with counting, as with *not* counting. Andreas and Greenhill (2010) observe:

> If there are no 'data', an issue or problem will not be recognized, defined, prioritized, put on the agenda and debated. Therefore, to measure something – or at least claim to do so – is to announce its existence and signal its importance and policy relevance. (p. 2)

[5]For a discussion of these dehumanising processes unfolding in other contexts, and that also impact refugee testimony, see Szoreyni (2009a).

In this vein, there is a strong emphasis on enumerating those people that the Australian government *desires to claim* that it has been able to stop from arriving. Such figures are deployed as a demonstration of the success of border protection laws and policies and as meeting 'performance targets' (Andreas & Greenhill, 2010, p. 269). This is even as we simply do not know the numbers of those who might have died in attempting to cross the border, or those who attempted to do so and were turned back. Counting at the border is thus a political act that is 'shaped by who does the counting' (Weber & Pickering, 2011, p. 37). There is inevitably a judgement or choice made about what and who to count and who to leave out, as well as how to interpret what is measured in the counting process (Weber & Pickering, 2011).

The irony then, is that even while some lives and deaths are situated outside of the gaze of government and its public, as the 'most guarded' structure 'in the world', borders

> are the object of unparalleled technological and human investment, to such an extent that they have become 'smart' and mobile, that is to say, capable of adapting to the mobility of individuals in order to follow them, tracing their routes, using carnal and vital markers such as heart rate or fingerprints, and verifying their identities almost in real time. (Bentouhami, 2021, p. 236)

This hyper-surveillance of surplus or unwanted bodies, as a 'racial necropolitics ... makes the bodies of living foreigners and their involuntary internal movements the very sites of the evidence against them' (Bentouhami, 2021, p. 235): This evidence is routinely hidden and the surveillance is targeted in the Australian case, not at individual bodies and 'lives lost' but at boats (Australia Senate, Commonwealth of Australia, 2002a, p. x; Weber & Pickering, 2011, p. 35). The surveillance of boat arrivals, in the waters north and west of Australia and the Mediterranean and north of the African continent, as with the digital surveillance of migrant movement within the border, reveal the 'mobility and dispersion of the border' (Bentouhami, 2021, p. 236) beyond the walls of the state.

Surveillance and Numbering

There is another side to this process, which is less about counting, but relates to the use of identification numbers in Australian immigration detention centres. In contemporary social life, the use of numbering practices provides a pathway into recognition of sorts, even while denying recognition as being uniquely human. Numbering is a bureaucratic process, motivated by a logic of control through processes of classification and administration, rendering those subjected to it 'psychologically invisible' (Bauman, 1989, p. 25). In contrast with those who are dying at the border, with no gravesite to mark their deaths, those who are brought into the system – notably a system of punishment and social exclusion – are recorded and documented through the assignation of numbers (Szörényi, 2004): that is, they are counted only as *a number*. Like counting, numbering is an exercise in statecraft: it enables governance (Weber & Pickering, 2011). At the time of his 'impending death' former Iranian refugee, Hamid Khazei was referred to centrally as GDD059, his boat identification number and his case, as he became fatally unwell, was described in government reports as the 'GDD059 issue' (Doherty, 2016).

It is clear that the use of numbers instead of names, has been a widespread practice over many years in immigration detention and especially in offshore processing. An unaccompanied child interviewed by the Australian Human Rights Commission (Ozdowski, 2004, p. 388) stated that:

> I often asked myself and so did the others 'why did we come here?' … My parents would regret their decision. … I feel like I did something wrong, like I was being punished. … Sometimes I feel like the ACM [Australasian Correctional Management] staff treated us like animals. They don't know how much my mother loves me. … They yell for us to line up, do this, do that. They call you by your number. (Ozdowski, 2004, p. 388)

In a personal account, former refugee Ali Kharsa, described how one of the most difficult and confronting moments of being sent by the Australian government to the offshore processing centre at Nauru, was when he was given an ID card: 'There was a number on it. I was like, "What is this?" And they were like, "This is your name. From now on this is the ID you have to use"' (Ryan, 2020). Numbering, then functioned as a *naming* practice. Experiences of dehumanisation are already endured as an effect of mandatory detention. However, to be addressed or interpellated as a number, inaugurates a level of dehumanisation that is profoundly violent, while not registering as the direct hit of violence (Loughnan, 2022a, 2022b). In Zygmunt Bauman's (1989) compelling analysis, the very possibility of the Holocaust was enabled by a set of practices that enabled the 'disappearance of violence from the horizon of daily life' (p. 107). Testifying to this process, Kurdish Iranian writer and former refugee Behrouz Boochani recounts:

> And then they call out my number: MEG45. Slowly but surely I must get used to that number. From their perspective, we are nothing more than numbers. I will have to forget about my name. My ears start ringing when they call out my number. I try to use my imagination to attribute some new meaning to this meaningless number. For instance: Mr MEG. But there are a lot of people like me. (Boochani, cited in Gessen, 2019)

'I will have to forget my name': that statement from Boochani reveals the embodied and internalised processes of dehumanisation as the simple effect of one's name becoming a number and a number which is, he says, 'meaningless'.[6]

[6]See also Boochani's (2018) incisive accounts of bureaucratic systems of control in the Australian immigration detention complex.

In their critical analysis of the use of ID numbers in immigration detention sites, Bacon and Hussein (2023) call this practice of identifying people by numbers rather than their names a 'numbering' process. Numbering, they state, 'connects a body to a row in a database, or a record in an archive' which enables this record to be utilised and 'retrieved' in ways that reflect the 'institution's logic' (Bacon & Hussein, 2023, p. 222). Numbering – like counting – is a mechanism through which people are made to be known or unknown (Bacon & Hussein, 2023). As Bauman's (1989) analysis of the Holocaust detailed, such classificatory processes are enacted through a bureaucratic logic, that is often experienced as viscerally violent, while appearing as the neutral application of a rule. This is common practice in carceral sites. In prisons, numbering processes are part of the 'formal and informal rituals of abasement, mortification and identity stripping that are designed to reshape the person into a manageable carceral subject' (Warr, 2020, p. 29).

While detained, the use of numbers ensures that those so numbered are recognisable only as subjects within the detention system. Like the failure to count deaths at sea and deaths within immigration prisons that the government claims to have no knowledge of, the Department of Home Affairs has claimed that there is no document that exists that explains the introduction of boat identifiers and affixing such numbers to people (Bacon & Hussein, 2023, p. 225). Yet such numbers are regularly called upon for processing of visa applications and access to services long after their release from detention. As Hartley and Fleay (2012) found in their analysis, release from detention does not equate to freedom. The pains of punishment remain embodied and manifest in poor mental and physical health. Similarly, those formerly detained are made to continue feeling the 'presence of the biopower' of the number, in which they remain as a 'body to be acted upon and made accountable to the institution' (Bacon & Hussein, 2023, p. 226).

Like other carceral ID numbers, Boat IDs travel and stick to people long after they have left detention. Many immigration documents, forms and processes require people to state their Boat ID as their identity. The Boat ID links these processes together, tracking the person. We are aware of cases of people being confronted with a Boat ID over ten years after it was first allocated and after being free from detention for many years. Indeed, when people call the immigration department for an update on their visa status or applications, reportedly, the first question they are asked is: 'how did you come to Australia?' Then: 'what's your Boat ID?' (Bacon & Hussein, 2023, p. 231).

Numbering is always, Bacon and Hussein (2023) observe, a 'situated action', that is, its 'meaning is particular to the institutional logic it enacts' (p. 226). These numbers ensure that the logic of the border continues to be felt by those interpellated as a number, whether detained, or not detained, whether living in community or out of it.

Counted and Uncounted Lives: Spectatorship and Mourning at the Border

Attending to counting/uncounting and numbering practices in the field of border studies, provides an understanding of the way that contemporary societies rely upon the exclusion of others at their own borders. However, it also requires a critical reflection on the effect of these processes. Despite the important aims of documenting border deaths to honour and mourn those who died as a result of border violence, there is a risk that the representation of such deaths will cluster around a uniform experience, even where these deaths are all singular deaths. Citing a single (large) number renders appreciable the scale of border deaths. But accounting practices are not only political in the sense that there is a decision made about what and who *counts* in being counted: in enumerating life in this way, they tend to reduce 'the complexity of worldwide refugee movements to a single number' (Rose, 1999, pp. 204, 198). Accordingly, such deaths are subsequently effectively (even if not intentionally) communicated through the lens of 'flows' (Weber & Pickering, 2011, p. 35). This is a common trope in the visual representation of migration and refugees in particular, with by now familiar images of the 'mass refugee exodus' or of crowded refugee camps (Szörényi, 2004, p. 6) communicating an image of 'compounded misery' (Szörényi, 2004, p. 17). Numbering and counting can replicate the effects of such images, reinforcing a representation which also effaces representation. For my purposes here, following Anna Szörényi (2004), the documentation and 'simple reportage of numbers' is the 'textual equivalent' of such images, which further distils the experiences of refugees into a 'vast amorphous mass' (p. 6). At the same time, there is 'an inverse relationship between numbers and distance': greater numbers appear necessary to generate a response the further one is away from the other. This impacts representation, since any 'sensitivity in representing the plight of others diminishes as geographical and cultural distance increases' (Szörényi, 2004, p. 96, 2009b, 97). In this respect, the location of death is also critical. When infant Alan Kurdi's body was found washed up on the Turkish coastline and similarly when over 50 asylum seekers died on the rocks and seas off Christmas Island, there was a collective outpouring of grief by Western states. This physical proximity enhanced the likelihood of their deaths being interpreted by Western spectators as a tragedy.

But whether reduced either to the one or the many, there remains the possibility of violence in the moment of representation. Perera (2006) describes this namelessness of the bodies as a reflection of contemporary political violence, rendering the dead as the unnamed collateral damage of border wars. For refugee advocate Marg Sutton:

> As long as these victims remain nameless it is easy to discount this huge tragedy that took place on our doorstep a year ago. 71 children, 142 women, 65 men – their bodies were never recovered from the ocean; they were never buried. Every single number represents a person. We need to know their names. (cited in Weber & Pickering, 2011, p. 72)

'They were never buried'. To leave a body unburied leaves it without grieving. The remarkable repository of testimony and documentation on the SIEV-X.com site – a non-government, community-driven site – ensures that the preventable drownings on the SIEV-X are remembered and honoured.[7] This work has been supported and extended by a project that established a permanent memorial to those on the SIEV-X who died, in Canberra, Australia's capital city (Gibbings, 2010).

However that documenting border deaths bears no equivalence with honouring those lives as grievable lives (Weber & Pickering, 2011) since the recognition of these deaths, as grievable, is obstructed not just by physical distance, but an ethical distance (Szörényi, 2009b). As with the SIEV-X.com site, the project *Deathscapes* has not sought to map deaths numerically, instead providing a site for the memorialisation of deaths that result from the violence of settler colonial states. Addressing the need for ethical recognition, the *Deathscapes* project exemplifies an engagement with deaths along a continuum of state violence:

> By documenting the lethal histories and legacies of settler states, Deathscapes privileges the lives and contributions of the dead that echo in the voices and experiences of the bereaved and their communities. It demands time and attention to follow its stories, drawing on a range of material, including media reports, community resources, songs, videos, photographs, poetry, artworks, interviews and institutional resources, including coronial findings. (Scott-Bray, 2020, p. 95)

In resisting erasure, Deathscapes (n.d.) works to 'instantiate agency in contexts in which it is often so brutally denied; they amplify, through their visual languages, the key analytical and political concerns articulated in the various case studies of racialised deaths'. The project responds to the question of how such deaths can be made to matter, not only as countable deaths, but as the deaths of those who *demand to be named*, in ethical terms. It is an affirmation of individual lives as grievable.

There remains however a residual risk in some settings that focussing on one face and the ethical command of the singular story could foster the fetishisation of one person's narrative, through attempts to 'humanise' through an individual narrative' (Szörényi, 2004, p. 6). The images of the suffering of the other interpellates the white viewer 'as a member of a community whose primary relationship to suffering is as spectator' (Szörényi, 2009b, p. 94). Such a position enables the

---

[7]See SIEV-X.com http://sievx.com/. As noted on the site: 'SIEVX.com is a comprehensive archive of all aspects of the SIEVX incident – the grossly overloaded asylum seeker vessel which foundered in the Indian Ocean en route to Australia on 19 October 2001, drowning an estimated 146 children, 142 women and 65 men. The website has been online since 2002 and contains a wealth of information, including news articles written at the time of the tragedy, the evidence and report of the Senate Committee that investigated the sinking in 2002, Parliamentary Questions on Notice from 2002 onwards, notes and articles on Abu Quassey, Khaleed Daoed and Maythem Radhi, the men who allegedly organised the smuggling venture as well as a collection of audio files connected with the incident and commentary exclusive to this site'.

white viewer to 'take for granted' that only some lives are characterised by suffering, that the suffering of others is remote from 'us', even when it might instead be a cause for reflecting on 'our own lives and subjectivities' (Szörényi, 2009b, p. 94). The capacity of contemporary governments and their publics, to respond to the suffering of others, is thus split between two calls: the individual call of the unique face and suffering of the other (Szörényi, 2009b) and the sheer weight of numbers in signalling the enormity and significance of human injury that demands attention and action as an effect of *scale*.

Yet the grief expressed at the discovery of the body of Alan Kurdi and by the Australian government after the deaths at Christmas Island, was promptly directed away from the state as responsible for the lethal policies that led to border deaths. In the first case, it led to the prosecution of people smugglers, a convenient way to direct attention away from the inherent violence of border protection regimes. In Australia, the tears shed in Parliament House for those who drowned off Christmas Island, led paradoxically to harsher border protection measures which were framed as necessary to prevent further deaths. What is the work being done through physical displays of grief doing then? Disturbingly, such displays perform care and compassion at the very moment that they are accompanied by policies that will lead to great suffering (Silverstein, 2023). Naming practices and honouring these deaths is not an automatic 'antidote to policies of dehumanisation' (Szörényi, 2004, p. 18). Despite the observation that 'counting and classifying a death is a translation that has the social, legal and political meaning' that can 'contest political inertia around death' (Scott-Bray, 2020, p. 94), such attempts to highlight the human cost of border enforcement are no guarantee that nation states will abandon their lethal policies.

Resistance

Numbers both grant entry to society and deny it (Bacon & Hussein, 2023). As a mode of governance, they can enable or prevent one from appearing as a 'valid' human subject. In an ironic twist, one of the men at the Manus Island detention centre recounted his experience of being numbered as one of identity-making.

> I came from Iran. The Kurdish province of Ilam. I'm stateless. I have no identity. A lot of the guys here don't like it when the officers refer to them by their numbers'. They say it's like being a prisoner, but I like it, because now I have some kind of identification. When I go to sleep, I place my ID card under my pillow. (Afshar, 2018)

However as is clear in many of the Australian immigration detention sites, numbering practices are often used and experienced in dehumanising ways, functioning as biopolitical apparatuses of carceral recognition (Bacon & Hussein, 2023). Against this, the databases and projects that are dedicated to documenting border deaths, comprise a mode of resistance to the refusal to acknowledge and honour such deaths. Likewise, those represented and interpellated only as numbers, are not inevitably 'helpless or hopeless victims of circumstance' (Scraton, 1999, p. 10). They resist. While detained, some refugees refused to show their ID and to state their boat number, when ordered to do so by Migration officers. At these moments of refusal 'the precision of the system faltered – it could not precisely see what it wanted to act on–and so control had to be rearticulated by other means', including through naming the behaviour (resistance) as 'abusive/aggressive' (Bacon & Hussein, 2023, p. 234).

Kurdish Iranian journalist and writer Behrouz Boochani, who was detained for seven years in an offshore immigration prison, exercised his own internal resistance to the dehumanisation of numbering practices:

> This system is trying to take people's personalities by calling them by a number and humiliating them. After a long time they think, they are not human. But fortunately I didn't lose my personality – I think I became a better man. I didn't forget that I am Behrouz, I am a Kurdish journalist. I didn't forget where I came from and what my mission is, my duty as a journalist. (Behrouz Boochani, cited in Bacon & Hussein, 2023, pp. 236–237)

For Kurdish refugee Mostafa 'Moz' Azimitabar, an artist, musician, writer and human rights activist, art is an avenue for resistance to the dehumanisation of numbering. Born in Iran in 1986, he was detained at Manus Island for several years. He describes one of his self-portraits in this way:

> My face looks outwards, showing the suffering I have experienced, but also my strength and determination. I painted it with a toothbrush using coffee and acrylic because I wasn't allowed to have art supplies in detention, so I used a toothbrush and coffee to make paintings on paper or whatever else I found. I chose the title KNS088 because for eight years I was called by this number instead of a name. (Art Gallery of New South Wales, 2022)

In this way, Azimitabar reflects the violence of the state back to itself. His work is a public reminder of the dehumanisation of the numbering practices embedded within the immigration detention system. But detention staff also recounted their efforts to refuse this systemic dehumanisation. Former migration worker Nicole Judge, reflects:

> We were told to use the ID numbers of those detained there, instead of their names. The rationale was that this was quicker and easier – I was told that this was because their names were 'too long and hard to pronounce'. Instead, I tried hard to memorise names, meanwhile attempting to keep my job, and not be seen as a 'troublemaker'. (Judge & Loughnan, 2022)

Cartoonist, Ali Dorani, who created work under the name 'Eaten Fish' was incarcerated at Manus Island Prison for four years. During that time, he began to develop connections with artists and advocates in Australian, including with Janet Galbraith[8] and cartoonist Andrew Marlton.[9] Like Azimitabar, in a number of his cartoons, including those published by 'Researchers Against Pacific Black Sites', Dorani inverts the violence of the system back to the community of the state that perpetrates it. Those complicit in this system are called to be a witness to these numbering processes by Dorani:

> Dorani's work commonly features an autobiographical avatar, Eaten Fish himself, whose appearance varies between drawings but is characterized by his skinny limbs, round, popping eyes, a bulbous nose, and a frizzy blob of hair perched on his forehead. He wears thong sandals, shorts, and a tee-shirt branded with Dorani's immigration processing number, RUF115. (Humphrey, 2020, p. 444)

Dorani's work is more than a call to be named, it is a call for freedom from such 'systems of domination' that are materialised through numbering (Bacon & Hussein, 2023, pp. 224–229).

Conclusion

For those who attempt to cross borders and who die in the act, the moment of mourning is limited by the failure to document deaths. These bodies are the disappeared, but their disappearance is too often not brought into view (Vallely, 2019). The failure to count such lives and deaths communicates a message that the (racialised) lives of those deemed to be border transgressors are lives not worthy of being grieved or acknowledged. Ironically those who are caught within the immigration detention system, are subject to extensive control and recognition: however, any acknowledgement of them as subjects tends to occur only within the frame of a bureaucratic system of numbers. This practice is designed to create an ethical distance between those imprisoned in immigration detention and the state and its citizens, including among those working in these sites. For both the uncounted and those subject to the numbering and classification processes of border regimes, the practices I have described above are characterised by terms

---

[8]Janet Galbraith is a Melbourne-based writer who has worked extensively with refugees in immigration detention, and was founder of 'Writing through Fences' an organisation of 'people who create – write or make art. Most of the members are, or have been, incarcerated in Australia's immigration detention regime'. *Source*: https://www.writingthroughfences.org/.

[9]Andrew Marlton is an Australian cartoonist and illustrator, often working under the pseudonym 'First Dog on the Moon'. He worked with Dorani to have Dorani's work published.

of *non*-relation. Like the failure to count and to grieve border deaths, assigning numbers as a substitute for names also erases the uniqueness of the other.

Critical criminologists have long sought to illuminate the complicity of state and organisational harms, bringing their analytical focus to the deaths of people in the prison complex (Carlton & Sim, 2018; Cohen, 2001; Scraton, 1999). From a state crime/state harm perspective, numbers can help shine a light on the state and its institutions as accountable for and complicit in, border deaths. A key concern has also been to ensure that such deaths are not decontextualised from the structures that produce them (Scraton, 1999). In recording lives and deaths at the border, a 'view from below' (Scraton, 1999, p. 10) or as Boochani (2017) describes it, a 'history from down below,' is critical. This is simply because it amounts to nothing more nor less than the appropriate recognition of this knowledge as coming from those who deliver the greatest insights into the continuum of border violence, because they have lived (and died) from it. Such a view from below is exemplified in the *Deathscapes Project* examined above.

Yet those in power often engage in techniques in which they fool themselves about the truth and engage in a complicated system of denial of culpability for the harms they produce (Cohen, 2001, p. 279). The failure to count and the deployment of numbers, as exercises in 'statecraft' are both designed to erase our own complicity in border violence. Whether through the failure to acknowledge deaths, or through the 'bureaucratic operations' (Bauman, 1989, p. 102) of detention management, the individual is situated outside the universe of moral obligations and the capacity for the state to maintain control at the border is affirmed. As Neil Vallely (2019) has remarked:

> This is the central logic of the necropolitical era in which we find ourselves, where putting unknown others to death, making them disappear, reinforces the desired attributes of national sovereignty and invulnerability. Importantly, disappearance here does not mean simply the killing of unknown others. It also includes those others who do not appear in my life, but whose existence enables me to live the life I do. (p. 38)

The border is a deathscape. But these deaths are often unseen and unmourned. At the same time, those who do manage to cross the border, exist but do not appear as lives. This is a politics of erasure of both lives and deaths at *and* within the border. Aside then from the effacement of those who die at the border, something else unfolds for those who become trapped in internal systems of border control. Where their lives are counted by the system that processes them, it is often only as a number. Such classificatory practices reduce a person to a technical rather than ethical concern. Once so categorised, humans no longer have a face and simply become a 'nuisance' (Bauman, 1989, p. 104). People start to lose their distinctiveness (Bauman, 1989, p. 103) even to the point of self-referencing as a number. A 2013 report (Ferrell, 2013) revealed numbering as a practice that was so widespread and systematic (Ozdowski, 2004), that many of those detained only knew each other by their number, not name. In both instances then, whether counted or uncounted, these are bodies that are, in Suvendrini Perera's (2006) words 'by decree unnamed, disposable casualties, whose value as 'deterrents' resides in their very anonymity' (p. 648). The effects of both counting/uncounting and of numbering, appear necessary both for the maintenance and endurance of border violence *and* the concealment of that violence.

References

Afshar, H. (2018). *Remain*. https://www.hodaafshar.com/remain-video

Andreas, P., & Greenhill, K. (2010). *Sex, drugs and body counts: The politics of numbers in global crime and conflict*. Cornell University Press.

Armbruster, S. (2021, October 19). *SIEV-X anniversary: Cover up claims remain 20 years after 353 asylum seekers drowned*. SBS News. https://www.sbs.com.au/news/article/siev-x-anniversary-cover-up-claims-remain-20-years-after-353-asylum-seekers-drowned/2o91e7enq

Art Gallery of New South Wales. (2022). *Mostafa Azimitabar KNS088H (self-portrait)*. Sydney, Australia. https://www.artgallery.nsw.gov.au/prizes/archibald/2022/30409/

Australian Senate, Commonwealth of Australia. (2002a). *Select committee for an inquiry into a certain maritime incident*. https://www.aph.gov.au/parliamentary_business/committees/senate/former_committees/maritimeincident/report/index

Australian Senate, Commonwealth of Australia. (2002b). Transcript of evidence, CMI 1325. Submission No. 2A. Select committee for an inquiry into a certain maritime incident. https://catalogue.nla.gov.au/catalog/2335047

Bacchi, C., & Goodwin, S. (2016). Making politics visible: The WPR approach. In C. Bacchi & S. Goodwin (Eds.), *Poststructural policy analysis* (pp. 13–26). Springer.

Bacon, L., & Hussein, A. (2023). Numbering and boat IDs: The dehumanizing use of ID numbers in Australia's border regime. *Design and Culture: The Journal of Design Studies Forum*, *15*(2), 221–241.

Bauman, Z. (1989). *Modernity and the holocaust*. Polity Press.

Bentouhami, H. (2021). *The life strike disobeying borders in the era of surveillance biotechnologies*. https://www.artgallery.nsw.gov.au/prizes/archibald/2022/30409

Boochani, B. (2017, December 6). I write from Manus Island as a duty to history. *The Guardian*. https://www.theguardian.com/commentisfree/2017/dec/06/i-write-from-manus-island-as-a-duty-to-history

Boochani, B. (2018). *No friend but the mountains* (O. Tofighian, Trans.). Picador.

Border Crossing Observatory. Monash University. https://www.monash.edu/arts/border-crossing-observatory/research-agenda/australian-border-deaths-database

Butler, J. (2003). *Precarious life: The powers of mourning and violence*. Verso.

Carlton, B., & Sim, J. (2018). Deaths in sites of confinement: A continuum of routine violence and terror. In S. Read, S. Santatzoglou, & A. Wrigley (Eds.), *Loss, dying and bereavement in the criminal justice system* (pp. 54–63). Routledge.

Cohen, S. (2001). *States of denial: Knowing about atrocities and suffering*. Polity Press.

Daulatzai, A., & Ghumkor, S. (2023). Afghanistan, racial melancholia and loss that exceeds loss. *Critical Times*, *6*(2), 202–211.

Deathscapes. (n.d.). *Mapping race and violence in settler societies*. https://webarchive.nla.gov.au/awa/20201103065140/http://pandora.nla.gov.au/pan/173410/20201103-1648/www.deathscapes.org/index.html

Doherty, B. (2016). Delay to treatment of Hamid Kehazaei before he died. The Guardian. https://www.theguardian.com/australia-news/2016/nov/28/delay-to-treatment-of-hamid-kehazaei-before-he-died-revealed-in-leaked-files

Ferrell, P. (2013, October 30). Officer disciplined for calling asylum seekers by numbers instead of names. *The Guardian*. https://www.theguardian.com/world/2013/oct/30/officer-disciplined-for-calling-asylum-seekers-by-numbers-instead-of-names

Fiske, L. (2015). *Human rights and refugee protest against detention*. Routledge.

Gessen, M. (2019, September 11). Behrouz Boochani is one of Australia's most celebrated writers, but he can't step onshore. *The New Yorker*. https://www.newyorker.com/news/our-columnists/behrouz-boochani-is-one-of-australias-most-celebrated-writers-but-he-cant-step-onshore

Giannacopoulos, M. (2006). Mabo, Tampa and the non-justiciability of sovereignty. In S. Perera (Ed.), *Our patch: Enacting Australian sovereignty post-2001* (pp. 45–60). Network Books.

Gibbings, B. (2010). Remembering the SIEV-X: Who cares for the bodies of the stateless, lost at sea? *The Public Historian*, *32*(1), 13–30.

Hartley, L., & Fleay, C (2012). *Released but not yet free: Refugees and asylum seekers in the community after long term detention*. Centre for Human Rights Education, Curtin University.

Humphrey, A. S. (2020). Drawing out of detention: The transnational drawing practices of Eaten Fish, refugee cartoonist. *a/b: Auto/Biography Studies*, *35*(2), 435–458. https://doi.org/10.1080/08989575.2020.1763569

International Committee of the Red Cross. (2022). *Counting the dead: How registered deaths of migrants in the Southern European Sea Border provide only a glimpse of the issue*. https://missingpersons.icrc.org/sites/default/files/2022-11/COUNTING-THE-DEAD-FINAL.pdf

Judge, N., & Loughnan C. (2022). Witnessing violence: Stories from a migration support worker. *Incarceration: An International Journal of Imprisonment, Detention and Coercive Confinement*, *3*(2). https://doi.org/10.1177/26326663221103442

Loughnan, C. (2022a). Active neglect and the externalization of responsibility for refugee protection. In A. Dastyari, A. Nethery, & A. Hirsch (Eds.), *Refugee externalisation policies: Responsibility, legitimacy and accountability externalisation* (pp. 105–123). Routledge.

Loughnan, C. (2022b). The scene and the unseen: Neglect and death in immigration detention and aged care. *Incarceration*, 3(2), https://doi.org/10.1177/26326663221103444

McKinnon, C. (2020). Enduring indigeneity and solidarity in response to Australia's carceral colonialism. *Biography (Honolulu)*, *43*(4), 691–704.

Missing Migrants Project. (n.d.). *International Organization for Migration*. https://missingmigrants.iom.int/

National Immigration Forum. (2022, September 12). *Explainer: Migrant deaths at the border*. https://immigrationforum.org/article/explainer-migrant-deaths-at-the-border/

O'Connor, A. (2010, December 20). *Christmas Islanders still shocked by drownings*. ABC Radio. https://www.abc.net.au/listen/programs/am/christmas-islanders-still-shocked-by-drownings/2381098

Ozdowski, S. (2004). *A last resort: National inquiry into children in immigration detention*. Human Rights and Equal Opportunity Commission.

Parish, G. (2002, July 17). *SIEV-X. Dateline, SBS*. http://sievx.com/articles/challenging/20020717Dateline.html

Perera, S. (2006). They give evidence: Bodies, borders and the disappeared. *Social Identities: Journal for the Study of Race, Nation and Culture*, *12*(6), 637–656.

Rose, N. (1999). Numbers. In N. Rose (Ed.), *Powers of freedom* (pp. 197–232). Cambridge University Press.

Ryan, H. (2020, December 10). Are they just gonna dump us here? Refugees given a number for a name. *The Guardian*. https://www.theguardian.com/australia-news/2020/dec/10/are-they-just-gonna-dump-us-here-refugees-given-a-number-for-a-name-on-nauru

Scott-Bray, R. (2020). Contested deaths and coronial justice in the digital age. *International Journal for Crime, Justice and Social Democracy*, *9*(4), 90–103.
Scraton, P. (1999). *Power conflict and criminalisation*. Routledge.
Silverstein, J. (2023). *Cruel care: A history of children at our borders*, Monash University Press.
Szörényi, A. (2004). The face of suffering in Afghanistan: Identity, authenticity and technology in the search for the representative refugee. *The Australian Feminist Law Journal*, *21*(4), 1–21.
Szörényi, A. (2009a). Till human voices wake us: Responding to refugee testimony. *Life Writing*, *6*(2), 173–191.
Szörényi, A. (2009b). Distanced suffering: Photographed suffering and the construction of white in/invulnerability. *Social Semiotics*, *19*(2), 92–109.
Vallely, N. (2019). The relationality of disappearance. *Angelaki: Journal of the Theoretical Humanities*, *24*(3), 38–52.
Warr, J. (2020). 'Always gotta be two mans': Lifers, risk, rehabilitation, and narrative labour. *Punishment and Society*, *22*(1), 28–47.
Weber, L., Newitt, R., & Loughnan, C. (2023). Place, borders and the decolonial. In C. Cunneen, A. Deckert, A. Porter, R. Webb, & J. Tauri (Eds.), *Routledge international handbook on decolonizing justice* (pp. 67–77). Routledge.
Weber, L., & Pickering, S. (2011). *Globalization and borders: Death at the global frontier*. Palgrave MacMillan.

Chapter 6

Die Trying: Asylum Seeker Deaths at Sea

Michelle Jasmin Dimasi

As the sun rises over the Hindu Kush Mountains after early morning prayers, movement on Kabul's streets gathers momentum. Roadside, men pushing street carts announce their sale of pomegranates from Kandahar and apples from Wardak province. Money exchangers congregate on street corners with wads of banknotes while others sell Roshan and Etisalat phone cards. Traffic escalates and cars are soon bumper to bumper as police officers blow whistles furiously directing traffic, their instructions often ignored by Kabul's manic drivers.

While listening to the chaos of movement, I cannot ignore my own personal reflections about 'migratory movements'. As the car horns beep and the frenetic nature of Kabul daily life inflates below my room in Sharenaw, a neighbourhood once popular with foreigners before the Ashraf Ghani-led government collapsed in 2021, I contemplated a phone call an Afghan colleague had made earlier that week. The call was to a relative of Torpekai Amarkhel, a female Afghan journalist who drowned in the Mediterranean Sea several months earlier in February 2023. She had registered on a waitlist for a humanitarian visa to Australia but in desperation had attempted to flee to Europe (Glaister, Alikhil & Theodosiou, 2023).

My colleague and I had planned to interview Afghan families such as Torpekai's, who had lost relatives on the perilous sea journey across the Mediterranean in search of safety. When my colleague phoned Torpekai's relative, the heaviness of grief was still ever present. When he answered the phone and spoke about the family's loss, painful howls echoed in the background as fellow family members who overheard the conversation broke down in tears. As the family's grief and pain was still so raw, we did not pursue requesting an interview.

Torpekai drowned when a boat carrying up to approximately 200 people mainly from Afghanistan, Pakistan, Iraq and Iran became distressed before smashing into rocks off the southern Italian coast of Calabria. Boat wreckage washed up near Steccato di Cutro, a Calabrian seaside resort town. Some of the town's 450 inhabitants helped with the search and rescue with one later stating, 'The beach is like a cemetery. Look at the sea – it's beautiful, but deceptive' (Giuffrida, 2023).

However, there is nothing beautiful about the loss of innocent lives at sea. Afghans such as Torpekai, once hopeful about finding safety as they boarded a wooden boat called *Summer Love*, became lifeless bodies flown back to the place they had fled.

Deter, Detain, Dehumanise: The Politics of Seeking Asylum, 99–105

Published under exclusive licence by Emerald Publishing Limited
doi:10.1108/978-1-83753-224-720241008

Under the Taliban's leadership, the Ministry of Foreign Affairs, held a funeral ceremony for the dead once they arrived 'home' from Calabria. Sadly, it was not the first time I witnessed the impact of asylum seeker deaths at sea. In the following sections, I share my reflections on the tragic impact loss of life at sea has on both asylum seekers and the communities who bear witness in places such as Italy and Australia.

Lampedusa and Liquid Graveyards in Italy

Strong winds had gathered momentum as I walked along via Grecale in the evening. The sand stung my face as I hurried across the arid plateau leading to the entrance of Dammusi Borgo Cala Creta, my hotel while on Lampedusa Island. The weather had quickly deteriorated on the Sicilian island located 200 km from mainland Italy. As the Mediterranean Sea swell grew, so did my concerns about possible asylum seekers travelling by boat who were now at its mercy.

Italy's southernmost point and only 100 km from Tunisia, Lampedusa is home to 4,500 islanders. Since the early 2000s, it has been a primary entry point for asylum seekers coming to Italy from North Africa, in an attempt to make Europe a place of refuge. Claiming 28,000 lives en route to Europe since 2014, the Mediterranean Sea is the largest mass grave in the world. Some have described it as a 'liquid graveyard' (Tondo & Giuffrida, 2023). In 2023, 78,000 asylum seekers and migrants traversed its waters, landing in Italy. In early August 2023, it took another 70 victims when two boats sank off Lampedusa (Tondo & Giuffrida, 2023).

A whirring noise, reminiscent of a bathtub plug being removed as the water is sucked down the drain, reverberates from Lampedusa's cliff face. I had come to the island to research asylum seeker deaths at sea. Neither the subject nor the noise were unfamiliar to me. On Christmas Island, during its monsoon seasons, a similar sound could be heard that I had come to know well: a turbulent sea filled with danger. After visiting Christmas Island for over a decade, this Australian outpost in the Indian Ocean that was a destination for many asylum seekers, was not dissimilar to Lampedusa.

Remembering Deaths at Sea on Christmas Island

Memories of a terrible boat crash on Christmas Island in 2010 flooded my consciousness throughout the night in Lampedusa. That tragic event on 15 December 2010, saw 50 asylum seekers drowned outside my parents' home that faced the ocean. The world watched on as graphic media images showed *Janga*, an asylum seeker boat that crashed against the razor-sharp rocks and bodies, including small children, that floundered in the water.

Only 42 people survived, including 3 now orphaned children. Survivors later gave thanks to the 1,500 Christmas Islanders whose rescue efforts were heroic. Islanders had clambered down onto the rocks, some cutting their legs open while making a human chain to throw life vests and pull people ashore.

Days after the boat crash, remnants of the *Janga* floated on the sea. Boat fuel that dispersed into the Indian Ocean could be smelt around the settlement area of the island. I experienced wafts of it in my family's home. The island's atmosphere was dark and dense. Everyone from asylum seekers, to islanders to Australian Navy personnel involved in the rescue mission were traumatised.

Asylum seekers survivors who were now detained in the Phosphate Hill camp tried to piece together what had happened, most still in shock. Some were escorted by detention guards to the island's hospital to identify drowned relatives, including those stored in shipping freezer containers on the roadside as the local morgue had run out of space for the dead.

While asylum seekers personally experienced nothing short of a nightmare, islanders spoke of haunted dreams where they repeatedly saw images of the drowned. A decade later, when I posted a photo of the *Janga* tragedy to commemorate the anniversary on my social media account, a local islander commented that she still hears the screams of asylum seekers.

Acts of God or 'Die Trying'

Several days after the boat tragedy, an Islamic service was held at the detention camp for the deceased. The Australian Immigration Department, which was responsible for detaining asylum seekers, permitted me access given my then role as a refugee advocate. When the imam recited Quranic verses for the deceased, survivors cried and some screamed. Harrowing sounds of pain and loss echoed through the camp. They wept for losing everything, including their dreams of a safe passage and resettling in Australia with their families.

The following week, I spoke with Gordon Thomson, the island's mayor who also attended the service and frequented the camp. We both agreed that since the service, the atmosphere at the camp was 'lighter'. We'd both had conversations with *Janga* survivors who informed us that the tragedy was an act of God, a higher plan as God moves in mysterious ways.

Rational explanations sometimes give little comfort to people, especially during moments of loss and death. This is often when people turn to God, needing him most or to simply cope. For these asylum seekers who had lost everything – their homelands, their only possessions now in the sea and their loved ones – all that remained was God.

Death is the common denominator for asylum seekers. Its near possibility drives people's choices between staying in their homelands where the threat of persecution is imminent. Death is still the undercurrent for many as they flee, including taking to the seas even when the high stakes of dying are well known. But, as an Afghan unaccompanied minor once explicitly told me, 'I would prefer to die trying than not try at all'.

Exploring Asylum Seeker Deaths on Lampedusa

On Lampedusa, asylum seekers, both the living and the dead, are embedded into the island's 20 km^2 sparse landscape. In the Imbriacola district, where the port is located, sits the 'Hotspot', a first reception centre managed by the Italian Red Cross. Here, asylum seekers are offloaded from docked Guardia di Finanza or Italian Coast Guard vessels that intercepted their leaky boats. New arrivals are detained at the Hotspot for up to five days before being transferred to the Sicilian mainland. The reception centre was designed to accommodate only several hundred people though numbers often surpass 1,000. By April 2023, a migrant state of emergency was declared and maritime transport increased to move surging numbers to the mainland and manage overcrowding at the Hotspot (ANSA, 2023).

Not far from the island's small airport on a road that juts off from the Old Harbour stands the Porta d'Europa, translated as the 'Gateway to Europe'. Designed by Italian sculptor Mimmo Paladino, this five-metre-tall monument was erected in 2008 to acknowledge those who perished in the Mediterranean Sea on their way to Europe. The monument's significance grew when more than 360 people drowned off the island on 3 October 2013. Every year, on the tragedy's anniversary, a commemoration is held at the Porta d'Europa to acknowledge this maritime atrocity. Other anniversary events also take place such as a reunion of Tunisian mothers whose children are still missing in the sea. They publicly retell the stories of their loss, while wearing large photographs of their children draped around their necks.

In the second year of the COVID-19 pandemic, tourism, one of the island's main industries along with fishing, picked back up on the island. But holiday makers couldn't help but notice a large cruise ship continuously circling the island. Upon arriving on Lampedusa, the Italian government mandated adult asylum seekers' quarantine on the cruise ship for two weeks (see e.g. Image 2). This was quite possibly a traumatic experience for those who had survived dangerous sea journeys to only be put back on the ocean. While this practice has now stopped, the detention of people at sea continues elsewhere. Currently, the UK government detains asylum seekers on migrant barges, evoking memories of past colonial maritime incarceration (Langton, 2023).

Mediterranean Hope is a non-governmental organisation that was established in response to the 3 October 2023 tragedy. The organisation supports newly arrived asylum seekers in Lampedusa, including directing them to legal services and informing them of their rights. Marta, a Mediterranean Hope employee, informed me about asylum seeker deaths and Lampedusa. She explained that the

Image 2. Cruise Ship Quarantining Asylum Seekers on Lampedusa.
Source: Michelle Jasmin Dimasi.

Image 3. Unmarked Asylum Seeker Graves in the Lampedusa Cemetery. Source: Michelle Jasmin Dimasi.

island's cemetery is home to deceased asylum seekers, many unnamed and it was essential I visit it to comprehend the extent of lives lost at sea.

Later that day when the strong Sicilian sun started to set and the heat subsided, I made my way to the cemetery by foot. Cutting across the rocky outcrops that lead from Cala Creta to Cala Pisana, I arrived at the cemetery. Wandering the narrow pathways, all I could see were names of Italians: Giuseppe, Maria, Giovanni … but no evidence of asylum seekers. I texted Marta saying, 'I can't seem to find the graves' to which she responded, 'It's a bit of a game of hide and seek'.

With little luck finding the graves and about to call it quits, Francesco, an Italian refugee advocate and artist whom I had briefly met at Mediterranean Hope that morning appeared in the cemetery accompanied by a refugee researcher from Rome. I said I couldn't find the asylum seeker graves. He responded that it was he who painted the graves of asylum seekers and had brought the researcher to the cemetery to show him how he gave the drowned 'deaths with dignity'.

'This is not a quiet cemetery', Francesco said as we went from grave to grave, him recalling the tragic stories. One unnamed young woman's grave revealed how the Italian government had uncompassionately dealt with her death. Scribbled on a concrete slab that covered her grave was '2008: Ex-communicare' meaning 'a person outside Europe' (see Image 4). Francesco retaliated by painting the image of a large plume encased with barbed wire representing that she deserved freedom yet Europe's draconian migration policies made this unachievable. Many asylum seeker graves revealed plume imagery. Francesco explained that these plumes represented the 'souls' of those lost at sea.

Francesco showed us the grave of Welela, a young African woman who was severely burned in a Libyan prison, after a gas cylinder exploded. By the time she arrived in Lampedusa her burnt body could not sustain the sea journey and she was dead upon arrival. Some months later, her brother turned up on the island

Image 4. Grave Featuring Plume and Barbed Wire Imagery and Concrete Ex-communicare Inscription. Source: Michelle Jasmin Dimasi.

with a photo of Welela telling locals he was searching for his dead sister. The community showed him where they had laid her to rest.

Asylum seeker children have also been victims of the Mediterranean Sea. Francesco pointed out the tiny grave of baby Yuseuf. Displayed was his photo and underneath was written, 'Why so soon my child, mumm [*sic.*] and daddy love you forever' (see Image 3). Every grave, despite many unnamed, represented someone's family member whose life was taken by the ocean.

An Ocean of Seasons: Politics and Compassion

There are 'seasons' when it comes to boat migration. On both Lampedusa and Christmas Island, from approximately November to March, the weather changes dramatically with high seas making the journey more dangerous. Countries' responses to asylum seekers are also dictated by seasons of political will and compassion or manipulation of the populus to win anti-immigration votes. Sometimes, when disturbing yet evocative images hit social media, public attention gravitates to a season of empathy. For example, in 2015 when Alan Kurdi, a young Syrian boy washed up on the shores of Turkey, the public responded with compassion and financial donations. Many related to this image as an innocent little boy that could have been their own son or little brother rather than a nameless *ex-communicare* who had drowned in the ocean.

In *An Ocean without Shore*, Ibn Al-Arabi, the Sufi mystic writes about an endless faith in God: 'I marveled at an ocean without shore and at a shore that did not have an ocean; And at a morning light without darkness and at a night that was without daybreak'. For over 15 years, asylum seekers have told their personal stories to me about their journeys across the sea. Despite the risks, they often felt they were surrendering the outcome of their lives over to God in an attempt to escape death in their homelands.

This summer, Sicily has experienced extreme heat waves while the hot topic of irregular migration still rages on and people keep drowning in the Mediterranean. Kheit Abdel Hafed, an iman and President of the Islamic Community of Sicily has given countless burial ceremonies for the nameless dead. He also attempted to lobby the Italian government to create a cemetery space called 'Martyrs of the Sea' as Sicilian cemeteries were running out of space to bury the drowned (Burdeau, 2022). Meanwhile, the European Union (EU) recently signed off on a EURO1 billion deal with Tunisia aimed at stopping asylum seekers and migrants departing by boat from Tunisia and travelling to Italy (O'Carroll, 2023).

However, asylum seekers and the underground networks they engage in will always find new ways to take to the sea. Politics and policies are irrelevant when people are fleeing for their lives. Asylum seekers like Torpekai will continue to die trying to cross the Mediterranean Sea, as they search for a better life that they've now placed in the hands of God, while the families of the dead will continue to mourn in war-torn countries like Afghanistan.

References

ANSA. (2023, June 13). *Ship to transfer 2,800 migrants a week from Lampedusa*. Infomigrants. https://www.infomigrants.net/en/post/49619/ship-to-transfer-2800-migrants-a-week-from-lampedusa

Burdeau, C. (2022, July 2). *Forlorn and unnamed, refugee graves in Italy evoke tragedy of deadly sea crossings*. Courthouse News Service. https://www.courthousenews.com/forlorn-and-unnamed-refugee-graves-in-italy-evoke-tragedy-of-deadly-sea-crossings/

Giuffrida, A. (2023, February 27). 'The beach is like a cemetery': Italian village grapples with shipwreck aftermath. *The Guardian*. https://www.theguardian.com/world/2023/feb/27/italy-shipwreck-calabria-migration

Glaister, S., Alikhil, A., & Theodosiou, P. (2023, March 10). *Former SBS Pashto journalist Torpekai Amarkhel was on a processing list for Australian asylum when she died*. SBS Australia. https://www.sbs.com.au/language/pashto/en/article/former-sbs-pashto-journalist-torpekai-amarkhel-was-on-a-processing-list-for-australian-asylum-when-she-died/uunahtwk9#

Langton, J. (2023, August 11). Why UK's migrant barge evokes memories of its shameful history of maritime incarceration. *The National*. https://www.thenationalnews.com/weekend/2023/08/11/why-uks-migrant-barge-evokes-memories-of-its-shameful-history-of-maritime-incarceration/?utm_source=Weekender+newsletter&utm_campaign=0cb96399c3-EMAIL_CAMPAIGN_2022_09_21_11_10_COPY_01&utm_medium=email&utm_term=0_c8e6f9226d-0cb96399c3-58874153

O'Carroll, L. (2023, July 16). EU signs off €1bn deal with Tunisia to help stem irregular migration. *The Guardian*. https://www.theguardian.com/world/2023/jul/16/eu-deal-with-tunisia-help-stem-irregular-migration#:~:text=EU%20signs%20off%20€1bn%20deal%20with%20Tunisia%20to%20help%20stem%20irregular%20migration,-Ursula%20von%20der&text=The%20EU%20has%20signed%20off,to%20have%20equity%20in%20life

Tondo, L., & Giuffrida, A. (2023, August 9). More than 40 feared dead after boat sinks in Mediterranean near Lampedusa. *The Guardian*. https://www.theguardian.com/world/2023/aug/09/people-feared-dead-boat-sinks-near-lampedusa

Chapter 7

Manus Prison Theory, Art and the Politics of Refugee Representation: Contesting the 'Deserving Refugee' Narrative

Anthea Vogl

University of Technology Sydney, Australia

Abstract

This chapter considers the modes and politics of refugee representation, and the function of art and literature as sites of resistance to, or the reinforcing of, dehumanising or idealised tropes of people seeking refugee protection. Specifically, the chapter addresses the connection between dehumanised representations of the imagined refugee and the violence and 'logic' of Australia's offshore detention regime in Nauru and Papua New Guinea. In engaging with these issues, the chapter draws on Manus Prison Theory and its focus on who gets to represent refugee experience, and to generate knowledge about it and on what terms. It considers these questions through an examination of two contrasting art projects, which alternately raise and contest the idea of the 'deserving refugee'. In exploring these questions, the chapter also engages with the temporalities of refugee representation and the role of crisis in generating 'stock' refugee representations. It ultimately argues that the politics of refugee representation are central to questions of refugee and migrant justice, and further, that we cannot separate contemporary forms and representations of violence against refugees from colonial and neocolonial acts of sovereignty and expulsion.

Keywords: Offshore detention; counter-storytelling; refugee narratives; refugeeness; colonial logic; representation

Deter, Detain, Dehumanise: The Politics of Seeking Asylum, 107–120

Published under exclusive licence by Emerald Publishing Limited
doi:10.1108/978-1-83753-224-720241009

Introduction

In early 2018, the art exhibition *All We Can't See* opened at The Yellow House, a gallery located in the gentrified, inner-city Sydney suburb of Potts Point. The exhibition was made up of about 50 works across mediums, each of which responded to a specific report or notification contained within the Nauru Files (All We Can't See – Illustrating the Nauru Files, n.d.). The Nauru Files are 'the largest ever leaked set of documents published from inside the Australian detention system' (Evershed et al., 2016). Leaked to *The Guardian* in 2016, they detail 2,116 mandatory 'incident reports' about refugees imprisoned in 'offshore detention' on the island nation of Nauru. The reports were written and filed by case workers, guards, social workers and teachers working for the companies privately contracted and funded by the Australian Government to operate the detention centre (Evershed et al., 2016).[1] Using an immense, interactive, searchable database, *The Guardian* published redacted versions of the leaked files in full in August 2016. Individual incident reports were the 'subjects' and basis of the *All We Can't See* artworks (Evershed et al., 2016).

In explaining why they put together the *All We Can't See* exhibition, curators Daniel New and Arielle Gamble stated: 'In the absence of media access to the island, our objective is to illustrate these [Nauru Files] stories through creative expression, using art to shed light on all we can't see' (All We Can't See – Illustrating the Nauru Files, n.d.). As Gamble further explained, '[l]anguage isn't working … the stories in the Nauru files are dehumanised, removed, redacted' (Dumas, 2018).

The reports in the Nauru Files detail the extreme physical and sexual violence experienced by refugees incarcerated in Nauru, and include accounts of child abuse, self-harm, suicide attempts and severe mental illness. They are intimate and distressing, but written in the cold, disinterested, perfunctory style of mandatory incident reporting. As explained in the Nauru Files database, 'critical incidents' were required to be reported verbally within 30 minutes and in writing within three hours; 'major incidents' had to be reported verbally within an hour and in writing within six hours; and for 'minor incidents', a written report was required within 24 hours and no verbal report was mandated (Farrell & Evershed, 2016). Whilst the leaked reports were headline national and international news following their release, the detention centre continued to operate as previously.

I went to see the exhibition with a friend on a quiet weekday afternoon in 2018. The gallery in which it hung was small, bright and airy. Numerous high-profile and celebrated Australian artists contributed work to the exhibition. Other works not hung in the gallery, but included on the exhibition's website, are by 'ordinary' members of the community who responded to the curators' open call to illustrate an incident report. After the first couple of web pages of the artworks

[1]The incident reports were filed from 2013 to 2015. At that time, the organisations and for-profit companies holding contracts with the Australian government to operate offshore processing on Nauru included Broadspectrum (formerly Transfield), Wilson Security, International Health and Medical Services and Save the Children.

online, visitors are able to click through page after page of tessellated, yet-to-be-illustrated incident reports. Every artwork in the gallery was accompanied by the particular incident report it was responding to, complete with official redactions, and the incident's categorisation and risk rating (critical, major or minor). Risk ratings and mandatory reporting requirements were set out in the contract between the Australian Government and Transfield Services, the for-profit company running the detention centre, and failure to meet them could trigger financial penalties. Each report is unique and harrowing.

In the exhibition space, I read each of the redacted files before I looked at the artwork. One work, by Luke Storrier, is a sculpture of a slanted, white and partially wrapped chair. The chair is partially suspended, connected by just one leg to a plinth, and at the base of the chair's foot, there is a small puddle of red paint, resembling a pool of blood. It is accompanied by a report which reads:

> MINOR. Incident: Complaint ... [REDACTED] informed case worker that his son [REDACTED] was walking through Area 9, felt dizzy (he had sewn his lips together at the time) and sat on the chair near the guard station. Guard stated Do not sit in front of me I don't want to see you and kicked the chair.

A thickly layered abstract oil painting, of relentless and saturated reds, yellows, oranges and whites by Aida Tomescu, illustrates an 'unclassified' incident report, dated 15 August 2014, which reads:

> WRITER WALKS/RUNS ON CRUSHED CORAL. KNEE LIGAMENTS ARE DETERIORATING DUE TO SURFACE. HAS BEEN GIVEN VARIOUS SUPPORTS WHICH DO NOT HELP. EXPERIENCING BACK PAIN.

An oil on board painting of a dark burning mass of everyday furniture and other detritus, rendered in tea-stain browns, muted yellows and blacks by Peter Gardiner, illustrates the following report, dated 20 September 2014 and classified as 'minor':

> [REDACTED] TOLD SCA STAFF THAT HER ALONG WITH MANY OTHER YOUTHS WERE CONSIDERING A MASS SELF HARM WITH RAZOR BLADES, DETERGENT AND CIGARETTE BUDS [*sic.*].[2]

A number of the artworks in the gallery illustrated reports that detail group or mass suicide plans or attempts. As we wandered the gallery, my friend broke

---

[2]SCA: Save the Children Australia. Save the Children was contracted to provide education and welfare services to minors detained on Nauru. The contract was valued at AUD36,740,058.53: (Whyte, 2017).

our mainly silent viewing to mention that none of the press or publicly available accounts of offshore detention that she had seen had ever mentioned or documented this.

On our way out of the gallery, we chatted briefly to the two curators. We asked what led them to curate the exhibition, did they do 'other stuff' in the visual art world or as part of the refugee rights campaigns? No, they told us, they were book designers who wanted to do something in response to Australia's policy of offshore detention and the Nauru Files. The response to the exhibition during and after it was first shown was immense, and a small campaign raised funds to allow it to be exhibited in Melbourne, Victoria later that same year (Gamble & New, 2018).

In the remainder of this chapter, I consider the modes and politics of refugee representation, and in particular the function of art and literature as sites of resistance to, or the reinforcing of, dehumanising *or* idealised tropes of people seeking refugee protection. The chapter also addresses the connection between representations of the imagined refugee and refugeehood, and the violence and 'logic' of Australia's offshore detention regime. In engaging with these issues, I draw on Manus Prison Theory and its recurring focus on the question of who gets to represent refugee experience, and to generate knowledge about it and on what terms. Alongside presenting two contrasting exhibitions, which alternately raise and contest the idea of the 'deserving refugee', the chapter presents Manus Prison Theory's direct engagement with the critical role of art, literature, and poetry in depicting, analysing and resisting tropes of refugeehood, and in turn Australia's 'offshore' prison regimes in Nauru and Papua New Guinea (PNG). Finally, I consider not just the content but the temporalities of refugee representation and the role of crisis both in generating 'stock' refugee representations, as well as in separating contemporary forms of violence against refugees from colonial and neocolonial forms of sovereignty and expulsion.

***

In 2015, a different kind of exhibition (and media campaign), *I Came by Boat*, was launched across Australia (*I Came By Boat*, n.d.). The campaign aimed to highlight the positive contribution of refugees and asylum seekers to Australia by profiling 'successful' refugees and presenting their stories across social media platforms, as well as on billboards and posters around capital cities (SBS Staff, 2015). The *I Came by Boat* website is still live and displays 12 of the campaign posters as an online gallery. The images are beautiful. Each one features a front-on, three-quarter-length photograph of a refugee living in Australia. In each portrait, the refugee is openly smiling or has smiling eyes. The posters each include a grab quote, and on the website, there is a longer description of each refugee's story for visitors to click on and navigate. The exhibition directly interrupts public and political discourse that only 'bogus' or opportunistic refugees come by boat. Each refugee depicted in the campaign did come by boat and is confirmed by the accompanying text as both a genuine and 'successful' refugee.

One of the images is of Dr Fern White, described as a dentist and a yoga teacher. Her profile explains that after 10 months in refugee camps, Fern's family were settled in Port Pirie; that Fern would sacrifice birthday parties and her school holidays 'to help her parents sew shoulder pads into garments' before she went on to pursue a medical career (*I Came by Boat*, n.d.). In another poster, Zakarya from Afghanistan is described as starting with a basic knowledge of the alphabet and 'since his release from [Australian] detention having been happily employed at the Berry King jam factory, working his way up to assistant production manager' (*I Came by Boat*, n.d.). Zakarya is quoted as dreaming of having his own business and loving the St Kilda Football Club. The other refugees depicted are described as a classical concert pianist, a kitchen hand, a restaurant owner and a surf lifesaver and an entrepreneur.

I wrote about these posters for research I was doing into how refugees' stories, personal credibility and oral evidence of persecution in their home countries are tested and judged by legal decision-makers in Australia (see Vogl, 2017) – but they came to mind again when I went to the *All We Can't See* exhibition. It was almost impossible to line up the images of the *I Came by Boat* refugees, succeeding, teaching, doing yoga, performing world-first surgery and generally excelling, with the people incarcerated in offshore prisons or the lives of refugees as surveilled, redacted, recorded and illustrated in *All We Can't See*. The poster-people in *I Came by Boat* are not waiting. They are successful refugee-citizens who live – and contribute economically and socially – in the present. They are incredible people who have achieved so much under at times horrific conditions, some of which were imposed by Australia upon arrival in their new home state.

The *I Came by Boat* poster-people are the kind of extraordinary refugees that author Dina Nayeri (2017) describes when she notes that '[w]ith the rise of nativist sentiment in Europe and America', there has been a 'troubling change in the way people make the case for refugees'. She observes that

> even those on the left talk about how immigrants make America great. They point to photographs of happy refugees turned good citizens, listing their contributions, as if that is the price of existing in the same country, on the same earth.

I'm with Nayeri (2017) when she asks, frustrated: 'Is the life of the happy mediocrity a privilege reserved for those who never stray from home?'. In Australia, these expectations of the good refugee citizen, of something far more than mediocrity, apply at the *same time* as the Government prosecutes policies of mandatory detention, social exclusion, and for those on offshore detention, out and out torture as a form of deterrence against the very refugees whom we expect to succeed and then to celebrate, against all odds.

Art, Representation and Manus Prison Theory

Manus Prison Theory, a theoretical framework and movement articulated by Behrouz Boochani and Omid Tofighian, has as one of its core themes the critical role of art, representation, literature, and poetry in depicting, analysing and resisting Australia's 'offshore' prison regimes in PNG and Nauru. Manus Prison Theory as a whole is a 'response to the illegal detention of refugees on Manus

Island in PNG and functions as a unique and multi-faceted discourse about border politics, colonialism and intersecting forms of domination in contemporary Australia' (Tofighian, 2020, pp. 1138–1139). The intersecting ideas and components of the theory developed by Boochani and Tofighian, alongside an international community of scholars, artists and activists, frequently return to critical questions of how 'refugees' are represented and by whom, and the erasure of refugees themselves in these processes. Another of the theory's orientating frames is the profoundly 'colonial logic conditioning and driving Australia's border regime' (Tofighian, 2020, p. 1140), which is in turn connected to who has the authority to define and represent the refugee experience. The role of Australia's colonial present and the ongoing dispossession of First Nations people in Australia is central to its analysis of violent acts of Australian sovereignty, as addressed in this book's Introduction.

Woven throughout writings on Manus Prison Theory is the insistence that literature, art and new genres of storytelling are essential to documenting, analysing and resisting the violent and racist regimes of sovereign control exercised by successive Australian governments. Connected to this claim is the assertion that journalism, the epistemology of everyday reporting on refugee issues, and the dehumanising language of the state and official discourse, are direct impediments to both understanding and contesting such regimes, and what Tofighian and Boochani theorise as the kyriarchal system of oppression (or system-e hākem) (Boochani & Tofighian, 2019, p. 280). As Boochani (2020) puts it, 'the language of journalism was incapable of telling this story, incapable of communicating this tragedy' (pp. 11–12). In explaining further the failure of journalism and official discourse and language, he writes:

> What I always try to do is create my own language to represent this situation, to challenge the system. So this language is not only words; I also use musical elements, and I create new concepts … I use terms like 'exile policy' and 'systematic torture', and other terms. What is important and necessary to understand about these words is that they help think about this exile policy in relation to a colonial system and a colonial mentality. That is why these words are not only about refugees; they are also about the local Indigenous population on Manus, people who are victims under this exile policy. (Tofighian & Boochani, 2020, p. 179)

Boochani articulates the need to relocate and recast discussion and analysis of Manus Prison (as one element of the border regime more broadly), 'to reclaim this issue from the many organisations involved and from the media and reposition it in different places such as universities, intellectual circles and arts communities' (Boochani & Tofighian, 2019, p. 277). As he argues, 'it's very important that we create a new language to be able to communicate with new groups of people –with artists, academics and others' (Boochani & Tofighian, 2019, p. 277). Or as Gamble put it, expressing a similar idea in explaining their motivations for curating *All We Can't See*, 'language isn't working' (Dumas, 2018).

The purpose of Manus Prison Theory and its interventions, amongst other things, is to create new forms of authority and of knowledge – new ways of knowing – about so-called refugees and 'shattering' the unity and uniformity of refugeehood as a category (Boochani & Tofighian, 2019, p. 287). Together Tofighian and Boochani draw a direct connection between the racist ideologies that hold up colonial border regimes, national assertions of sovereignty, and the epistemic basis for dehumanising tropes associated with refugees and displaced peoples, which seek to justify their punishment. These contradictory tropes include the 'desperate supplicant'; the 'trickster'; the 'tragic and miserable victim'; and the 'struggling [and battling] overcomer' (Boochani, 2018, pp. 365–366; Tofighian, 2018a, p. 535). These characterisations and expectations have been cast as a measure of one's 'refugeeness', an awkward term which in its capaciousness captures the demanding, contradictory and regularly dehumanising ways in which Global North states define and judge those seeking access to the category of refugee, and determine how 'acceptable' refugees ought to behave (Lacroix, 2004; Luker, 2015).

Evaluating the sources and forms of knowledge that govern refugees and 'refugeehood' is about more than challenging stereotypes, which proliferate both amongst refugee supporters (of 'good', innocent, deserving refugees) and within government rhetoric (of refugees as dangerous, deceitful, opportunistic and security threats). It is about knowledge production by people who have experienced and endured the force of sovereign borders, and about reshaping the landscape of 'expertise' about the nature of Australia's policies of imprisonment, torture and racialised deterrence. The 'new' sources of understanding in turn give rise to new modes and forms of expression, representation and analysis.

This resonates strongly in research on the form and content of state-enforced narratives of 'the good refugee' (and conversely of the 'bogus' or 'inauthentic' refugee) that structure processes for refugee status determination and the judgement of refugee credibility (Vogl, 2013; Vogl, 2024). The dehumanising harms of these narratives, which cast refugees as *already* racialised, deceiving and opportunistic (Razack, 2000), is both a question of the content of the narratives (good refugees do not travel illegally; 'bogus' refugees exploit white benevolence) and of the genre and form of the story, which dictates *how* the authentic, acceptable refugee story must be told. Nayeri's argument in favour of refugees' right to be boring and mediocre is also an expression of the right to be part of something like an anti-story. A life that does not involve linear moves from suffering, persecution and adversity in one's home country through to brave resolution of such adversity and a triumphant, fulfilled and successful existence in a new Global North state. Whilst the *I Came by Boat* refugee portraits are clearly a celebration of such success, they also function to reinforce the demand for it.

Language and genres that challenge stock refugee stories, however, do exist, as do forms of art and expression that resist tropes of suffering refugees, refugee innocence or indeed suffering refugees-come-economic success stories. Writing and research at the intersection of literature and the politics of asylum have held open the possibilities of literature and 'the arts' more broadly as a means of recasting the epistemologies and standard stories of the refugee experience

(Barsky, 1994; Woolley, 2017). This is not just about a kind of counter-storytelling but also about the potential of counter-genres. Even though the *All We Can't See* exhibition illustrates 'state' accounts of offshore detention (in the very unique form of incident reports), it simultaneously reinterprets and resists the dehumanising genre of these documents. Omid Tofighian, for example, has put forward the idea of an 'anti-genre' for refugee writing and knowledge, as well as 'horrific surrealism', to best interpret Boochani's book *No Friend but the Mountains*, which is (amongst other things) an extended and polyphonic critique of the stifling range of refugee stories that can be told by or about people seeking safety and protection (Tofighian, 2018b, p. xxix; see also Tofighian & Boochani, 2020). Tofighian applies the horrific surrealism genre to Boochani's narration and analysis of imprisonment and torture in Australia's offshore detention regime on Manus Island. Anna Poletti also considers the genre of Boochani's writing; she argues that *No Friend but the Mountains* and Boochani's writing more generally represent a 'new form of transnational life writing', which is both a work of theory and life writing that 'responds to and seeks to understand the logics of the nation state' (Poletti, 2020) based on an account in real time of the lived experience of refugees incarcerated on Manus Island.

Boochani's writing and Manus Prison Theory each recast the 'refugee story' as a story of colonial state violence, imprisonment, humour and solidarity. *No Friend but the Mountains*, as both a non-reconciliatory anti-genre and a political analysis of offshore processing, demonstrates that state violence, systemic torture and incarceration are part of an asylum-seeker's experience of arrival in Australia. Indeed, experiences of state violence are part of the so-called refugee story, but certainly are not a part of the refugee story addressed within state narratives or depictions of 'good' or authentic refugeehood and their reconciliatory narrative frames (Slaughter, 2007; Tofighian, 2018b). Indeed, the erasure of Global North state violence in the good refugee narrative is crucial to both its structure and success.

Crisis, Time and Offshore Detention

The temporality of representations of refugeehood, that is how time is invoked and presented within refugee imagery, has also defined and shaped mainstream refugee representation. Indeed, one striking aspect of the images illustrating the incident reports in *All We Can't See* was the way they represented and marked the time and history of Australia's extraterritorial detention centres and long colonial presence in Nauru. Or more accurately, the way they marked the very long time of offshore detention, and Australia's refugee prison camps in Nauru and PNG. The paint is dry. The sculptures are cast. The works are here and now, but they also suggest their own longevity, and a future in which they represent and explain Australia's abhorrent policy of systematic offshore torture of refugees. Carefully framed, thoughtfully lit artworks are not the standard medium used to represent or to protest refugee policy in Australia. Poll posters, pamphlets, website fact sheets and online petitions are the forms we associate with 'information' about, knowledge or exposure to the camps. These documents are short-lived. They are usually urgent in tone and form, because of the urgency of bringing these policies to an end. The artworks in *All We Can't See* do not comfort us with the immediate present of offshore detention or with the possibility of an imminent end to the policy, but the artworks and the documents so clearly demonstrate why the policy should be immediately dismantled.

Saskia Sassen (1996), amongst others, has long critiqued the language of crisis and the sense of emergency in relation to migration. States might have less control than they would like over their borders, but there is nothing to equate this with a crisis. She has written about how the language of crisis is used to justify reams of migration policy-on-the-run. Governments invoke crises to implement extreme and exceptional but supposedly short-term policy responses to long-term, predictable and patterned movements of people across borders. The short-term responses become long-term ones, but the frame of crisis and urgency remains.

It is not only the government that represents migration in terms of crisis and emergency. The media, non-governmental organisations, advocates and those running emergency fundraising for refugees and asylum seekers, all invoke crisis in various ways and to various ends. The language of humanitarian crisis is an effective call to action. This framing infects how we think about these policies. They must be short-lived. They are so horrific they must be unsustainable. But the artworks on the wall in the gallery, the moments of violence and resistance that they represent, confirm the deceit of 'crisis' and impermanency. So-called offshore detention has now featured at the heart of Australia's 'refugee policy' (on and briefly off) for over 20 years.

It is of course a luxury not to be wholly aware of the long, slow time of offshore detention – to need art or literature to comprehend its horrors and endurance. Anthropologist Shahram Khosravi (2014) has written about waiting as 'a particular experience of time' (p. 66). Undocumented migrants and refugees are very frequently forced to wait for periods unimaginable for many (though not all) citizens and their experiences of waiting. Non-citizens and refugees live through protracted periods defined more than anything else, by waiting: for papers, for a decision, for deportation, for access to a service and for policy change. Waiting in this way means 'not being in-time with others' (Khosravi, 2014, p. 66). And usually, as Schwartz (1974) has written, it also means that 'one's own time (and therefore, one's social worth) is less valuable than the time and worth of the one who imposes the wait' (p. 856). Hage (2009) has described this as a state of 'stuckedness' or existential immobility for certain groups who are denied the sense of 'going somewhere' in their lives, and which has been intensified by the social condition and state of permanent crisis (p. 97). Indeed, the stuckedness of indefinite waiting could not be further from the temporality of emergency and crisis.

For those privileged enough to be outside the temporality of border violence and exclusion, state-driven discourse and stock representations of refugees *en masse* produce and naturalise the idea of a migrant and/or refugee crisis, based on looming threats to state borders, and in Australia's case, what Aileen Moreton-Robinson (2004) has theorised as a white, possessive nationalism. Only through creating new languages, narratives and modes of representation and analysis can we seriously begin to challenge the stock narratives and standard representations of refugeehood.

This includes shifting the temporality and conception of offshore detention as a refugee policy, in order to historicise its violence. This aim is shared by, and lies at the heart of, Manus Prison Theory in its insistence on the explicitly neocolonial nature both of Australia's racist expulsion of asylum seekers from its own territory and its exploitation of the sovereignty of PNG and Nauru in the operation of Manus and Nauru prisons (Boochani & Tofighian, 2020). Indeed, as Ingrid Matthews and James Arvanitakis observe, offshore detention is not 'merely a 9/11 politic'. Instead, the island prison is 'a prototype of the imperial ethno-state … [which] sits on a continuum from British colonialism to Australian coloniality, from 1770 to the present' (Matthews & Arvanitakis, 2019, p. 20). In considering these 'colonial connections', Maria Giannacopoulos (2022) has argued that a key challenge for those thinking and writing about refugee policy and law is not only to contest:

> contemporary exclusionary laws that prevent entry and deny human rights to refugees but also to actively foreground as an object of study the coordinates of the [colonial] legal regimes producing the exclusions for which remedy and justice are being sought. (p. 159)

Representations and critiques of offshore processing regimes are incomplete as siloed studies of isolated refugee policies. Giannacopoulos (2022) argues they must include and bring into the picture 'the indissociable and colonially constituted connection that holds between the illegitimate assertion of colonial sovereignty and the exclusionary and violent practices that, at once, dispossess Indigenous peoples and target refugees and migrants' (p. 159).

***

Numerous works within the *All We Can't See* exhibition connect Australia's white possessive sovereignty and nationalism (Moreton-Robinson, 2004) with both dehumanised representations of refugees as a dangerous and invading mass, as well as with the extreme violence perpetrated by Australia on Manus Island. One of the many other illustrated Nauru incident reports reads as follows:

> CSO's guarding the SAA were doing a routing check on UAM [REDACTED] at approx. 1am. CSO noticed UAM was attempting to conceal her right wrist. When CSO's entered the room and investigated more closely, they noticed blood on UAM's right wrist. She then surrendered a small razor blade. UAM agreed to go to IHMS.[3]

The accompanying artwork by Abdullah M. I. Syed is a depiction of the Southern Cross, a Southern hemisphere constellation and symbol (amongst other things) of Australian nationalism and the British colonising of Australia. The

[3]CSO: Client services officer (at this time, usually a Wilson security guard); SAA: supported accommodation areas; UAM: unauthorised maritime arrival; IHMS: International Health and Medical Services.

constellation is pictured against a bright blue circle and every arm of each of the constellation's six stars is represented with a small, domestic razor blade.

Enduring Arrangements

Before the conservative Liberal Party Coalition led by Scott Morrison won the Australian Federal election in 2019 against almost all predictions and polls, the Australian Labor Party (ALP) made clear that, if elected, it was firmly committed to maintaining its support for offshore processing. This commitment came despite the steady stream of information flowing out of Nauru and Manus Island, evidencing the horrors of both offshore prisons including the Nauru Files. At the ALP's national conference in 2018, which preceded the election and determined the party's policy platforms, the *All We Can't See* exhibition was part of the conference's 'fringe program'. The exhibition was hung in the foyer of the Adelaide Convention Centre, where the ALP conference took place. The decision to host the exhibition was reported to have 'stunned' senior Labor figures who 'do not want to open up major differences with the Coalition on border protection prior to the election' (Bramston, 2018). Labor MPs walked through the foyer and exhibition on their way to uphold, by majority vote, the policy that had generated the abject harm that the artworks depicted. During that same party conference, the ALP also voted in favour of upholding the existing policy of forcible refugee boat 'turnbacks' on the high seas. Whatever effect the exhibition may have had, it did not disrupt the bipartisan agreement on refugee deterrence or offshore processing, which has marked Australian refugee policy since at least the introduction of the policy of mandatory detention of all unauthorised arrivals in 1992.

***

In 2021, the Liberal Coalition Government signed a new agreement with the Nauruan government to establish an 'enduring form' of offshore processing in Nauru. In distinction to previous time-limited agreements and justifications of the policy using the rhetoric and politics of crisis (as justified, for example, the *Migration Legislation Amendment (Regional Processing and Other Measures) Act 2012*), the new arrangement was described as permanent and as creating 'enduring regional processing capacity' (Burke, 2021). The Nauruan president at the time, Lionel Aingimea, also praised the permanent nature of the agreement as taking 'regional processing to a new milestone' (Doherty, 2021).

As well, at the time of writing, refugees still being held on Nauru reported to the Australian media that the Government, finally, was arranging the transport to Australia of all remaining refugees on the island (Gillespie, 2023). The Labor Government has reiterated, though, that their transfer will not affect the policy or enduring arrangements for offshore processing on Nauru; indeed, despite the absence of refugees on Nauru, these arrangements 'will continue to cost at least AUD350m a year as a "contingency"' (Karp & Shepherd, 2023). Further, the refugees being brought to Australia are not arriving to any form of security, residency, or resettlement. Instead, like many refugees 'transferred' from offshore detention, they may initially or indefinitely be held in hotels designated as alternative places of detention, and then only ever granted short-term bridging visas with no access to permanent status in Australia, under current law and policy settings (Gillespie, 2023). If they are ever released from permanent insecurity and limbo, and granted anything other than short-term vias, they too will be expected to fulfil the good refugee trope and to be deserving of potential citizenship.

Conclusion

This chapter has sought to think through the modes and politics of refugee representation, and to consider the function of art and literature as sites of resistance to, or reinforcement of, the violence and logic of regimes of refugee deterrence and Australia's offshore detention and processing. The tropes and standard imagery that shape refugee discourse, including those that represent both illegal *and* good asylum seekers, shape the politics and logic of refugee deterrence. The dehumanising of refugees begins with the idea of refugees as an undifferentiated group, represented and described again and again as 'hoards', and depicted as adjacent to or crossing state borders and almost always in crisis. Good refugees, by contrast, must overcome this depiction to become successful, contributing individuals, and thereby become both deserving and accepted. In contrast to both depictions are the mundane, devastating and daily incident reports and accounts of state violence and indifference released in the Nauru Files, as well as the *All We Can't See* artworks that interpreted them. The tropes that emerge in these 'refugee stories' include the routine nature of extreme state violence, the daily resilience, strength and degradations endured by refugees within Australia's extraterritorial processing policy and the cruel neocolonial regime of refugee deterrence which has kept it in place.

References

All We Can't See—Illustrating the Nauru Files. (n.d.). Retrieved May 23, 2023, from https://allwecantsee.com/

Barsky, R. F. (1994). *Constructing a productive other: Discourse theory and the convention refugee hearing*. John Benjamins Publishing.

Boochani, B. (2018). *No friend but the mountains: Writing from Manus prison* (O. Tofighian, Trans.). Picador.

Boochani, B., & Tofighian, O. (2019). Manus Prison Theory: Borders, incarceration and collective agency. *Griffith Review, 65*, 275–288. https://doi.org/10.3316/informit.576901127941717

Boochani, B., & Tofighian, O. (2020). No friend but the mountains and Manus Prison Theory: In conversation. *Borderlands Journal, 19*(1), 8–26. https://doi.org/10.21307/borderlands-2020-002

Bramston, T. (2018, December 1). ALP fringe dwellers won't be silent on asylum. *The Australian*. https://www.theaustralian.com.au/search-results?q=ALP+fringe+dwellers+won%E2%80%99t+be+silent+on+asylum

Burke, H. (2021, September 24). *Blow for asylum seekers seeking refuge*. News.Com.Au. https://www.news.com.au/national/politics/asylum-seeker-processing-in-nauru-cemented-by-new-agreement/news-story/2d333c5d488b1b2a230e941e27123256

Doherty, B. (2021, September 24). Australia signs deal with Nauru to keep asylum seeker detention centre open indefinitely. *The Guardian*. https://www.theguardian.com/australia-news/2021/sep/24/australia-signs-deal-with-nauru-to-keep-asylum-seeker-detention-centre-open-indefinitely

Doherty, B., & Gillespie, E. (2023, June 25). Last refugee on Nauru evacuated as Australian government says offshore processing policy remains. *The Guardian*. https://www.theguardian.com/australia-news/2023/jun/25/last-refugee-on-nauru-evacuated-as-australian-government-says-offshore-processing-policy-remains

Dumas, D. (2018, February 2). *"Language isn't working": Artists illustrate leaked Nauru files in new exhibition*. SBS Voices. https://www.sbs.com.au/voices/article/language-isnt-working-artists-illustrate-leaked-nauru-files-in-new-exhibition/lpjiy8dg9

Evershed, N., Liu, R., Farrell, P., & Davidson, H. (2016, August 9). The Nauru files: The lives of asylum seekers in detention detailed in a unique database. *The Guardian*. https://www.theguardian.com/australia-news/ng-interactive/2016/aug/10/the-nauru-files-the-lives-of-asylum-seekers-in-detention-detailed-in-a-unique-database-interactive

Farrell, P., & Evershed, N. (2016, August 9). What are the Nauru files? How to read and interpret them – explainer. *The Guardian*. https://www.theguardian.com/news/2016/aug/10/explainer-how-to-read-and-interpret-the-nauru-files

Gamble, A., & New, D. (2018). *All we can't see tour—Kickstarter*. https://www.kickstarter.com/projects/237240050/all-we-cant-see-tour

Giannacopoulos, M. (2022). Nomocide or the nonperformativity of colonial law. In S. Little, S. Suliman, & C. Wake (Eds.), *Performance, resistance and refugees*. Routledge.

Gillespie, E. (2023, June 13). Australia to transport last asylum seekers off Nauru within weeks, refugees say. *The Guardian*. https://www.theguardian.com/australia-news/2023/jun/14/australia-to-transport-last-asylum-seekers-off-nauru-within-weeks-refugees-say

Hage, G. (2009). Waiting out the crisis: On stuckedness and governmentality. In G. Hage (Ed.), *Waiting* (pp. 97–106). Melbourne University Publishing.

I Came by Boat. (n.d.). Retrieved May 23, 2023, from https://www.icamebyboat.com.au/

Karp, P., & Shepherd, T. (2023, May 23). Nauru offshore processing to cost Australian taxpayers $485m despite only 22 asylum seekers remaining. *The Guardian*. https://www.theguardian.com/australia-news/2023/may/23/nauru-offshore-detention-immigration-processing-to-cost-australia-485m-22-asylum-seekers

Khosravi, S. (2014). Waiting. In B. Anderson & M. Keith (Eds.), *Migration: The COMPAS anthology* (pp. 66–67). ESRC Centre on Migration, Policy and Society, COMPAS.

Lacroix, M. (2004). Canadian refugee policy and the social construction of the refugee claimant subjectivity: Understanding refugeeness. *Journal of Refugee Studies*, *17*(2), 147.

Luker, T. (2015). Performance anxieties: Interpellation of the refugee subject in law. *Canadian Journal of Law and Society*, *30*(1), 91–107. https://doi.org/10.1017/cls.2014.13

Matthews, I., & Arvanitakis, J. (2019). Whose island home? *Courts of Conscience*, *13*, 19–25.

Moreton-Robinson, A. M. (2004). The possessive logic of patriarchal white sovereignty: The high court and the Yorta decision. *Borderlands E-Journal*, *3*(2), 1–9.

Nayeri, D. (2017, April 4). The ungrateful refugee: We have no debt to repay. *The Guardian*. https://www.theguardian.com/world/2017/apr/04/dina-nayeri-ungrateful-refugee

Poletti, A. (2020). Introduction: A forum on Behrouz Boochani's no friend but the mountains: Writing from Manus prison. *Biography*, *43*(4), 685–691.

Razack, S. H. (2000). Simple logic: Race, the identity documents rule and the story of a nation besieged and betrayed. *Journal of Law and Social Policy*, *15*, 181–210.

Sassen, S. (1996). *Losing control?: Sovereignty in an age of globalization*. Columbia University Press.

SBS Staff. (2015, December 9). Former refugee launches "I Came by Boat" campaign to highlight migrant contribution. *SBS News*. https://www.sbs.com.au/news/article/former-refugee-launches-i-came-by-boat-campaign-to-highlight-migrant-contribution/qx1vxx1p1

Schwartz, B. (1974). Waiting, exchange, and power: The distribution of time in social systems. *American Journal of Sociology*, *79*(4), 841–870.

Slaughter, J. R. (2007). *Human Rights, Inc.: The world novel, narrative form, and international law*. Fordham University Press.

Tofighian, O. (2018a). Behrouz Boochani and the Manus Prison narratives: Merging translation with philosophical reading. *Continuum*, *32*(4), 532–540. https://doi.org/10.1080/10304312.2018.1494942

Tofighian, O. (2018b). Translator's tale: A window to the mountains. In B. Boochani (Ed.), *No friend but the mountains: Writing from Manus Prison*. Picador.

Tofighian, O. (2020). Introducing Manus Prison Theory: Knowing border violence. *Globalizations*, *17*(7), 1138–1156. https://doi.org/10.1080/14747731.2020.1713547

Tofighian, O., & Boochani, B. (2020). Narrative, resistance and Manus Prison Theory. *Review of Middle East Studies*, *54*(2), 174–195. https://doi.org/10.1017/rms.2021.25

Vogl, A. (2013). Telling stories from start to finish. *Griffith Law Review*, *22*(1), 63–86. https://doi.org/10.1080/10383441.2013.10854767

Vogl, A. (2017). The genres and politics of refugee testimony. *Law & Literature*, *30*(1), 81–104.

Vogl, A. (2024). *Judging refugees: Narrative and oral testimony in refugee status determination*. Cambridge University Press.

Whyte, S. (2017, January 30). *Save the Children workers removed from Nauru receive compo*. ABC News. https://www.abc.net.au/news/2017-01-31/save-the-children-workers-government-pays-compensation/8217686

Woolley, A. (2017). Narrating the "Asylum Story": Between literary and legal storytelling. *Interventions*, *19*(3), 376–394.

Chapter 8

People and Places that Matter: Racialised Assemblages in Nauru's Hyperextractive Asylum Regime*

Julia Morris

University of North Carolina Wilmington, USA

Abstract

In recent years, many Western states have moved towards funding the asylum processing and resettlement systems of countries in the Global South. These forms of outsourced migration governance are upheld by a vast industry of state and non-state actors. This chapter draws on fieldwork conducted in the Republic of Nauru to look at the people and places on the frontlines of the extractive asylum industry. Using Alexander Weheliye's (2014) concept of 'racialising assemblages', the author argues that outsourced asylum regimes exacerbate the continuous subjection of Indigenous and migrant communities to toxic practices and discourses. Outsourced asylum is a contemporary practice of resource extraction (much like other forms of mining) that builds on colonial extractive projects that disproportionately target communities of colour. Ongoing processes of dispossession and displacement are occurring as people and places are rendered into resources and frontline sites for the extractive asylum industry. This chapter also shows how humanitarian and liberal democratic discourses are part of the mechanics of racialised geopolitical ordering. Racialised refugees are

*Some sections of this chapter are taken from my book *Asylum and Extraction in the Republic of Nauru* and article 'As Nauru Shows, Asylum Outsourcing Has Unexpected Impacts on Host Communities' in *Migration Information Source*. Thank you to the editors of Cornell University Press and *Migration Information Source* for the permission to republish the material.

Deter, Detain, Dehumanise: The Politics of Seeking Asylum, 121–142

Published under exclusive licence by Emerald Publishing Limited
doi:10.1108/978-1-83753-224-720241010

made into destitute victims, whereas locals become brutish villains, rather than political subjects. In attending to the politics of refusal, where Nauruans and refugees refuse ingrained racialising assemblages that deny them personhood, the author stresses the importance of intersectional advocacy that highlights the toxic effects of extractive asylum regimes on local and migrant populations alike.

Keywords: Nauru; asylum; offshore; refugees; extraction; racism

Introduction

Rory, a Nauruan teenager, sits together in his bedroom in Nauru's Nibok District with his friend Taj, a young Afghani refugee.[1] They are putting together the final touches to their music video on an impressive music technology set-up (a big-screen Mac and the latest music recording and production software) funded by the Australian government as a way of integrating refugees in Nauru. Rory is well-versed in the music software, often recording birthday remixes for family and friends around the island. Taj is a keen beatboxer and rapper, contributing his vocal flair to the collaboration. They proudly show me their latest version with its edited sound and colours, which vividly captures Taj as he raps in the ocean surrounds of Anibare boat harbour. But Taj and Rory's lyrics do not celebrate the multicultural harmony of refugees living in Nauru, as the Australian Immigration Department envisaged. Instead, in their rhythmic and vocal mix, they voice shared hopes that refugees in Nauru receive asylum in Australia. Standing tall on the harbour walls, Taj raps about the troubled situation he left behind. The expanse of azure blue waters stretches infinitely beyond the horizon. A group of their Nauruan, Afghani and Iranian friends converge by his side, punctuating his verses with a backing chorus that denounces the unfairness of the offshore asylum policy that sent asylum seekers to Nauru. Rory turns to look at me from his editing work, saying, 'I really want to help Taj. Hopefully, get the Australian government to change their mind. This isn't right what's happening here'. Taj is quick to add, 'Nauruans also experienced this from Australia. I don't blame them. Phosphate mining, then their government almost bankrupt the island, then this. Now we're pushing back together'.

These kinds of solidarities are not commonly visible in media and scholarly accounts of Nauru's asylum processing and resettlement regime. Moments such as these, when Nauruans and refugees joined forces to push back on the Australian government's draconian policy, which saw asylum claimants sent to the 21 km^2 Pacific island of Nauru (see Image 5) and Papua New Guinea's (PNG)

[1]All names have been changed throughout this chapter and some individuals have been given composite identities to confer anonymity.

Image 5. The Republic of Nauru. Source: Julia Morris.

Manus Island from 2001 to 2008, then again from 2011 to 2023.[2] Instead, the overwhelming representation of Nauruans in the Australian and Western media draws on long-standing tropes of Indigenous populations as savage. Nauru is all-too-often depicted in Conradian terms such as a 'hell hole', where 'refugees [are] attacked "on a daily basis"' (Davidson, 2016) and subject to 'violent beatings' by islanders (Mathiesen, 2015). Meanwhile, refugees are positioned by mostly white Australian media and solidarity campaigners on a victim-villain binary. In leftist framings, migrants become racialised Third World victims fleeing despotic regimes. Alternatively, in right-wing press and political discourse, refugees are typically racialised terrorists, criminals and/or economic scroungers. Both are othering discourses that evoke a white salvational fantasy of protecting charitable subjects (Dawned, 2017) or utilise tropes of racialised refugee threat (Gray &

[2]Across the course of the on-and-off policy, migrants claiming asylum by boat were sent to Nauru and Manus Island for refugee status determination. Those successful in their asylum claims received refugee visas and basic resettlement support to live and work on that island. From 2013 to 2016, just over 1,200 asylum seekers were in Nauru; most came from the Middle East or South Asia. In June 2023, the last refugees held by Australia left Nauru, finally ending the controversial offshore asylum policy. In the years shortly prior, some refugees were resettled in the United States of America (USA), Canada, and New Zealand. The regional processing centre itself is still standing under an 'enduring capability' arrangement. Nauru may once again host asylum seekers, depending on the Australian government's immigration policy directions. And indeed, has since been used as such on an intermittent basis. In 2016, the Manus Island facility was ruled unlawful by PNG's supreme court and shut down. Some refugees were resettled elsewhere, but a small number of refugees remain in PNG.

Franck, 2019; Gutiérrez Rodríguez, 2018). These portrayals of Nauruans and refugees speak in different ways to the racial character of the people and places that are wrapped into outsourced asylum regimes. They extend from early racial classifications of Nauruans in terms of primitivism and barbarism and refugees as voiceless victims or as threats to social cohesion. Such patronising colonial narratives once motivated humanitarian missions to civilise and save Black and Brown populations (Behlmer, 2018). They convey a whole range of prejudiced assumptions about inferiority and underdevelopment associated with non-Western peoples in European colonial-racial logic.

This chapter examines the racialised assemblages that subject people and places to the massive upheavals of outsourced asylum regimes. In recent years, many politicians have found political purchase from discourses around border protectionism, investing enormous amounts of money into the governance of migration. The incorporation of human movement into market regimes has resulted in the emergence of new industry segments, often termed the 'migration industry' (Gammeltoft-Hansen & Nyberg Sørensen, 2013) or 'immigration-industrial complex' (Golash-Boza, 2009). Several Western states have moved towards a model of funding the asylum processing and resettlement systems of countries in the Global South (Dastyari et al., 2022; FitzGerald, 2019; Gazzotti et al., 2023; Morris, 2023a). The European Union (EU) has adopted this policy in Eastern Europe, Turkey, North Africa, and Central Asia (Follis, 2012; Gazzotti, 2021; Lambert, 2021), as has the United Kingdom (UK) in their attempted arrangement with Rwanda, which until now has been blocked by the courts (Morris, 2023b). Many of these forms of containment retrace the fault lines of colonial-era extractive practices (Morris, 2021a). Migration governance regimes zigzag from Global North to South, as well as in the peripheries of rural impoverished regions (Besteman, 2020). They exhibit what is often referred to as 'environmental racism', whereby Black, Indigenous, and people of colour communities are disproportionately exposed to environmental harms (Taylor, 2014). This concept is typically used to make visible toxic environmental exposures, such as air and water pollution and chemical exposure. In my work, I expand the toxicological conversation to consider the health impacts of exposure to destructive asylum legal systems: a form of unseen violence that affects millions (Morris, 2019, 2023a). Extractive asylum practices also have immense impacts on local populations, who similarly experience the corrosive effects of uneven migration governance geographies. Such understandings account for the ways in which Black and Brown bodies remain entangled with the forces of capital, subject to – and destinations for – outsourced asylum systems, penetrated by both toxic practices and toxic discourses.

Over the last decade, I have been tracking the extractive dynamics related to outsourced asylum regimes. This chapter draws on ethnographic fieldwork conducted in Nauru and Australia for a total of fifteen months between 2015 and 2016. It extends my previous work into outsourced asylum as a contemporary practice of resource extraction (much like other forms of mining) that builds on colonial extractive projects. Here, I argue that outsourced asylum regimes exacerbate the ongoing subjection of Indigenous and migrant communities to racialising assemblages fraught with damaging effects. Critical race studies scholar

Alexander Weheliye (2014) uses the concept of 'racialising assemblages' to consider how 'uneven global power structures defined by the intersections of neoliberal capitalism, racism, settler colonialism, immigration, and imperialism are predicated upon hierarchies of racialized, gendered, sexualized, economized, and nationalized social existence' (p. 1). Weheliye describes race as 'a set of sociopolitical processes that discipline humanity into full humans, not-quite-humans, and nonhumans' (Weheliye, 2014, p. 4). People marked by dehumanising racial assemblages are routinely abused or killed, and often have little standing before the law. These dynamics reveal how outsourced asylum regimes render individuals subhuman. But this is not to say that asylum seekers are marked as disposable to the value system of capitalism, as is often argued to be the case (Bauman, 2004). Rather, in their categorisation as asylum seekers and refugees, migrants are also made integral to the amassment of the wealth of capitalist accumulation of the refugee industry (Morris, 2021b). Ongoing processes of dispossession and displacement are occurring as people and places are rendered into resources and frontline sites for the extractive asylum industry.

This chapter is divided into three main sections, each of which thinks through Nauru as a site of colonial encounter or 'contact zone', where 'disparate cultures meet, clash, and grapple with each other, often in highly asymmetrical relations of domination and subordination' (Pratt, 2008, p. 7). Throughout, I take up Eva Haifa Giraud's (2019) call to centralise and politicise the exclusions in these extractive entanglements. The first section focusses on the contemporary extractive industry that brings Nauruans and refugees together in shared conditions of exploitation. I ask what forms of affiliation emerge when, in Mel Chen's (2011) words we 'think and feel with toxicity' (p. 265): here, the toxic effects of migration governance regimes. The second section considers the racialised representations that frequently regard Nauruans and refugees as racially inferior. I examine how racialised and gendered discourses travel across the transimperial terrains of other countries that take on outsourced asylum arrangements. The final section details the grounded consequences of Nauru's outsourced asylum regime on migrants claiming asylum, as well as local populations. In Nauru, different people's bodies remain connected to global commodity chains, to uneven relations of colonial and post-colonial relations of power and to racial capitalist world systems. Such a differential exposure to contamination in the service of maximum profit, what Elizabeth Povinelli (2006, p. 1768) terms 'biosocial spacing of environmental harm', reveals the uneven ways in which these governance regimes unfold.

In this chapter, I draw on the conversations I had with Nauruans, asylum seekers, and refugees on the island, who highlighted these interconnections and their colonial-capitalist undergirding.[3] As Taj makes clear, solidarity moments

---

[3]In this chapter, I refer to 'asylum seekers' as those awaiting asylum claims and 'refugees' as those who have received them. I often use 'migrant' to refer interchangeably to asylum seekers and refugees. In doing so, I remain cautious that all these terminologies are heavily racialised categorisations of people who move (Crawley & Skleparis, 2017). Such categorisations produce forms of value specific to migration control regimes, which Lauren Martin (2021) calls 'status value' (p. 747).

draw attention to the neocolonial logics of a shared condition, in what Behrooz Boochani (2022) terms a *system-e hākem* or 'kyriarchal system'. The offshore asylum regime is indissociable from histories of colonialism, capitalism, and racism. Asymmetries of power manifest in its geographies, the uneven relations of Nauruans and refugees to largely white settler Australians, and the paternalistic – often racist – rhetoric of civilisational humanitarianism: by which I mean a white supremacist language bound up in humanitarian work (Pallister-Wilkins, 2021). In attending to the politics of refusal, where Nauruans and refugees refuse ingrained racialising assemblages that deny them personhood, I close by stressing the importance of intersectional advocacy. Currently, Nauru is no longer in extensive use as an asylum processing and resettlement hub. Instead, it is funded by the Australian government to maintain 'an enduring regional processing capability', which can be activated when required (Australian Government Department of Foreign Affairs and Trade, 2021, p. 1). Meanwhile, evermore countries are outsourcing forms of migration governance, upheld by a vast industry of state and non-state actors (Gazzotti et al., 2023). Alliances that highlight the toxic effects of extractive asylum regimes on local and migrant populations alike are all-the-more pressing.

Extractive Entanglements

It is not happenstance that Taj and Rory found themselves together in Nauru as people and places on the frontlines of migrant extractivism. Taj astutely recognised the shared histories of imperial exploitation that undercut the political economies of Afghanistan and Nauru. The two grew up almost 11,000km from one another in worlds that, at first glance, were quite different. While Rory spent most of his younger life between Fiji and Nauru, Taj was born in Afghanistan's southern Helmand Province: an area of intense military occupation. The stories they share of their childhoods hold similarities; even as the respective forms of imperial interventionism played out differently. Taj was born into a country torn apart by Soviet and US strategic interests. At the crossroads between Central Asia, the Middle East, and South Asia, Afghanistan's geopolitical location has long rendered the country and its peoples subject to invasions and absorption into numerous empires and dynasties (Ewans, 2002). Massive land grabs, fighting over access to natural gas resources, and ideological one-upmanship have all generated huge out-migrations in recent years.[4] Taj's family is Hazara, an ethnic and religious minority, who faced overt discrimination. Every day, Taj recalls, was spent in fear of gunshots and explosions, with school haphazard at best. After brutally losing his father, Taj found himself the breadwinner for his family. Food and fuel prices constantly rose, yet economic opportunities were minimal for young people. These compounding insecurities and pressures pushed him to

[4]See Rashid (2010) for a discussion into Soviet and American interventionism in Afghanistan.

save money so that, with the support of family and friends, he could purchase a flight to Kuala Lumpur. His intention was to relocate to Australia via Indonesia, find employment, and eventually bring his mother, brother and sisters to join him.

Taj's movements were shaped by the racialising assemblages of contemporary border regimes. Instruments of mobility restriction and control are, as E. Tendayi Achiume (2022) points out, configured by deep imperial inequity, and are inherently racial. Coming from Afghanistan, Taj fell on the wrong side of the 'mobility divide', whereby citizens of countries in the Global North and elites in the Global South overwhelmingly experience privileged mobility (Mau et al., 2015). Unable to obtain a visa to Australia, Taj travelled to Malaysia and then Indonesia because he could access a short-term visa. In Indonesia, he found himself imbricated in a 'clandestine economy of mobility' (Lucht, 2022, p. 18). Undocumented migrants and those on tenuous visas looking to move to Australia, like Taj, have become a source of income locally. Under the pressure of heightened border controls, including Australian investments in immigration detention centres and other policies to criminalise migration, an elaborate network of landlords, drivers, brokers, and boat captains has developed in Indonesia (Missbach, 2015; Nethery & Gordyn, 2014). Migrants, such as Taj, are subject to racial categorisation and violence, rendered into sources of profit and predation. Taj shuttled between overcrowded hostels on the fringes of Jakarta. Racially profiled as a 'transit migrant', he often experienced altercations with the police, who would ask for bribes to turn a blind eye to his presence locally. Taj found himself constantly on edge, in fear of arrest or confinement in an immigration detention centre. At the time, surveillance and raiding by national and local police and immigration offices dramatically increased. Taj could not work legally or obtain any further education or vocational training. Even though he knew it was a dangerous and costly proposition (AU$10,000 back then), Taj decided to pursue his original plan of boarding a small fishing boat bound for Australia.

Extractivism does not stop at the point of generating out-migrations from a region. Taj was subject to the extractive systems of legal technologies, whereby myriad legal procedures track individuals' movements across territories (Morris, 2021b). Australia has long developed border control technologies that attempt to achieve – and profit from – racialised migrant exclusion (Morris, 2023c). Lower-income migrants from the Global South are often restricted to guest-worker and related migrant-labour regimes (Tazreiter & Burridge, 2022). Within this racialised immigration regime, asylum has become another means of subordinate inclusion in the neocolonial empire (Behrman, 2019). Despite being posited as emancipatory, the refugee regime is a part of what Barnor Hesse (2007) calls 'governmental racialization' (p. 656). Regulatory administrative power exercised 'by Europeanized ('white') assemblages over non-Europeanised ('non-white') assemblages' (Hesse, 2007, p. 656) is socially routinised and institutionalised as a natural arrangement of races. Racialisation is baked into the governance of nation-states, including 'who is included and who excluded, culturally, racially and legally' (Ticktin, 2008, p. 864). The asylum system is characterised by immense racial hierarchies. Non-western and largely people of colour are subject to an administrative regime that demands they prove suffering to move elsewhere. An emphasis on the refugee regime's emancipatory power occludes these colonial and racial hierarchies.

For Taj, claiming asylum was one of his limited means of obtaining legal status in Australia. He certainly met the requirements of this form of border entry. However, the asylum legal regime placed him in a particular juridico-political position in relation to economic circuits (Coddington et al., 2020). Not only would he have to prove his suffering through the performative economy of asylum legal systems (Morris, 2023d), but he also held value for others – non-governmental organisations (NGOs), corporations, state agencies, activists, academics, and more – in the system of production and circulation that is the international refugee regime (Morris, 2021b). Seven days in, his boat was intercepted by the Australian coastguard in the Indian Ocean. Under the hardline immigration policies of the time, Taj and his fellow passengers were taken to Christmas Island, before eventually being sent to Nauru.

Arriving in Nauru marked the next step in a clear instance of practices exploiting people's mobility as a raw material. By then, Nauru's economy revolved around the asylum industry, whereby refugees substituted phosphate as a new human commodity (Morris, 2023a). In Nauru, asylum claimants were subject to the intimate extractions of asylum legal practices, upheld by a spectrum of state and non-state actors. Offshore contracts for NGOs and corporate firms carrying out a range of asylum processing and refugee resettlement provisions topped the multi-millions. Fly-in-fly-out Australian and foreign workforces carried out asylum adjudication and refugee resettlement. Local business ventures such as land leasing, car rentals, accommodation, supermarkets, and cocktail bars made the island abuzz with economic activity (see Image 6). Meanwhile, the Nauruan government received over AUD5 billion across the course of the offshore asylum policy. A new hospital, school, courthouse, and road system packaged on as

Image 6. A New Accommodation Compound for Asylum Industry Workers in Nauru. Source: Julia Morris.

Image 7. Promoting Refugee Resettlement to Islanders in Nauru.
Source: Julia Morris.

development support to convince islanders of the benefits of this form of extraction in their backyard (see Image 7).

The choice of sending migrants to Nauru is part of a historical and ongoing imperial terrain. The uneven racialised geographies, which have brought together migrants and Pacific islanders, reveal how racial and colonial logics structure the people and places entangled in outsourced migration governance regimes. In Nauru, the island's strategic location and natural phosphate resources have resulted in decades of colonial-esque occupations and ecological destructions (Williams & Macdonald, 1985). These histories of violent dispossession set the stage for the emergence of capitalist accumulation, which compelled islanders to enter the global marketplace for their survival (Morris, 2021a). Only a few years old, Rory did not remember the island blackouts of the early 2000s when Nauru's central bank went bankrupt and basic infrastructure collapsed. Other islanders recalled stories to me of that time, of sitting around by candlelight and fishing on the reef to survive. Many Nauruans, like Rory, also battle with the toxic effects of phosphate mining on the island. Nauru's healthcare system is wracked with the consequences of colonial interventionism (McLennan & Ulijaszek, 2014), including one of the highest diabetic rates worldwide. Respiratory conditions, in particular the acute bronchitis that Rory suffers, are the leading cause of hospital admissions locally.

Like asylum seekers sent to Nauru, the eleven thousand islanders of this fence-line community (a term used to describe those living immediately adjacent to hazardous industries) have once again found themselves the playthings of political, economic, and environmental misfortunes that, for many, were not of their own making. Theirs is a story, common to other territories ravaged by extractive industries, which illustrates the short shrift given to local desires. Initially, the asylum processing and resettlement arrangement was agreed to in desperation by Nauru's spendthrift President René Harris. Nauruans were not consulted about the coming of the asylum industry. Many Nauruans I spoke with held complex feelings about the arrangement. Some, such as Rory, were passionately against the policy, considering it to be unethical: ill-gotten money that, like the 'bitter money' Parker Shipton (1989) once described among the Luo in southern Kenya, would be dangerous to its holder. Others were scared about who might be sent to their island. They were plugged into Australian media reports of asylum seekers as unknowable and high-risk. Some wondered why the Australian government did not want these potentially risky new arrivals in their country. Many islanders also believed that they were providing a safe haven to people in need: an angle that was enthusiastically promoted by the Nauruan government at the time. As part of the efforts to market the asylum industry locally, school children were encouraged to write poems about refugees and World Refugee Day was instated as an annual holiday, not long after Phosphate Commemoration Day.

This trade and substitution of migrants from minerals is an example of a literal bioeconomy that is meted in long-standing relation to racial capitalism and colonial violence. When showing how geology is structured by white supremacy, Kathryn Yusoff (2018) draws attention to the entanglement of Blackness and minerals as empty signifiers for capital accumulation and value. In Nauru, this is quite a literal practice, where, in Yusoff's (2018) words, 'bodies become gold, emptied of the sign of the human, reinvested with the signification of units of energy and properties of extraction' (p. 83). Here, racism supplies the precarious and exploitable lives needed by capitalism for the extraction of land and labour. Migrants, such as Taj, are forced to embark on lengthy journeys and the intimate labours of making an asylum claim. Much like the toxicological body burden, whereby harmful substances accumulate in the body (Agard-Jones, 2013), claiming asylum entails demonstrating past trauma, which wreaks havoc on many migrants' bodies (Ticktin, 2008). Simultaneously, historical geographies of extraction and environmental racism structure where the unwanted industry is located (Auyero & Swistun, 2009). Practices of contemporary migrant extraction are 'predicated on the presumed absorbent qualities of black and brown bodies to take up the body burdens of exposure to toxicities' (Yusoff, 2018, p. 792).

These forms of affiliation that bring Nauruans and refugees into inhuman proximity are reliant on racist settler colonial discourses. The next section turns to the toxic discourses that render certain populations and geographies exploitable.

Section 2: Racialised Representations

> 'Fat. Lazy. Refugee beaters. That's all they say', says Judith, a caterer at one of Nauru's primary schools. She references the latest headlines in the Australian and international media circulating about Nauru's 'torture complex' (2016), sighing, 'Most of these people have never even been to Nauru'! On a regular basis, Nauruans contended with representations of their home as an 'island

> of despair' (Amnesty International, 2016) outside the rule of law. Media reports about violent altercations, where refugees are 'attacked "on a daily basis" on Nauru' (Davidson, 2016), regularly featured in the Australian news. During my fieldwork, the Australian Broadcasting Corporation (ABC) released a *Four Corners* programme, *The Forgotten Children*. This included claims of a local culture in Nauru of rape, savagery, and violence, where Nauruans sexually assaulted refugee children. 'Regular – we're not talking several incidents. Regular, systematic attacks from local population. People are hacked with machetes', said Amnesty's Anna Neistat an interview on National Public Radio on 11 August 2016, after flying to Nauru on a three-day 'refugee mission'. 'Every single woman I spoke to told me that they cannot go out because now they're absolutely at the mercy of the locals'.

Such narratives of Nauruan savagery dominate popular understandings of the island. Many Nauruans I spoke with were upset with characterisations that drew on racist colonial tropes of Pacific islanders as violent, cannibals, and hostile to outsiders (see e.g. Davidson 2016; Edwards 2015). These contemporary media portrayals are set within a long colonial history of attempts to diminish islanders and ultimately establish European control in the region (Said, 1978).[5] Nauru's historiography is suffused by an exoticised imaginary of Pacific cannibalism, including early European books such as *Life and Laughter 'Midst the Cannibals* (Collinson, 1926) and *Cannibals and Coconuts* (Collinson, 1929). *A Wild Place Indeed*, wrote the white Australian explorer Louis Becke (1897). 'Their German masters try to keep a tight rein upon their blood-letting proclivities, and the seven clans with which the island is peopled are no longer allowed to slaughter each other with a free hand' (p. 65). Racialised characterisations like these are paradigmatic for the region (Kabutaulaka, 2015; Smith, 1992; Stella, 2007). Ethnographic accounts of Pacific peoples often depict islanders in perpetual warfare, calling for colonial missions to pacify, modernise, and Christianise local populations. In Nauru, these portrayals have shaped contemporary Western representations that continue to regard Nauruans as inferior and inherently violent.

Asylum seekers and refugees in Nauru also contended with their own dehumanising representations. Sitting on the boat harbour wall in Nauru's Anibare District, Imran, a middle-age Iranian refugee, discussed 'the political and media storm' that enveloped refugees in the Australian media. 'It's either this or that', he said. 'The bad guy or the poor refugee'. What Imran highlights is characteristic of Australian media, where asylum seekers are typically constructed along a villain-victim binary (Haw, 2021). Racialised refugees are portrayed as threats to Australian society, justifying border securitisation; or as helpless victims fleeing

[5]See Michelle Nayahamui Rooney's (2022) excellent discussion of similar representations of Manutians that build on exoticised colonial portrayals of foreign Others.

the wretched third world (Lippi et al., 2020).[6] Like the discourses levelled at Nauruans, such mutually dependent representations of refugee threat and vulnerability are underpinned by neocolonial logics (Gray & Franck, 2019). Across colonial spaces, humanitarian sentiments surrounding the protection of colonised subjects were part of legitimising but also seemingly emancipating individuals from forms of colonial violence (Lester & Dussart, 2014). These discursive practices ensured the continuation of a white Western superiority complex that continues to manifest in humanitarianism today, and especially that of international refugee law and solidarity campaigns (Pallister-Wilkins, 2021; Picozza, 2021).

The meteoric rise of the refugee industry has also been essential to the capitalist modes of commodification that see migrants categorised as vulnerable refugees (Morris, 2021a). As the refugee regime morphed from one centred on Eastern Europeans to migrants from Africa, Asia, and the Middle East, so too have popular images of refugees (Johnson, 2011). Forced migrants are no longer framed as heroic white male Europeans with political agency, but rather as poverty-stricken voiceless victims of colour from the Global South. Such marketing techniques have become essential to the refugee industry for whom refugees have become a popular marketable commodity, in terms of both financial rewards and the feel-good worth of moral capital.

To this day, Orientalist fantasies of the Other define the portrayals of racialised migrants promoted by refugee solidarity campaigners in Australia. High-profile campaigns at the time of my fieldwork focussed on a #RefugeesWelcome and #LetThemStay narrative, imbued with racialised hierarchies. Within the rhetorical and visual framings of these campaigns, migrants, and the places from which they come, are often characterised as backwards. The West is, in comparison, represented as the space of civilisation and progress. Racialised migrants are depicted as uniquely vulnerable refugees in need of rescue from their 'barbaric' cultures – a colonial construction that justifies Western imperial interventionism (Abu-Lughod, 2013), which ironically pushes more people to migrate. As Ida Danewid (2017) argues in the context of refugee solidarity campaigns in Europe, dynamics of hospitality in the 'saving of refugees' erase imperialist histories and present-day complicities. Instead, 'Bring Refugees to Australia'-style campaigns allow for the reconstitution of 'the west' as ethical and good, and the maintenance of what Gloria Wekker (2016) terms 'white innocence'. Visual and rhetorical illusions of staggering numbers of desperate refugees 'flooding' across western borders converge with the moral panics stoked by right-wing campaigners. Such apocalyptic narratives, framed within humanitarian or securitisation agendas, relegate migrants as objectified figures to protect or fear (Bettini, 2013). Refugee solidarity campaigns about Nauru also reinforce the racial stereotypes of people (refugees as threats, Nauruans as savage) and places (refugee origin countries and Nauru as Conradian 'hearts of darkness') that have, in the past, bolstered the depiction of offshore

---

[6]The favourable reception of white Ukrainians in Western countries over Black and Brown victims of conflict shows the significant role that race plays in mobility regimes and solidarity campaigns (Bajaj & Stanford, 2022). Ukrainians did not have to go through the refugee legal system, instead receiving temporary visas in many western countries, including those within the EU.

asylum as a strategy of deterrence. This only serves to rile local populations – an exasperation I often encountered among islanders in Nauru – rather than producing the kind of alliances that Taj and Rory created in their rap collaboration.[7]

Asylum seekers and refugees in Nauru were placed in a tense situation: unable to move beyond the island confines, except, at the time of my fieldwork, through a resettlement offer to Cambodia. Depictions of islanders as savage and refugees as victims, who need to be 'saved' by heroic white Western humanitarians, also fostered performances of 'idealized refugeeness' among some migrants as part of a 'politics of survival' (Fiddian-Qasmiyeh, 2014). Twinned images of savage native and vulnerable refugees combined with the dehumanising prerogatives of the international refugee system. Migrants must utilise gendered, racialised, and class-based discourses to produce 'pictures' of lives eligible for protection that fit templates of victimhood and vulnerability (Cabot, 2013). In Nauru, some asylum seekers and refugees took on these constructions publicly as a counterhegemonic strategy of self-representation to capture the attention of Australian media and public. Subject to vicious politics and humanitarian power imbalances, they utilised tropes of Nauruans as violent and refugees as victims in social media posts and collaborations with Australian activist campaigners. 'Well, what else can we do to get there?' Jamil, a young Iranian refugee, asked me in Nauru on one occasion. This is not to imply that Jamil is somehow not a 'real refugee', that he was creating 'fake news', or that altercations did not occur between some Nauruans and refugees or among some refugees. Rather, it is to make the point that migrants and Nauruans were imbricated in a racialising assemblage. Migrants also played a part in the ongoing commodification of refugee identities, 'helping to soothe the troubled souls of white folk concerned with both the well-being of Black and Indigenous populations and their own security at the top of racial hierarchies' (Pallister-Wilkins, 2021, p. 101). Meanwhile, fights that happened between some Nauruans and refugees were leapt on as evidence of Nauruan savagery and the need to evacuate refugees from Nauru: rather than the effects of the Australian government's policy. These rhetorical misrepresentations obscure the shared conditions of Nauruan and migrant exploitation endemic to the extractive offshore arrangement.

The final section turns to some of the impacts of outsourcing asylum in Nauru. The horrifying experiences of those in the asylum industry, which I go on to describe, illustrate how Nauruans and migrants were mutually subjected to dehumanising racialising assemblages. But the power of a liberal #RefugeesWelcome discourse, which pits suffering refugees against savage Nauruans, obscures the emergence of a shared oppositional consciousness and collective action surrounding the asylum industry's toxicity. Humanitarian and liberal democratic discourses are part of the mechanics of racialised geopolitical ordering.

[7]Another example of a coordinated challenge to the offshore processing regime is the successful legal case in the PNG Supreme Court in 2016 led by the PNG lawyer Ben Lomai and Australian lawyers, which mandated the closure of the Manus detention centre. However, most Australian and international press coverage glossed over Lomai's involvement and the risks he took to do so.

Section 3: Toxic Impacts

Despite the economic promises, the asylum industry had disquieting effects in Nauru. These impacts were even more pronounced than other toxic industries in that humans were the commodities in the production process. Migrants were subject to an immensely dehumanising regime where they had to prove the legitimacy of their asylum claims to receive a refugee visa for Nauru. With the support of refugee defence lawyers (or claims assistance providers) from the Sydney-based firm Craddock Murray Neuman, asylum seekers were required to collate evidence (photos, maps, and medical and psychological reports) that emphasised the dangers they faced in their home regions. In lengthy screenings at Nauru's regional processing centre, asylum claimants were quizzed on their fear, harm, and threat of persecution by fly-in-fly-out Australian immigration officers. Numerous studies and oral histories chronicle the experiences of individuals who live with this type of human extraction: having no work rights, subjected to demeaning NGO representations, and in a waiting game – sometimes for several years in various forms of detention – before any decision is made. In Australia, psychiatrists designated 'protracted asylum seeker syndrome' (Sundram & Loi, 2012) as a pathological condition connected to the lethal effects of asylum. Powerlessness, depression, and identity crises characterise this condition, exasperated by the uncertainty of people's situations and the demands of demonstrating traumatic experiences.

Asylum claimants in Nauru also described the retraumatising effect of having to collate past dreadful experiences into an objectified form. 'Intense', 'exhausting', and 'scrutinising' were some of the many words I heard used to describe refugee determination in Nauru. These experiences were all-the-more acute in Nauru, where asylum claimants were subject to an unknowable future. Although first envisaged as a temporary arrangement, migrants successful in their asylum claims received refugee visas for Nauru on a five-year then ten-year then perpetually extending basis. Many lived each day with uncertainties around their futures, rumours surrounding what the Australian government's latest policy might be, and fears of living in an unknown locale. Refugees were then expected to set up small business ventures in Nauru, which largely catered to fly-in-fly-out Australian personnel connected to the asylum industry (see Image 8). Many refugees questioned the point of this kind of arrangement run by Australian NGO workers from Connect Resettlement Services: an amalgamation of Melbourne's Australian Multicultural Education Services and the Brisbane based Multicultural Development Association Ltd. Some described it as 'patronising', highlighting the ludicrousness of Australian resettlement workers, themselves new to Nauru, resettling refugees on the island. These resettlement efforts involved cultural orientations and a regular programme of activities and events (including Rory and Taj's music project, aerobics classes, film nights, and even a World Refugee Day Nauru) designed to encourage local refugee integration. Outside this twilight zone, many refugees described how they felt 'physically trapped' by the restrictions that barred them from moving beyond Nauru. These limitations produced an immense claustrophobia that affected several refugees' desires to leave their resettlement compounds or, for some, to keep going. Many suffered the aftereffects of trauma, which had

Image 8. Australian-funded Refugee Business Ventures in Nauru.
Source: Julia Morris.

included abuse and economic deprivation in their homelands, compounded by harrowing boat journeys and unknowable futures in Nauru. Meanwhile, contracts in Nauru topped the multi-millions as asylum seekers and refugees remained connected to the racial capitalist world system. From refugee legal claims and medical services to operational security and child welfare, numerous organisations buoyed Nauru's asylum processing and resettlement operations.

Race-making practices were crucial not only to the *people* subject to the extractive asylum regime but also to the *place* where the asylum arrangement was sited. The arrival of the asylum industry in Nauru is set within a long (neo)colonial history of extractive industries (Morris, 2023a). This pattern of placing environmental risks near the path of least resistance, where communities have minimal political, economic and social capital, is repeated time and time again (Pulido, 2017). In Nauru, with its recent history of toxic phosphate mining and colonial violence and exploitation during the Australian and later Japanese occupation, this path has resulted in the arrival of yet another toxic extractive industry. Research details how slave plantations in the American South 'provided the blueprint for future sites of racial entanglement' (McKittrick, 2011, p. 949). The phosphate extractive landscape of Nauru, with its historical topology of pit mining sites and forms of environmental and health pollution, can be read in close parallel. The exchange of land use from phosphate to refugees has exposed residents and migrants to the harmful effects of a human extractive regime. As Hannah Appel (2019) found in her ethnographic work on the oil industry in Equatorial Guinea, the asylum industry in Nauru has not created new racial practices, but rather ensured their continuity.

Like other toxic industries, disproportionately sited in communities of colour, Nauru's outsourced asylum regime deeply impacted local islanders. Well-connected landowners and political leaders profited exponentially, but poor islanders without access to land, did not equitably share in the lifestyle and educational benefits that the Australian and Nauruan governments promised would accompany asylum processing and resettlement activity. Instead, residents witnessed the loss of local workforces to the asylum industry (as security guards, facility managers, drivers, teachers, and social workers). Nauruans and Australian personnel described these dynamics as a 'brain drain'. Typically, this concept characterises the emigration of well-educated professionals out of the country, but here it represented the concentration of Nauruan workers leaving jobs in the government and other public-facing sectors to work for Australian and foreign contractors paying much larger salaries. While remaining in Nauru, their skills were nonetheless diverted to serving foreign interests rather than their own population. During my fieldwork, there was a dearth of Nauruan professionals to administer local policies, particularly in the education and medical fields. The processing centre and resettlement compounds where asylum seekers lived became enclaves, isolated from essential sectors of the economy.

Other crucial sectors were left to decay. Often, development aid went unspent because no trained staff were there to ensure money was allocated effectively. Nauru remained reliant on foreign expertise, with almost all institutions led by foreign advisors in managerial positions. High school dropout rates increased, locals attributing the disenrollment to easily obtainable low-level employment with refugee contractors. Younger locals dropped out of teacher-training courses because they could easily access jobs within the asylum industry as security guards and drivers. While there is no doubt that the asylum policy has brought the country significant wealth, the benefits have limited reach. And as the asylum industry moves on, those who chose it over other career paths are finding themselves with short-lived gains.

The toxic discourses that circulated in Australian and global media about the island deeply affected local islanders. Gregory, an older Nauruan man, characterised these mixed feelings of anger, sadness, and humiliation, saying, 'I go to Australia and people laugh when I say I'm from Nauru. Bird-shit island, now this refugee business', in what became a familiar conversation locally. However, racist discourses that depicted Nauruans and their country in derogatory terms were crucial to the Australian government's use of Nauru for the asylum arrangement. Nauru was envisaged as a place of deterrence to reduce the number of migrants taking a boat to Australia. For the Australian government and its corporate contractors, housing the asylum industry in Nauru also reduced their accountability. Allegations of violence or sexual assault could be blamed on local personnel, already subject to racist representations of savagery, rather than as the effects of a destructive policy arrangement.[8]

---

[8]Rooney (2022) discusses these accountability politics in relation to allegations of sexual assault and the tragic death of Reza Barati on Manus Island, which was attributed to the violent actions of Manutian security guards, who were sentenced to 10 years in jail in PNG. The Australian government reached a confidential settlement with Barati's family in 2023.

Yet, powerful solidarities also existed between some refugees and locals. The music project advanced by Rory and Taj was one such creative formulation from those in the throes of a dehumanising regime. The project was a striking example of just one of several moments where Nauruans and refugees circumvented the extractive asylum system. Through song and solidarity, Rory and Taj recognised the policy's colonial fault lines and the mutual exploitation it engendered. The rap collaborators were all keen to upload their music videos to YouTube to publicly protest the asylum arrangement. Weeks of work and thousands of Australian dollars had gone into the project, and they were galvanised into action. Yet, despite the success of the project in engaging local youths with the moral value of refugee resettlement – albeit for Australia, not Nauru – the Australian Immigration Department would not authorise the video upload. Unfortunately, for Rory and Taj, their efforts remained caught up in the Australian government's spectacle of deterrence, and so the videos were not allowed airplay outside the island. The Australian government brought offshore processing to Nauru in the first place as a Debordian spectacle – a 'circuit breaker' (Expert Panel on Asylum Seekers, Commonwealth Government of Australia, 2012, p. 12) – that would dissuade future boat arrivals. Funding music collaborations that voiced the injustices of exclusion from Australia – not to mention sound systems for World Refugee Day celebrations, pop aerobics classes, yoga, and the like – sat uneasily with the Australian government's presentation of hardened maritime deterrence. As a result, the images of Nauruan-refugee solidarities were not aired beyond the island. This, I was told by islanders, was similarly the case when they contacted Australian media and activists to give nuance to the local impacts of the asylum regime. Their perspectives were constantly dismissed in favour of normative refugee solidarity campaigns that emphasised Nauruan violence and refugee victimhood.

The erasure of these experiences of solidarity, and discourses that elevate tropes of savagery and suffering, is part of the project of racialisation imbricated in the governance of belonging to the nation-state. Media headlines such as 'We Will F*****g Kill You: Beaten Nauru Refugees Fear for Their Lives' (SBS News, 2014) and 'Refugees on Nauru plead for resettlement' (Ferrie, 2018) through the recent language of 'evacuation' (Doherty & Gillespie, 2023), when referring to the remaining refugees in Nauru eventually leaving for Australia, depoliticise refugees as voiceless victims saved by mostly white Australian activists in developed countries. The voices of refugees and Nauruans calling together for an end to offshore asylum are stifled, fading away amid the cacophony of white salvation. These discourses inform the hierarchies that enable certain bodies to be subjected to practices of asylum rarely experienced by others. White Western citizens and elite non-westerners on the move are positioned at the pinnacle of the 'human' continuum, while migrants such as Taj are forced to undergo dehumanising asylum. Such practices serve to enrich former colonial centres, strengthening the border zones between the first and third world. Meanwhile, migrants and Nauruans bear the tolls of the destruction attendant with these forms of human extraction and exploitation.

Conclusions

Global practices of exterritorialising asylum follow related contours of colonial extractivism and epistemic intervention such as those operating in Nauru. Similar discursive framings are also present in refugee solidarity campaigns targeting non-western countries in outsourced asylum arrangements. This is the situation with campaigns against the UK government's attempted third-country asylum deal with Rwanda. There are certainly well-founded concerns of the Rwandan government, however, some advocates and media have stigmatised Rwanda as an underdeveloped conflict zone. This chapter has argued that such uncritical representations can undermine possibilities for political action. They fail to recognise the potential of shared relations of exploitation that could push back on outsourced asylum arrangements. Refugees are depicted as destitute victims, whereas locals become brutish villains, rather than political subjects. This construct can marginalise local and refugee populations. Instead, others (largely white westerners) speak on their future, leaving little room for contestation.

Giraud (2019) argues that we should move beyond an ethics based on uncritical celebrations of relationality to an ethics of exclusion. Rather than realising relational modes of ethics, we should pay more attention to 'ways of being that are foreclosed when other entangled realities are materialized' (Giraud, 2019, p. 2). Such a way of centralising and politicising shared exclusions could be invaluable for those seeking to shed light on the impacts of asylum regimes, including in the Global North (Morris, 2023c). Instead of creating hierarchies of humanity that pit migrants against native, which Nandita Sharma (2020) points out was fundamental to colonial rule, this approach pays attention to intersectional inequalities. It moves away from an activist ethics based on upholding the international refugee system, rather than seeing it as a racialised practice of migration governance. By recognising the 'everyday exclusions and processes of marginalization' (Giraud, 2019, p. 25) that enable late capitalism's arrangements to appear natural, we can instead contest liberal orderings of life that reproduce the border regime. At the same time, centralising exclusions avoids highlighting refugee-local alliances in ways that can be used by governments and their corporate and non-governmental contractors to rose-tint asylum regimes. Certainly, there were quiet moments of human connection in Nauru, when islanders and refugees formed close friendships, shared meals, and celebrated special occasions together. These relations were often promoted as 'positive refugee stories' in local industry newsletters. But this kind of uncritical celebration negates the immense power imbalances that lurk throughout such asylum arrangements. Unlike their islander companions, refugees could not move beyond the island perimeter nor did they want to be in Nauru. Both were entangled in a racialising assemblage that saw migrants immobilised beyond demeaning practices of asylum and Pacific islanders once again having their worlds upended to benefit Australian politicians, contracted workforces, and local elites.

Making visible the shared exclusions experienced by refugees and local populations in the context of outsourced asylum regimes can form a powerful ethico-political practice. Nauru might no longer be an offshore asylum industry hub, but similar practices are taking hold in diverse locations around the world. It is essential that we bring to the fore the people and places entangled in asylum to foster the conditions for advancing meaningful political change.

References

Abu-Lughod, L. (2013). *Do Muslim women need saving?* Harvard University Press.

Achiume, E. T. (2022). Racial borders. *Georgetown Law Journal, 110*(3), 445–508.

Agard-Jones, V. (2013). Bodies in the system. *Small Axe, 17*(3), 182–192.

Amnesty International. (2016). *Australia: Island of despair: Australia's "processing" of refugees on Nauru*. https://www.amnesty.org/en/documents/asa12/4934/2016/en/

Appel, H. (2019). *The licit life of capitalism: US oil in Equatorial Guinea*. Duke University Press.

Australian Government Department of Foreign Affairs and Trade. (2021, September). *Memorandum of understanding between the Republic of Nauru and Australia on the enduring regional processing capability in Republic of Nauru*. https://www.dfat.gov.au/sites/default/files/mou-nauru-enduring-regional-processing-capability-sep-2021.pdf

Auyero, J., & Swistun, D. A. (2009). *Flammable: Environmental suffering in an Argentine shantytown*. Oxford University Press.

Bajaj, S. R., & Stanford, F. C. (2022). The Ukrainian refugee crisis and the pathology of racism. *British Medical Journal, 376*, 0661. https://doi.org/10.1136/bmj.o661

Bauman, Z. (2004). *Wasted lives: Modernity and its outcasts*. Polity Press.

Becke, L. (1897). *Pacific tales*. Routledge.

Behlmer, G. K. (2018). *Risky shores: Savagery and colonialism in the Western Pacific*. Stanford University Press.

Behrman, S. (2019). Refugee law as a means of control. *Journal of Refugee Studies, 32*(1), 42–62. https://doi.org/10.1093/jrs/fey016

Besteman, C. (2020). *Militarized global apartheid*. Duke University Press.

Bettini, G. (2013). Climate barbarians at the gate? A critique of apocalyptic narratives on 'climate refugees'. *Geoforum, 45*, 63–72. https://doi.org/10.1016/j.geoforum.2012.09.009

Boochani, B. (2022). *Freedom, only freedom: The prison writings of Behrouz Boochani*. Bloomsbury Press.

Cabot, H. (2013). The social aesthetics of eligibility: NGO aid and indeterminacy in the Greek asylum process. *American Ethnologist, 40*(3), 452–466. https://doi.org/10.1111/amet.12032

Chen, M. Y. (2011). Toxic animacies, inanimate affections. *GLQ: A Journal of Lesbian and Gay Studies, 17*(2–3), 265–286. https://doi.org/10.1215/10642684-1163400

Coddington, K., Conlon, D., & Martin, L. L. (2020). Destitution economies: Circuits of value in asylum, refugee, and migration control. *The American Association of Geographers, 110*(5), 1425–1444. https://doi.org/10.1080/24694452.2020.1715196

Collinson, C. W. (1926). *Life and laughter 'midst the cannibals*. Hurst & Blackett.

Collinson, C. W. (1929). *Cannibals and coconuts*. George Philip & Son.

Crawley, H., & Skleparis, D. (2017). Refugees, migrants, neither, both: Categorical fetishism and the politics of bounding in Europe's 'migration crisis'. *Journal of Ethnic and Migration Studies, 44*(1), 48–64. https://doi.org/10.1080/1369183X.2017.1348224

Danewid, I. (2017). White innocence in the Black Mediterranean: Hospitality and the erasure of history. *Third World Quarterly, 38*(7), 1674–1689. https://doi.org/10.1080/01436597.2017.1331123

Dastyari, A., Nethery, A., & Hirsch, A. (2022). *Refugee Externalisation Policies*. Routledge.

Davidson, H. (2016, August 3). Refugees attacked 'on a daily basis' on Nauru, human rights groups say. *The Guardian*. https://www.theguardian.com/australia-news/2016/aug/03/refugees-attacked-on-a-daily-basis-on-nauru-says-amnesty-report

Doherty, B., & Gillespie, E. (2023, June 25). *Last refugee on Nauru evacuated as Australian government says offshore processing policy remains*. https://www.theguardian.com/australia-news/2023/jun/25/last-refugee-on-nauru-evacuated-as-australian-government-says-offshore-processing-policy-remains

Edwards, M. (2015, March 19). *Tensions on Nauru heightened after series of attacks on refugees by locals*. ABC News. http://www.abc.net.au/news/2015-03-20/tensions-high-on-nauru-after-attacks-on-refugees/6334234

Ewans, M. (2002). *Afghanistan: A short history of its people and politics*. Curzon Press.

Expert Panel on Asylum Seekers, Commonwealth Government of Australia. (2012). *Report of the expert panel on asylum seekers*. http://apo.org.au/research/report-expert-panel-asylum-seekers

Ferrie, J. (2018, September 5). *Refugees on Nauru plead for resettlement as regional leaders meet*. https://www.reuters.com/article/us-australia-refugees-nauru-idUSKCN1LL15Y

Fiddian-Qasmiyeh, E. (2014). *The ideal refugees: Gender, Islam, and the Sahrawi politics of survival*. Syracuse University Press.

FitzGerald, D. S. (2019). *Refuge beyond reach: How rich democracies repel asylum seekers*. Oxford University Press.

Follis, K. S. (2012). *Building fortress Europe: The Polish-Ukrainian frontier*. University of Pennsylvania Press.

Gammeltoft-Hansen T., & Nyberg Sørensen, N. (Eds.). (2013). *The migration industry and the commercialization of international migration*. Routledge.

Gazzotti, L. (2021). *Immigration nation: Aid, control, and border politics in Morocco*. Cambridge University Press.

Gazzotti, L., Mouthaan, M., & Natter, K. (2023). Embracing complexity in 'Southern' migration governance. *Territory, Politics, Governance*, *11*(4), 625–637. https://doi.org/10.1080/21622671.2022.2039277

Giraud, E. H. (2019). *What comes after entanglement? Activism, anthropocentrism, and an ethics of exclusion*. Duke University Press.

Golash-Boza, T. (2009). The immigration industrial complex: Why we enforce immigration policies destined to fail. *Sociology Compass*, *3*(2), 295–309. https://doi.org/10.1111/j.1751-9020.2008.00193.x

Gray, H., & Franck, A. K. (2019). Refugees as/at risk: The gendered and racialized underpinnings of securitization in British media narratives. *Security Dialogue*, *50*(3), 275–291. https://doi.org/10.1177%2F0967010619830590

Gutiérrez Rodríguez, E. (2018). The coloniality of migration and the "refugee crisis": On the asylum-migration nexus, the transatlantic white European settler colonialism-migration and racial capitalism. *Refuge*, *34*(1), 16–28. https://doi.org/10.7202/1050851ar

Haw, A. L. (2021). "Hapless victims" or "making trouble": Audience responses to stereotypical representations of asylum seekers in Australian news discourse. *Journalism Practice*, *17*(1), 5–23. https://doi.org/10.1080/17512786.2021.1930574

Hesse, B. (2007). Racialized modernity: An analytics of white mythologies. *Ethnic and Racial Studies*, *30*(4), 643–663. https://doi.org/10.1080/01419870701356064

Johnson, H. (2011). Click to donate: Visual images, constructing victims and imagining the female refugee. *Third World Quarterly*, *32*(6), 1015–1037. https://doi.org/10.1080/01436597.2011.586235

Kabutaulaka, T. (2015). Re-presenting Melanesia: Ignoble savages and Melanesian alternatives. *The Contemporary Pacific*, *27*(1), 110–146. https://doi.org/10.1353/cp.2015.0027

Lambert, L. (2021). Extraterritorial asylum processing: The Libya–Niger emergency transit mechanism. *Forced Migration Review*, *68*, 18–21.
Lester, A., & Dussart, F. (2014). *Colonization and the origins of humanitarian governance: Protecting Aborigines across the nineteenth-century British Empire*. Cambridge University Press.
Lippi, K., McKay, F. H., & McKenzie, H. J. (2020). Representations of refugees and asylum seekers during the 2013 federal election. *Journalism*, *21*(11), 1611–1629. https://doi.org/10.1177/146488491773407
Lucht, H. (2022). EU border control in Niger: From migrants to gold, drugs, and rare animals. *Cultural Anthropology*, *37*(1), 16–22. https://doi.org/10.14506/ca37.1.03
Martin, L. (2021). Carceral economies of migration control. *Progress in Human Geography*, *45*(4), 740–757. https://doi.org/10.1177/0309132520940006
Mathiesen, K. (2015, October 28). *For refugees like Abyan, Nauru even worse than detention*. Crikey. https://www.crikey.com.au/2015/10/28/for-refugees-like-abyan-nauru-even-worse-than-detention/
Mau, S., Gulzau, F., Laube, L., & Zaun, N. (2015). The global mobility divide: How visa policies have evolved over time. *Journal of Ethnic and Migration Studies*, *41*(8), 1192–1213. https://doi.org/10.1080/1369183X.2015.1005007
McKittrick, K. (2011). On plantations, prisons, and a black sense of place. *Social & Cultural Geography*, *12*(8), 947–963. https://doi.org/10.1080/14649365.2011.624280
McLennan, A. K., & Ulijaszek, S. (2014). Obesity emergence in the Pacific islands: Why understanding colonial history and social change is important. *Public Health Nutrition*, *18*(8), 1499–1505. http://dx.doi.org/10.1017/S136898001400175X
Missbach, A. (2015). *Troubled transit: Asylum seekers stuck in Indonesia*. ISEAS Publishing.
Morris, J. C. (2019). Violence and extraction of a human commodity: From phosphate to refugees in the Republic of Nauru. *The Extractive Industries and Society*, *6*(4), 1122–1133. https://doi.org/10.1016/j.exis.2019.07.001
Morris, J. C. (2021a). Colonial afterlives of infrastructure: From phosphate to refugee processing in the Republic of Nauru. *Mobilities*, *16*(5), 688–706. https://doi.org/10.1080/17450101.2021.1961289
Morris, J. C. (2021b). The value of refugees: UNHCR and the growth of the global refugee industry. *Journal of Refugee Studies*, *34*(3), 2676–2698. https://doi.org/10.1093/jrs/feaa135
Morris, J. C. (2023a). *Asylum and extraction in the Republic of Nauru*. Cornell University Press.
Morris, J. C. (2023b, March 24). *'A toxic policy with little returns' – lessons for the UK–Rwanda deal from Australia and the US*. The Conversation. https://theconversation.com/a-toxic-policy-with-little-returns-lessons-for-the-uk-rwanda-deal-from-australia-and-the-us-201790
Morris, J. C. (2023c). Necropolitics as accumulation: Enforcement and enclosure in Brisbane during COVID-19. *Political Geography*, *102*(102854), 1–11. https://doi.org/10.1016/j.polgeo.2023.102854
Morris, J. C. (2023d). (Im)mobility economies: Extractivism of the refugee as a human commodity. In F. Calvão, M. Archer, & A. Benya (Eds.), *The lives of extraction: Identities, communities, and the politics of place*, 249–269. Brill-Nijhoff. https://doi.org/10.4000/poldev.5430
Nethery, A., & Gordyn, C. (2014). Australia–Indonesia cooperation on asylum-seekers: A case of 'incentivised policy transfer'. *Australian Journal of International Affairs*, *68*(2), 177–193. https://doi.org/10.1080/10357718.2013.841122
Pallister-Wilkins, P. (2021). Saving the souls of white folk: Humanitarianism as white supremacy. *Security Dialogue*, *52*, 98–106. https://doi.org/10.1177/09670106211024419

Picozza, F. (2021). *The coloniality of asylum: Mobility, autonomy and solidarity in the wake of Europe's refugee crisis*. Rowman & Littlefield.

Povinelli, E. (2006). *The empire of love: Toward a theory of intimacy, genealogy, and carnality*. Duke University Press.

Pratt, M. L. (2008). *Imperial eyes: Travel writing and transculturation*. Routledge.

Pulido, L. (2017). Geographies of race and ethnicity II: Environmental racism, racial capitalism and state-sanctioned violence. *Progress in Human Geography*, *41*(4), 524–533. https://doi.org/10.1177/0309132516646495

Rashid, A. (2010). *Taliban: Militant Islam, oil and fundamentalism in Central Asia*. Yale University Press.

Rooney, N. M. (2022). *Weaponising alleged sexual assault on Manus: A gendered timeline of political discourse in the Australian media, 2012–2019* [Discussion Paper, 102, Development Policy Centre]. http://dx.doi.org/10.2139/ssrn.4172686

Said, E. (1978). *Orientalism*. Random House.

SBS News. (2014, October 29). *We will F*****g kill you: Beaten Nauru refugees fear for their lives*. https://www.sbs.com.au/news/article/we-will-f-g-kill-you-beaten-nauru-refugees-fear-for-their-lives/998vzmp6u

Sharma, N. (2020). *Home rule: National sovereignty and the separation of natives and migrants*. Duke University Press.

Shipton, P. (1989). *Bitter money: Cultural economy and some African meanings of forbidden commodities*. American Anthropological Association.

Smith, B. (1992). *Imagining the Pacific in the wake of the Cook voyages*. Melbourne University Press.

Stella, R. T. (2007). *Imagining the other: The representation of the Papua New Guinean subject*. University of Hawaii Press.

Sundram, S., & Loi, S. (2012, May 23). *Long waits for refugee status lead to new mental health syndrome*. The Conversation. https://theconversation.com/long-waits-for-refugee-status-lead-to-new-mental-health-syndrome-7165

Taylor, D. (2014). *Toxic communities: Environmental racism, industrial pollution, and residential mobility*. NYU Press.

Tazreiter, C., & Burridge, A. (2022). Fault-lines in temporary migration schemes: The case of Australia and the legacies of settler-colonial mentalities in the exploitation of temporary non-citizens. International Migration, *60*(4), 85–92. https://doi.org/10.1111/imig.13015

Ticktin, M. (2008). Sexual violence as the language of border control: Where French feminist and anti-immigrant rhetoric meet. *Signs*, *33*(4), 863–889. https://doi.org/10.1086/528851

Weheliye, A. (2014). *Habeas viscus: Racializing assemblages, biopolitics, and black feminist theories of the human*. Duke University Press.

Wekker, G. (2016). *White innocence: Paradoxes of colonialism and race*. Duke University Press.

Williams, M., & Macdonald, B. (1985). *The phosphateers: A history of the British phosphate commissioners and the Christmas Island phosphate commissioners*. Melbourne University Press.

Yusoff, K. (2018). *A billion black anthropocenes or none*. University of Minnesota Press.

Chapter 9

An End to Refugee Protection? The New Global Carceral Archipelagos of Exclusion and Possibilities for Alternative Futures

Claudia Tazreiter

Linköping University, Sweden

Abstract

This chapter offers a critical evaluation of the concept and application of global carceral archipelagos designed as punitive barriers to refugees. With a focus on policies and practices in Australia for over two decades, the chapter shows how more recently, the European Union (EU) and the United Kingdom (UK) are also adopting similar strategies to Australia in a pattern of Western countries turning their backs on their human rights obligations. The histories of colonial practices of the racialisation of certain minorities within and outside nation-state borders are an important aspect of understanding contemporary bordering regimes that exclude refugees. The chapter discusses examples of resistance, as well as alternative politics emerging from refugees who have suffered from the carceral border complex, drawing on creative and collaborative work and practices.

Keywords: Refugees; detention; human rights; racialisation; necropolitics; futures

Introduction

It is the middle of 2023 and in the UK, up to 500 asylum seekers whose claims for protection are still being assessed, are being moved onto a large barge,

Deter, Detain, Dehumanise: The Politics of Seeking Asylum, 143–156

Published under exclusive licence by Emerald Publishing Limited
doi:10.1108/978-1-83753-224-720241011

permanently docked in Portland Port in southern England. The barge is topped with an imposing three-storey structure resembling stacked shipping containers, each with a small window. The introduction of this form of housing for asylum seekers is part of the government's *Small Boats and Migration Bill* that came into law in July 2023. The UK is emulating and in some respects directly copying the policies, logics and political rhetoric used by the Australian government since 2001. This logic targets asylum seekers, particularly those arriving by boat, creating political rhetoric supported by new policy regimes of asylum seekers as problems and threats to society and instituting totalising systems of control and indeed, of punishment.

The context for this chapter is the geopolitics of contemporary bordering practices of states. These practices that detain, deport and deter asylum seekers and refugees are complex in administrative and legislative detail across Western states. These policies and practices aim to securitise unwanted arrivals. At the same time, these policies are communicated to citizens as shielding them from asylum seekers, as if asylum seekers pose existential threats. Despite the accumulation of much evidence by researchers over more than two decades of the human rights abuses and harms of such practices, borders and border regimes are hardening with the accumulation of more practices of exclusion and harms in contemporary border regimes globally, but particularly in, and by, Western states. The chapter first outlines the architecture of these practices, and then considers alternatives emerging from refugee activism, from critical race and decolonial researchers, and importantly, from the experiences of refugees that are subject to the racialised laws and administrative measures that give authority to border carceral practices.

The chapter begins with an outline of recent practices in the EU and the UK of instituting and hardening a global carceral archipelago that punishes asylum seekers who arrive spontaneously. These developments and new practices mirror earlier practices in Australia. I then turn to the Australian case and a chronology of the carceral archipelago that began in 2001. These harmful policies and practices do not go without opposition, resistance and proposals for alternative pathways. The chapter draws together some of these voices of resistance, focussing on Australia. The history of these practices is set against a theorisation of racialisation as historically embedded practices, that are normalised in the values and social attitudes linked to colonialism. Here, the concept of racial capitalism is also key to revealing the systems of power that build wealth through the impoverishment of people and ecology, through a system of hierarchies of life, worth and value. In conclusion, I draw together some key aspects of what can be learned and offer a modest diagnosis of the times, asking whether there is any hope for alternative futures towards a post-border world that would genuinely offer mobility rights.

The European 'Migration Crisis' of 2015 and Beyond

An important moment to consider in the recent history of new global carceral archipelagos of detention and deterrence of asylum seekers, is the so-called 'migration crisis' of 2015 in Europe. The year 2015 was typified as a migration crisis by political leaders, but also by many migration scholars, as the number of spontaneous migrants arriving in Europe reached numbers not seen since the end of the Second World War, with an estimated 1.3 million people arriving in the EU territories. Importantly, other scholars have problematised the use of crisis in relation to migration (De Genova, 2018; Ghosh, 2021; Tazreiter, 2019; Tazzioli et al., 2018).

In the period since the 'migration crisis', the EU has entered into numerous agreements to deter the arrival of spontaneous migrants (refugees, asylum seekers and other irregular migrants), as well as deporting many who are already within EU member states. Most recently, the EU signed an agreement with Tunisia to send asylum seekers there for their claims for protection to be processed (Wintour, 2023). This most recent deal in the geopolitics of migration borders follows a number of other deals struck by the EU, such as with Turkey and other North African states; the UK has sought a deal with Rwanda to move on asylum seekers; and many other Western states are implementing securitised borders to asylum seekers and refugees. Notable also is Australia, in its decades-long approach of sending asylum seekers to Manus Island, Papua New Guinea (PNG) and Nauru (a small Pacific island nation). The European responses to spontaneous arrivals are not unique. In many other parts of the world barriers for asylum seekers and refugees include removal to remote sites of detention, forced deportation to dangerous situations and the withdrawal of access to basic welfare provisions. In Australia, the use of third states to detain asylum seekers and refugees began in 2001, detailed later. The UK has more recently emulated Australia's laws, policies and administrative processes under the political slogan 'stop the boats', copied directly from the political campaign of Tony Abbott in the 2013 Federal election. The UK High Court has ruled the proposed agreement to send refugees to Rwanda unlawful, though the UK government is appealing the decision. Similarly, the UK courts have ruled the detention of unaccompanied minors in hotel rooms unlawful. In the United States (USA), the new policy of the Biden administration that came into force in early 2023, called Title 42, restricts the possibility to apply for asylum, targeting movements across the Mexico/US border.

It is important to contextualise the histories of racialisation, traced to colonial and imperial regimes, values and logics and to historicise the understanding of a radical policy change in the governance of forced migration and the global effects of this change. The EU deal with Turkey, signed in March 2016 in the aftermath of the EU hysteria of what was called a 'migration crisis', presents a new externalisation of the free movement of refugees. Denmark has pivoted towards sending refugees to Rwanda with a law passed in mid-2021 allowing the state to send refugees elsewhere. In Europe, the pivot to harsher restrictions towards refugees heightened after the influx of refugees in 2015 (Barker, 2018). The connections between Australian externalisation policies and more recent EU and UK approaches are evident with the outcome of increasing adoption of externalisation policies for the refugee protection system as a cooperative agreement between states.

These deals struck by Western governments to transfer their responsibilities for asylum seekers and refugees to impoverished third countries for a monetary payment amount to ethical traps. On the one hand, Western governments and intergovernmental and human rights organisations regularly wring their hands in public statements of regret at the tragedies of deaths at sea in the Mediterranean Ocean, the Pacific Ocean and many other sites of sinking vessels with asylum seekers aboard including babies and small children. Yet, on the other hand, the safe passage advocated as necessary for forced migrants to seek asylum is unavailable. Seemingly endless mountains of money are available for instituting restrictive policies aimed at refugees. Examples include deals with third countries, lucrative private contracts granted to multinational prison companies to run remote detention centres and court-mandated compensation payments where governments are found to have breached their obligations under national and international human rights standards. Yet, the lives of thousands of refugees and asylum seekers continue to be treated as political capital and remain the target for increasingly restrictive and punitive policies. It is noteworthy that states spend far more public funds on deterrence and punishment of refugees, than they do on finding durable solutions to displacement.

From this evidence, the chapter develops the argument that racial capitalism is an important critique to explain historically embedded systems and logics of laws, policies and everyday practices that are lived as global inequality and injustice in contemporary times. These histories require careful explication and unpicking to link the restrictions to asylum with global inequalities and injustice that have historical origins in coloniality, empire and racialisation. The international rules-based order that has the international human rights system as a pillar, is one key aspect of this system. With access to asylum curtailed through securitised borders across the global carceral archipelago, the international system of states faces a conundrum. The values of democracy and human rights, regularly espoused as fundamental by Western states, are not extended to refugees and asylum seekers. The concept of racial capitalism, along with Mbembe's (2019) articulation of *necropolitics*, provides the theoretical framework, discussed later in the chapter, for making sense of the empirical evidence of the withdrawal of the right to asylum as acts of injustice (Gleeson, 2016; Grewcock, 2017; Tazreiter et al., 2023, chapter 3).

I now turn to the Australian case of building a carceral archipelago of removal and harm aimed at asylum seekers arriving by boat. Later, these responses are linked to the racialisation of minorities that provides such a key framework for understanding state responses to asylum seekers and refugees.

The Tampa Crisis as Proxy for the Withdrawal from Refugee Protection: THE Australian Case

The year 2001 was a momentous year for the geopolitics of borders and migration. The events of September 11, with the attacks on the Twin Towers in New York and on the Pentagon in Washington, marked the beginning of the USA 'War on Terror', the related global rise in Islamophobia and an intensification of the racialisation of migrants and refugees, including the introduction of laws of exceptionalism. In the Asia-Pacific region, the Australian state carved out a punitive and exclusionary set of policies aimed at the arrival of asylum seekers. These policies gained widespread public support in the context of political justifications drawing on the 9/11 terror attacks. The Australian governance of refugee arrivals after August 2001 is important at regional and global levels of refugee protection because the refugee protection system relies on key norms in international law, including the 1951 Refugee Convention and the 1948 Declaration on Human Rights (McAdam, 2017; Tazreiter, 2017).

A key incident in the contemporary perpetuation of crisis narratives in Australia about asylum seekers arriving by boat is the *Tampa* incident of August 2001. The *MV Tamp*, a Norwegian cargo freighter, rescued 433 Afghani asylum seekers from their sinking vessel on August 24 in international waters close to the coast of Christmas Island which was at the time part of Australian territory. The Australian government refused the repeated requests of Tampa's captain to land the asylum seekers on Australian territory. Over several tense days, international negotiations failed to reach a solution. Eventually, the Australian Navy transferred the asylum seekers from *MV Tampa* to naval vessels on the high seas and in the weeks following, the first iteration of 'offshore' processing and detention of asylum seekers began with the *MV Tampa* asylum seekers moved to the island state of Nauru. From this first incident, the appearance of a war footing in responding to asylum seekers arriving by boat became evident, with heavily armed Special Service soldiers transferring asylum seekers from the *MV Tampa* onto naval ships. Following the *Tampa* incident, the Australian government passed a number of laws that created the legal framework for what came to be known as the 'Pacific Solution', with offshore detention of asylum seekers in both Nauru and Manus Island in PNG. The terrorist attacks of 11 September 2001, that followed only a few weeks after the *Tampa* incident, saw many political leaders, including the Australian government of John Howard, make links between these terrorists and the risks asylum seekers pose to society (Tazreiter, 2017).

The more than two decades of Australia's externalisation policies can be traced to these events of 2001. These include: the refusal of the Australian government to allow asylum seekers saved from drowning by the Norwegian freighter, the *Tampa*, to enter Australia; the 'children overboard' affair; and the beginning of 'offshore' detention of asylum seekers in Nauru and Manus Island (Gleeson, 2016; Grewcock, 2017; Juss, 2017; Tazreiter et al., 2023, chapter 3; Williams, 2016). It is beyond the scope of this chapter to review all the legal and policy developments during this 20-year period. I focus on key developments that have built and entrenched the carceral archipelago as totalising policies. The next key moment I now briefly refer to is in 2013, as one of the first acts of the newly elected conservative government of Prime Minister, Tony Abbott. After the election, a suite of policies were quickly announced under the banner of *Operation Sovereign Borders*, with the issue of asylum seekers arriving by boat defined as the key threat to the nation and the target of new policies (Huynh, 2023; Tazreiter, 2017, 2015). Included in this drive for border enforcement and security targeting the arrival of asylum seekers in small vessels on Australia's north-western shoreline, was the reintroduction of an 'offshore' processing and detention regime. Offshore processing had its first incarnation in 2001 under the conservative Howard government, and its second incarnation under the labor government of Julia Gillard in 2012. Under *Operation Sovereign Borders*, agreements were negotiated with the governments of Nauru, and PNG. Asylum seekers attempting to arrive in Australia by boat and engage Australia's protection obligations under the Refugee Convention were subsequently sent for processing of their protection claims to detention facilities on Nauru and Manus Island. As part of this policy, the Australian government negotiated a multi-billion dollar contract with the private company Transfield Services – renamed *Broadspectrum* in late 2015 – to manage the operations of the Australian Department of Immigration and Border Protection on Nauru and Manus Island. The contract was renewed in August 2015 for AU$2.2 billion.

From early in its tenure as a contractor to run detention centres, *Transfield/ Broadspectrum* faced criticism regarding the conditions of detention and high levels of abuse occurring in the centres: sexual, emotional and physical, including self-harm (Gleeson, 2016). However, the Australian government has attempted to hide these abuses by introducing federal legislation that restricts press freedom and prevents employees of detention centres from blowing the whistle on detention conditions. Infringements on press freedom have been introduced via amendments made in 2014 to the *Australian Security Intelligence Organisation Act 1979* (Cth), which, among other things, prohibit media reporting of 'special intelligence operations' and anything that 'relates to' them. It has been argued that the effect of this particular provision is to criminalise reporting that may be in the public interest, since it could reveal incompetence or wrongdoing on the part of the authorities (Williams, 2016).

For more than two decades, Australia's carceral archipelago has produced numerous sites of subjugation and death for displaced and exiled people. Australia's relationship with PNG and Nauru demonstrates a neo-colonial dynamic as aid and development are part of the equation, while developing nations remain dependent on richer nations to recover from the continuing legacies of colonialism. A key feature of Australia's border industrial complex of incarceration and violence is the multinational companies contracted to build, maintain, and manage the carceral sites. These companies include, Transfield/ Broadspectrum, Group 4 Securicor (G4S), Serco, International Health & Medical Services (IHMS), Paladin, and Pacific International Health (PIH). They have all secured remarkably lucrative contracts without oversight or accountability for the way they manage and care for the already traumatised refugees. In Paladin's case, the contract was not made available for public tender. The privatisation of immigration detention centres in Australia mirrors similar developments in other Western countries (Mountz, 2020) and is being challenged by new abolitionist demands and movements (Wilson Gilmore, 2022).

It is also noteworthy in assessing crises attached to migration, that Tony Abbott was consulted in a range of meetings by the UK government on their 'stop the boats' policies, now enacted in a way that emulates the Australian approach not only in law and administration, but in political rhetoric. The British Broadcasting

Corporation (BBC) reports that it is not only the 'stop the boats' slogan that is taken directly from the 2013 *Operation Sovereign Borders* policies of Tony Abbott, but broader rhetoric used in the securitised borders context. The UK Home Secretary, Suella Braverman, refers to her job as being 'about stopping the invasion on our southern coast' (Turnbull, 2023).

Influential counter voices in the UK have documented the human cost of 'everyday borders' in the suite of laws and administrative measures that operate at all levels of society to surveil and punish refugees, asylum seekers and other categories of migrant. For example, Nira Yuval-Davis et al. (2019), as well as Gargi Bhattacharyya (2018), detail the processes that create irregular and undocumented persons through the very processes of state rationalisation. In these practices, the state relies on crisis narratives, whether it is about refugees, or other issues facing society, to convince the domestic population that harsh measures are necessary.

Refugee Resistance and Alternative Voices

Over the more than two decades of Australia's policies and practices of the carceral archipelago, many interventions, critiques and alternatives have been formulated, published and shared through various digital and creative means. Of great importance are the voices of those with lived experience of the carceral archipelago. Here, I focus on a select number of examples from refugees detained on Manus Island. Many of these works and forms of resistance were collaborative, both among refugees and with people in Australia and in other parts of the world. One such example is the video work *Remain* created by photographer Hoda Afshar in collaboration with refugees who have been detained on Manus Island since 2013. The work, filmed on Manus Island, engages with the situation refugees face in being sent to a remote island by the Australian state where they sought protection. It is a layered work that addresses absence and invisibilities. The work depicts the ongoing mistreatment of refugees, including the remembrance invoked by the refugees of the murdered refugee, Reza Barati, beaten to death by detention centre guards. Yet, despite these horrors, the work depicts the beauty of the island setting, of the sand and the ocean and the resilient bodies of the refugee men. A haunting presence of the interwoven stories echoes through the work. One man recites poetry and another man sings in the seemingly idyllic tropical setting of the lush tropical rainforest setting of Manus Island. Afshar and Behrouz Boochani, one of the refugees on Manus Island, discuss their artistic practice and collaboration and the ideas on the aesthetic and political dimensions of their work in this way:

> by working with you guys to create something that was more incongruent with our usual expectations so that the audience would have to pause to confront what they think they know. There is already the disjunction between your surroundings, which seem to us like a tropical paradise but which you obviously see and narrate differently in the video because of the horror that you have

> experienced there. But we do not confront that horror directly or see the situation neatly laid out in linear fashion. Instead, what we get through your testimony is this brief glimpse into your world and its brute circularity – the cycle of death, trauma, boredom, anticipation – but in a way that resists our understanding. (Afshar & Boochani, 2019)

Behrouz Boochani is a Kurdish Iranian journalist, filmmaker and writer who was held in the Manus Island detention facility, Manus Prison as he calls it, for over six years. During the years, Boochani was incarcerated in Manus Prison, he regularly published in international media, gave speeches, posted and engaged in social media, participated in interviews, shot and co-directed a feature film, and wrote a book. These forms of intellectual and cultural production were written, prepared and created using a mobile phone, with all texts typed, saved and sent via WhatsApp text messages. Together with his translator Omid Tofighian, they worked across the seas on the book *No Friend but the Mountains* (Boochani, 2018), which was written and translated simultaneously, through the digital screen. The philosophical vision and intellectual framework captured in this collaboration continue to take shape and have benefitted from various working relationships and networks that are scholarly and artistic including collaborations with First Nations peoples (Boochani & Tazreiter, 2019; Boochani et al., 2021, 2023).

In 2017, Boochani and his collaborator and co-director Arash Kamali Sarvestani released the film *Chauka, Please Tell Us the Time*, which documents life in detention over time and pieced together with hundreds of mobile phone clips and written texts. Along with other forms of visual and material culture and communication, this has given the Australian public access to counter-narratives to the dominant government narratives that generate fear, mistrust, and hatred of refugees and asylum seekers. In the film, the stories of the men and boys living in the detention centre are presented in narrative form. The film is a meditation on what everyday life is like in the detention centre on a remote island like Manus and gives Australians a glimpse into the physical and psychological stresses and traumas of the detainees. The film is particularly powerful in the context of Australian policies that have made asylum seekers and refugees invisible to the Australian public – they have essentially 'disappeared' through media and information blackouts, which include visa restrictions on lawyers and human rights organisations.

With the release of the film, *Chauka*, Boochani received numerous invitations to appear at International Film Festivals for the premiere. However, the Australian government denied him a visa to enter Australia. Nevertheless, with the help of his translator, friend, and collaborator Omid Tofighian and his prosthesis, the mobile phone, Boochani appeared for interviews at numerous public events and at the screening of his film on social media. In this way, the Australian public and an international audience have come to know the work, the face, and the voice of Boochani and his fellow refugee detainees.

Other refugees detained in Manus Island prison who have written and addressed the public about the twenty-three-day siege of Manus Prison in 2017 include Hass Hassaballa and Mohamed Adam, whose posts detail the deliberate deprivation in which Australian authorities cut off food, water, medical supplies, and electricity as the refugees protested the conditions of their ongoing detention. Shaminda Kanipathi also published regularly while detained on Manus Island. Now that he has resettled as a refugee in Finland as part of the Australian government's third state resettlement, he continues to write about his experiences of incarceration.

In the foreword to a recent publication that gathers Behrouz Boochani's journalism while on Manus Island, the Australian First Nations author, Tara June Winch states in her foreword:

> Refugees and First Nations Australians share an affinity – we've taken control of our narrative and contributed to the retelling of time and space and linguistics, of the past and present and future. Behrouz speaks the language of testifying on our continent. Reading these words in their entirety, written at the edge of the jungle and in the aftermath, and from that uncomfortable position of being free, is not easy .... Here in these pages is everything we must face if we are to save ourselves from the horror of repetition. (Winch, cited in Boochani, 2023, p. xiii)

Racialisation and Racial Capitalism as Critique, Theory and Method

Irregular migration, and particularly the spontaneous arrival of refugees and asylum seekers has emerged for over two decades as the 'medium' of geopolitics (Bauböck, 2015; Hyndman, 2012; Mezzadara & Neilson, 2021). That is, irregular migrants, refugees and asylum seekers are securitised and excluded from Western states, creating totalising forms of state exceptionalism. Many scholars consider the contradictions of the international system of states with strong forces that denationalise states, while simultaneously renationalising tendencies are just as strong in the realms of border control and access to basic rights (Brown, 2019; Carens, 2013; Collins, 2019; Dauvergne, 2016; Sassen, 2006; Yuval-Davis et al., 2017). The crisis narratives used in relation to migration, referred to earlier in the chapter, are a key aspect of the racialisation that occurred through colonisation in many parts of the world and remain a social and political tool of division that embeds inequalities and is connected to border politics (Gilroy, 2005; Mbembe, 2017). Research of border externalisation policies (Barker, 2018; Hyndman, 2012; Juss, 2017; McAdam, 2017; Sassen, 2006; Tazreiter, 2017) contributes to the understanding and conceptualisation of border politics and protection of refugees.

The deeply racialised histories of colony and empire, and the connections between these histories and modernity, liberalism, and capitalism, demand attention to unpick contemporary bordering practices and logics that manifest in punitive borders (Grewcock, 2017; Juss, 2017; Tazreiter, 2017; Tazreiter et al., 2023, chapter 3). In a powerful recent book on colonialism and empire, Gurminder

Bhambra and John Holmwood (2021) show how modern social theory fails to account for the centrality of colonialism and empire in the modern world, normalising racism and racialisation. State racialisation of minoritised populations is evident in institutions such as hospitals, schools, and churches, which have been normalised over time as legitimate practices in governing populations (Braidotti, 2013; Haraway, 1989; Mbembe, 2017). In the Australian context, colonial settlers' systems and practices of governance directed against First Nations populations since violent colonisation in 1788 demonstrate systematic violence and annihilation of minoritised populations premised on racial hierarchies assigned to human life (Lake & Reynolds, 2008; Moreton-Robinson, 2015; Puar, 2017; Weheliye, 2014). Medical facilities, schools and orphanages as well as other institutions of the state have usually been the sites of such systematic practices carried out on First Nations Australians. It is perhaps no surprise that Australia as a country still to include First Nations Australians in the constitution or to strike a treaty, are applying the same harmful racial logic and practices of the colonial settler state to refugees that were previously applied to First Nations peoples.

The explanation of racialisation in human and nonhuman life is elaborated most clearly through the concept of necropolitics as the extraction of profit from the flesh of living entities (Mbembe, 2019). In this politics, death is not just an unintended by-product of the values that drive economic production and consumption, but a deliberative nihilism in creating suffering and death. In similar ways, the concept of racial capitalism commodifies life itself, with the legacies of colonialism deferring or indeed masking responsibility for crimes such as slavery, land theft, cultural genocide and while perpetuating gross violations of the fundamental rights of humans and other living entities – as 'human flesh' and other life forms are treated merely as resources (Mbembe, 2017, 2019; Weheliye, 2014). Racial capitalism is a series of explanations, arguments and evidence of the role of race at key moments in capitalist development (Bhattacharyya, 2018). Racialisation occurs when discrimination creates artificial hierarchies according to entirely arbitrary categories or identities. Over time, the systematised ways in which some living beings are treated as an expendable 'thing' or as waste become imprinted in systems of power and dominance, as well as in social attitudes and mentalities. Racialisation, then, refers to the myriad discriminations that create hierarchies of values that do real harm to the living entities devalued in these neo-colonial processes. The transformation of humans into flesh is perhaps most clearly seen in slavery (Robinson, 1983). Looking at Achille Mbembe's theory of necropolitics, we see that the multi-generational, and indeed, multi-species impacts of colonial practices of theft of living beings and resources through cycles of colonial expansion over the past centuries are still felt today in the form of contemporary inequalities, poverty and violence in many parts of the world.

The literature and approaches of scholars focussing on the histories of racialisation and racial capitalism, importantly connect with Indigenous and decolonial knowledge and methodologies (Campbell, 2022; Walsh, 2023). This scholarship and connections between different fields working on issues of justice and alternative epistemic frames, highlight the urgency of dis-embedding the dominance of settler/colonial ideas and methods. Research, creative works and activism in various ways rework racialised histories, (de)constructing the hierarchies of humans at the heart of racial capitalism and in so doing also offer alternative futures.

The harms that have occurred to refugees on Manus Island and Nauru as part of the Australian government's policies of exceptionalism in building a carceral archipelago in the Asia Pacific, exemplifies such a necropolitics. Both countries, Nauru and PNG, have been contracted and resourced by the Australian government to act as Australian prison guards for refugees in locations intentionally removed from the Australian mainland. Manus Island and Nauru are examples of how the geopolitics of borders can be used to abdicate responsibility for refugees. It shows what can occur when policies, laws, and everyday practices turn human life into flesh in cycles of dehumanisation and cruelty (Weheliye, 2014). Far from making life 'disappear' through sovereign exceptionalism (Tazreiter, 2017, 2020), these remote prisons have produced new forms of resistance as detainees create new life, coexistence and collaboration with far-flung people in many parts of the world.

Alternative Futures, Drawing Threads Together

From the cases developed at the beginning of this chapter, of state operations of carceral logics applied to vulnerable populations that ought to be protected and prioritised, I have shown the inversed logic of campaigns, policies and political rhetoric such as 'stop the boats'. What is created through totalising policies towards asylum seekers and refugee arrivals is the dismantling of the very framework and values of human rights cultures that undergird the liberal political systems themselves. Importantly, what is shown by the research and creativity of those that resist these policies and mark out alternative futures, is that the legal, administrative and rhetorical architecture of the security border applies not only to asylum seekers and refugees, labelled as external threats that the nation must be safeguarded against, but to marginalised and invisible minorities within the nation, the unemployed, First Nations people, disabled persons and trans persons.

From the histories of racialisation and the normalisation of created hierarchies, allocating differential value to humans according to scientific racism, the relationships between individuals and groups are also impacted, normalising the created divisions over time and arguably making them less visible. Ignorance and indifference to such harms are an important consequence of racial capitalism, able to be used politically at moments of crisis, risk or rupture. That is, how we decipher and respond to the traumatic pasts experienced by fellow humans, speaks to ignorance and indifference. There is an urgent intervention needed in response to the cases developed in this chapter in building resilient futures based on knowledge, understanding and empathy. Importantly, the creative force of testimony, art and storytelling from those of lived experience of the carceral archipelago in the Asia Pacific and globally that uncovers the systematised and normalised practices of harm (necropolitics) of the carceral border complex, also offers alternative visions of more just futures.

Understanding and transmitting the past to future generations, necessitates access to the heritage –artefacts, objects of ritual, performance and storytelling of the diverse histories created through colonialism and empire. And here there is also a challenge in creating access to the archives, both material and immaterial that store these histories. The material archives of the state, in libraries, museums, official archives and also public universities, have historically been the domain of a select elite group. More recently other forms of archiving, storytelling and intangible heritage are telling alternative histories. Importantly refugee camps constitute part of this intangible heritage as accumulated memories and stories that survive beyond the materiality of the camp or the detention centre, when it returns to the desert, to the jungle, or is deliberately dismantled to hide evidence of harm and crimes (Estudio et al., 2020; Hilal & Petti, 2018).

Conclusion

The activists and theorists I refer to in this chapter, and many others, collectively offer a powerful critique of the racial capitalist necropolitics that cause the pain I describe. A key aspect of the nihilism of the systems of domination and violence is aptly characterised by Brown's (2019) assessment of the end-stage of neoliberalism, which she summarises in the following way:

> Free, stupid, manipulable, absorbed by if not addicted to trivial stimuli and gratifications, the subject of repressive de-sublimation in advanced capitalist society is not just libidinally unbound, released to enjoy more pleasure, but released from more general expectations of social conscience and social comprehension. (p. 167)

The harms and pains described in this chapter are profound. They undo the world. The forms of resistance, often in creative forms, simultaneously point to new ways of making the world in collaboration.

References

Afshar, H., & Boochani, B. (2019). Beyond human: Artists in conversation. *UN Magazine, 13*(1). http://unprojects.org.au/magazine/issues/issue-13-1/behrouz-boochani-hoda-afshar/

Barker, V. (2018). *Nordic nationalism and penal order: Walling the welfare state*. Routledge.

Bauböck, R. (2015). Rethinking borders as membranes. In L. Weber (Ed.), *Rethinking border control for a globalizing world* (pp. 169–178). Routledge.

Bhambra, G. K., & Holmwood, J. (2021). *Colonialism and modern social theory*. Polity.

Bhattacharyya, G. (2018). *Rethinking racial capitalism: Questions of reproduction and survival*. Rowman & Littlefield.

Boochani, B. (2018). *No friend but the mountains: Writing from Manus Prison* (O. Tofighian, Trans.). Picador.

Boochani, B. (2023). *Freedom, only freedom: The prison writings of Behrouz Boochani* (O. Tofighian & M. Mansoubi, Trans. and Eds.). Bloomsbury.

Boochani, B., Tazreiter, C., & Tofighian, O. (2021). The multiple faces of the people smuggler. In R. Balint & J. Kalman (Eds.), *Smuggled: An illegal history of journeys to Australia* (pp. 176–190). New South Press.

Boochani, B., & Tazreiter, C. (2019). Notes on exile: Behrouz Boochani in conversation with Claudia Tazreiter. *Australian Journal of Human Rights, 25*(3), 370–375. https://doi.org/10.1080/1323238X.2019.1685768

Braidotti, R. (2013). *The posthuman*. Polity Press.

Brown, W. (2019). *In the ruins of neoliberalism: The rise of antidemocratic politics in the West*. Columbia University Press.

Campbell, L. (2022). Indigeneity, indigenous feminism and indigenization. In E. Lee & J. Evans (Eds.), *Indigenous women's voices: 20 years on from Linda Thuiwai Smith's decolonizing methodologies* (pp. 123–135). Zed Books. https://library.oapen.org/handle/20.500.12657/52483

Carens, J. (2013). *The ethics of immigration*. Oxford University Press.

Collins, J. (2019). Migration to Australia in times of crisis'. In C. Menjivar, M. Ruiz, & I. Ness (Eds.), *The handbook of migration crises* (pp. 817–831). Oxford University Press.

Dauvergne, C. (2016). *The new politics of immigration and the end of settler societies*. Cambridge University Press.

De Genova, N. (2018). The migrant crisis as racial crisis: Do black lives matter in Europe? *Ethnic and Racial Studies, 41*(10), 1765–1782.

Estudio, T. B., Bilbao, T., Greenberg, N., Ghosh, A. S., & Baan, I. (2020). *Two sides of the border: Reimagining the region*. Lars Müller Publishers.

Ghosh, A. (2021). The great uprooting: Migration and displacement in an age of planetary crisis. *The Massachusetts Review, 62*(4), 712–733.

Gilroy, P. (2005). *Postcolonial melancholia*. Columbia University Press.

Gleeson, M. (2016). *Offshore: Behind the wire on Manus and Nauru*. NewSouth.

Grewcock M. (2017). 'Our lives is in danger': Manus Island and the end of asylum. *Race & Class, 59*(2), 70–89.

Haraway, D. (1989). The biopolitics of postmodern bodies: constitutions of self in immune system discourse. *Differences: A Journal of Feminist Cultural Studies, 1*(1), 3–43.

Hilal, S., & Petti, A. (2018). *Permanent temporariness*. Art and Theory Publishing.

Huynh, K. (2023). *Australia's refugee politics in the 21st Century: STOP THE BOATS!* Taylor & Francis.

Hyndman, J. (2012). The geopolitics of migration and mobility. *Geopolitics, 17*(2), 243–255.

Juss, S. S. (2017). Detention and delusion in Australia's Kafkaesque refugee law. *Refugee Survey Quarterly, 36*(1), 146–167.

Lake, M., & H. Reynolds (2008) *Drawing the global colour line: White men's countries and the question of racial equality*. Melbourne University Press.

Mbembe, A. (2017). *Critique of black reason* (L. Dubois, Trans.). Duke University Press.

Mbembe, A. (2019). *Necropolitics* (S. Corcoran, Trans.). Duke University Press.

McAdam, J. (2017). The enduring relevance of the 1951 Refugee Convention. *International Journal of Refugee Law, 29*(1), 1–9.

Mezzadara, S., & Neilson, B. (2021). The geopolitics of labour. In L. Weber & C. Tazreiter (Eds.), *Handbook of migration and global justice* (pp. 14–25). Edward Elgar.

Moreton-Robinson, A. (2015). *The white possessive: Property, power, and indigenous sovereignty*. University of Minnesota Press.

Mountz, A. (2020). *The death of asylum: Hidden geographies of the enforcement archipelago*. University of Minnesota Press.

Puar, J. K. (2017). *The right to maim: Debility, capacity, disability*. Duke University Press.

Robinson, C. J. (1983). *Black Marxism*. Chapel Hill.

Sassen, S. (2006). *Territory, authority, rights: From medieval to global assemblages*. Princeton University Press.

Tazreiter, C. (2015). 'Stop the Boats!' Externalising the borders of Australia and imaginary pathologies of contagion. *Journal of Immigration, Nationality and Asylum Law, 29*(2), 141–157.

Tazreiter, C. (2017). *Asylum seekers and the state: The politics of protection in a security-conscious world.* Routledge.
Tazreiter, C. (2019). Crisis politics of asylum seekers and migrant arrivals in Australia. In C. Menjivar, M. Ruiz, & I. Ness (Eds.), *The handbook of migration crises* (pp. 619–634). Oxford University Press. https://doi.org/10.1093/oxfordhb/9780190856908.013.71
Tazreiter, C. (2020). Emotions, borders and the role of visual culture in refugee arrivals. *Critical Criminology, an International Journal*, *2*(28), 193–207.
Tazreiter, C., & Tofighian, O., Boochani, B. (2023). Spectres of subjugation/inter-subjugation/resubjugation of people seeking asylum: The kyriarchal system in Australia's necropolis. In P. Billings (Ed.). *Regulating refugee protection through social welfare: Law, policy and praxis* (pp. 68–90). Routledge. https://doi.org/10.4324/9781003298595-6
Tazzioli, M., Garelli, G., & De Genova, N. (2018) Autonomy of asylum?: The autonomy of migration undoing the refugee crisis script. *South Atlantic Quarterly*, *117*(2), 239–265.
Turnbull, T. (2023, March 18). *How Australia wrote the 'stop the boats' playbook*. BBC News online. https://www.bbc.com/news/world-australia-64898507
Walsh, C. E. (2023). *Rising up, living on: Re-existences, sowings, & decolonial cracks*. Duke University Press.
Weheliye, A. G. (2014). *Habeas viscus: Racializing assemblages, biopolitics, and black feminist theories of the human*. Duke University Press.
Wilson Gilmore, R. (2022). *Abolition geography: Essays towards liberation*. Verso.
Williams, G. (2016). The legal assault on Australian democracy. *QUT Law Review*, *16*(2), 19–41. https://doi.org/10.5204/qutlr.v16i2.651
Wintour, P. (2023, July 17). EU accused of whitewashing Tunisian regime in bid to stem migration. *The Guardian*. https://www.theguardian.com/world/2023/jun/26/eu-migration-aid-tunisia-betrayal-values-imprisoned-dissidents-children
Yuval-Davis, N., Wemyss, G., & Cassidy, K. (2019). *Bordering*. Polity.
Yuval-Davis, N., Wemyss, G., & Cassidy, K. (2017). Everyday bordering, belonging and the reorientation of British immigration legislation. *Sociology*, 52(2), 228–244. https://doi.org/10.1177/0038038517702599

Trenches of the Unknown

Hani Abdile

Poet

In distant lands where dreams are torn,
A refugee, in search, tripping in the trenches of unknown.
Leaving behind a world once known,
To seek solace, a new place to call home.

Displaced from homelands, torn apart,
Seeking refuge, peace to recover.
Fleeing from chaos, fearing for life,
We embark on this treacherous strife.
Through barren deserts and stormy seas
Holding onto hope, heart's unease
Shattered dreams float in the starlit night,
Memories fading, shadowed by the plight.

From shattered streets to foreign shores,
We yearn for a life with open doors
In the depths of our soul, we carry the weight
Of stories untold, burdened by fate.

So crowded where sorrows unite.

We find solace in each other's fight
From different lands, we form a sacred kin
United by the shared longing within.

We are more than just a lost soul
A refugee, in search of a home
We are survivors, resilient and strong,
With untapped potential, ready to belong.

Deter, Detain, Dehumanise: The Politics of Seeking Asylum, 157–158

doi:10.1108/978-1-83753-224-720241012

With each sunrise, a new day dawns,
With hope and dreams that carry on.
We weave our story, a tapestry untold,
With threads of courage, resilient and bold.

For in the depths of despair, we find our grace,
Embracing challenges we often face.
We may be a refugee, but we won't be confined,
For our spirit soars, boundless and undefined.

So, we can stand together, hand in hand,
Fighting for justice across each land,
Marking hope our guiding star.

Every human has a journey to tell, no matter how far.
We are not here to compare pain
We are here to heal
To understand this new path
To lend a hand to embrace the smell of a new land.

Printed and bound by CPI Group (UK) Ltd, Croydon, CR0 4YY

13/09/2026

14961026-0008